CHRIST AMONG THE NATIONS

The American Society of Missiology Series, published in collaboration with Orbis Books, seeks to publish scholarly works of high merit and wide interest on numerous aspects of missiology—the study of Christian mission in its historical, social, and theological dimensions. Able presentations on new and creative approaches to the practice and understanding of mission will receive close attention from the ASM Series Committee.

American Society of Missiology Series, No. 62

CHRIST AMONG THE NATIONS

*Narratives of Transformation
in Global Mission*

Sarita Gallagher Edwards
Robert L. Gallagher
Paul W. Lewis
DeLonn L. Rance

Maryknoll, New York 10545

ORBIS BOOKS
Maryknoll, New York 10545

Founded in 1970, Orbis Books endeavors to publish works that enlighten the mind, nourish the spirit, and challenge the conscience. The publishing arm of the Maryknoll Fathers and Brothers, Orbis seeks to explore the global dimensions of the Christian faith and mission, to invite dialogue with diverse cultures and religious traditions, and to serve the cause of reconciliation and peace. The books published reflect the views of their authors and do not represent the official position of the Maryknoll Society. To learn more about Maryknoll and Orbis Books, please visit our website at http://www.maryknollsociety.org.

Copyright © 2021 by Sarita Gallagher Edwards, Robert L. Gallagher, Paul W. Lewis, and DeLonn L. Rance

Published by Orbis Books, Box 302, Maryknoll, NY 10545-0302.

All rights reserved.

All Scripture quotations, unless otherwise indicated, are taken from the Holy Bible, New International Version®, NIV®. Copyright ©1973, 1978, 1984, 2011 by Biblica, Inc.™ Used by permission of Zondervan. All rights reserved worldwide. www.zondervan.com The "NIV" and "New International Version" are trademarks registered in the United States Patent and Trademark Office by Biblica, Inc.™

No part of this publication may be reproduced or transmitted in any form or by any means, electronic or mechanical, including photocopying, recording, or any information storage or retrieval system, without prior permission in writing from the publisher.

Queries regarding rights and permissions should be addressed to: Orbis Books, P.O. Box 302, Maryknoll, NY 10545-0302.

Manufactured in the United States of America

Library of Congress Cataloging-in-Publication Data

Names: Gallagher, Sarita D., 1977– author. | Gallagher, Robert L., author. | Lewis, Paul W., PhD, author. | Rance, DeLonn L., author.
Title: Christ among the nations : narratives of transformation in global mission / Sarita Gallagher Edwards, Robert L. Gallagher, Paul W. Lewis, DeLonn L. Rance.
Description: Maryknoll, NY : Orbis Books, [2021] | Series: American society of missiology; no. 62 | Includes bibliographical references. | Summary:
"Explores the specific identity of Christ as savior, sanctifier, healer, and king, using narratives, theological interpretation, and insights from anthropology and sociology"— Provided by publisher.
Identifiers: LCCN 2021016425 (print) | LCCN 2021016426 (ebook) | ISBN 9781626983700 (trade paperback) | ISBN 9781608338344 (epub)
Subjects: LCSH: Christian converts—Biography. | Missions. | Jesus Christ—Person and offices. | Christian biography.
Classification: LCC BV4930 .G348 2021 (print) | LCC BV4930 (ebook) | DDC 232—dc23
LC record available at https://lccn.loc.gov/2021016425
LC ebook record available at https://lccn.loc.gov/2021016426

To our spouses:

Thomas Edwards

Jayna Louise Gallagher

Eveline Susanto Lewis

Valerie Ann Rance

who have offered their unfailing support throughout our various missiological endeavors, reminding us daily of the true gifts of God in our lives.

It is to them that we dedicate this book.

Contents

Preface to the American Society of Missiology Series	xv
Foreword Paul W. Lewis	xvii
Introduction DeLonn L. Rance	xxi
The Transformative Power of the Full Gospel	xxiv
The Transformative Power of Narrative	xxvi
Missiological Foundations in the Missionary Narrative	xxviii
The Word of God	xxviii
Missionary People of God	xxix
Planting Communities of Faith	xxix
Songs of Pentecost	xxx
Pentecostal Experience	xxxi
A. B. Simpson's Missiology	xxxii
Indigenous Church Principles	xxxiii
Overview of the Book	xxxiv
Conclusion	xxxv

Part I
Christ Our Savior

1. Centrality of the Cross:
 God's Historic Plan of Salvation in Lukan Perspective   3
 Robert L. Gallagher

Not My Will, But Thine Be Done	4
Use of the Verb Dei	5
Salvation toward the Parousia	6
Now It Came about in Those Days	7
Secular History of Acts	8
Summary of the Argument	9
Overview of Christ Our Savior	9
Love that Saves a Harlot	9
Ziegenbalg and the Salvation of Souls	10
Salvation's Call in Papua New Guinea	11

2. **Holy Tears of a Weeping Harlot: Love that Saves**   12
   Robert L. Gallagher

A Notorious Life	12
Sleeping with the Enemy	13
Abandonment in Poverty	14
Shameless Entry	15
Invading the Party	16
Questioning Looks	18
Feelings of Devastation	19
What a Waste!	19
If Only He Knew	20
A Story in Silence	20
Do You See This Woman?	20
Where Is My Kiss?	21
Behold the Woman!	22
Jesus Ends the Story	23
Conclusion	23

3. **Seeking Nothing but the Salvation of Souls: The Story of Bartholomäus Ziegenbalg in Southern India**   25
   Robert L. Gallagher

Consecration to Christ	26
Missions to Tranquebar	27
Royal Danish Mission	29
Church and School Together	29

Bible in the Vernacular	30
Contextualized Gospel	32
Personal Conversion Is Paramount	33
Indigenous Leadership and Church	34
Drawing to a Close	36

4. **Salvation's Call in Papua New Guinea: How Can We Baptize All These People?**   39
   Robert L. Gallagher

Spiritual Background	40
Salvation's Call in Papua New Guinea	41
New Beginnings in Port Moresby	41
Pressure of Missions Reports	42
Lighting of Revival Fires	43
Historic Christianity	44
The Spirit's Open Door	45
Message of Salvation	45
Good News Spreading	46
Surprised by the Spirit	48

Part II
Christ Our Empowerer

5. **Biblical, Historical, and Contemporary Components of Empowerment**   53
   Paul W. Lewis

Biblical Components	54
Empowerment of the Holy Spirit	56
Empowerment to Be Witnesses	58
Empowerment of Creativity and Charismata	59
Empowerment of Ethical Dimensions	61
Historical Components	61
Empowerment to Proclaim the Gospel	62
Empowerment to Be Not of This World	63
Empowerment for Diversity of Proclamation	64
Contemporary Components	65
Overview of Christ Our Empowerer	65

	A Beloved Servant at Death's Door: Faith that Empowers	66
	St. Ephrem, St. Francis, St. Clare, Wesley, and Bonhoeffer	66
	Empowerment to Holiness, Service, and Witness	67
6.	**A Beloved Servant at Death's Door: Faith that Empowers** *Robert L. Gallagher*	68
	Magnificence of Rome	69
	Coming to Capernaum	70
	Religions of Rome	72
	Changing Allegiance	72
	Entertaining Unfired Passions	74
	Jesus Comes to Town	75
	Good News Spreading	77
	Power from Above	78
	Royal Army of Capernaum	80
	Conclusion	82
7.	**Historical Narratives of St. Ephrem, St. Francis, St. Clare, Wesley, and Bonhoeffer** *Paul W. Lewis*	83
	St. Ephrem (ca. 306–73)	84
	St. Francis (ca. 1181–1226) and St. Clare (1194–1253) of Assisi	87
	John Wesley (1703–1791)	89
	Dietrich Bonhoeffer (1906–1945)	91
8.	**Contemporary Stories of Empowerment to Holiness, Service, and Witness** *DeLonn L. Rance*	93
	Empowered to Holiness and Witness	93
	Empowered to Missionary Service	94
	Empowered to Cross-Cultural Ministry	96
	Empowered to Start Churches	98

Part III
Christ Our Healer

9. Healing as a Divine Testimony, Compassionate Act,
   and Coming Kingdom — 103
   Sarita Gallagher Edwards

   Themes in the Healing Narratives — 105
      Healing as a Divine Testimony — 105
      Healing as a Compassionate Act — 107
      Healing as a Coming Kingdom — 110
   Overview of Christ Our Healer — 113
      Christ Our Healer in First-Century Palestine — 113
      Healing Works of Thaumaturgus, Cuthbert,
        the Blumhardts, and Kuhlman — 114
      Contemporary Healings of Jennifer Matheny
        and Sarah Puckett — 114

10. Christ Heals the Paralytic and Demon Possessed — 115
    Sarita Gallagher Edwards

    Healing the Paralytic Man in Capernaum — 115
    Healing the Demon-Possessed Man in Gerasenes — 118

11. The Healing Stories of St. Thaumaturgus,
    St. Cuthbert, the Blumhardts, and Kuhlman — 125
    Paul W. Lewis

    St. Gregory Thaumaturgus (ca. 213–270) — 126
    St. Cuthbert of Lindisfarne (ca. 636–687) — 127
    Johann Christoph Blumhardt (1805–1880)
    and Christoph Friedrich Blumhardt (1842–1919) — 129
    Kathryn Kuhlman (1907–1976) — 132

12. Contemporary Stories of Christ Our Healer — 134
    Sarita Gallagher Edwards

    Christ Heals Jennifer Matheny — 134
       What Is Causing Jenny's Pain? — 135
       A Turn of Events — 136
    Christ Heals Sarah Puckett — 137

Daily Pain Remained 138
Following God's Mission Call 139
Prayer for Inner Healing 140
Jesus Washed Sarah's Feet 141
Enemy Attack 142

Part IV
Christ Our Hope

13. Living with Christ in Purpose, Hope, and Expectancy 147
DeLonn L. Rance

Living with Purpose: Serving Christ, the King 150
Living with Hope: The Promises of Christ 153
Living with Expectancy: The Soon-Coming King 156
Overview of Christ Our Hope 159
   Living with Purpose, Hope, and Expectancy in Biblical Narratives 159
   Living with Purpose, Hope, and Expectancy in Historical Narratives 160
   Living with Purpose, Hope, and Expectancy in Contemporary Narratives 161

14. Blessing Our World with Messianic Hope 162
Sarita Gallagher Edwards

Abraham, Sarah, and Hagar (Gen 16, 21) 163
Hannah and Samuel (1 Sam 1, 2) 166
Anna and Simeon (Lk 2:21–38) 170

15. Historical Glimpses into Christ Our Hope 174
Paul W. Lewis

St. Irenaeus (ca. 130–202) 175
Joachim of Fiore (ca. 1135–1202) 176
André Crouch (1942–2015) 177
Jürgen Moltmann (1926–) 179

16. Christ the King: Our Purpose and Hope 183
DeLonn L. Rance

Serving Christ with Purpose:
Miguel of El Salvador 183
Christ the Source of an Impossible Hope:
Carlos and Ruth of Nicaragua and Peru 185
    Your "Culture Shock" Is Six Weeks Old 186
    Isaac Adonai 187
    Entrusted with Two Children 188
Christ the Resurrection and the Life:
Katy, Roberto, and Christina of
Equatorial Guinea 188

Conclusion:
Communicating the Transforming Global Mission of Christ through Story 191
Robert L. Gallagher

Learning to Grow in the Scriptures 192
    Responsibility, Community, and Mission 193
    Principlizing Hermeneutics 195
    Missional Hermeneutics 196
    Viewing the Panorama 197
    Recovering the Scriptures as a Whole 200
    Tossing Morsels under the Table 202
Ziegenbalg Models Promotion of Mission
in Asia and Europe 204
My Identity in the Story of Christ 208
    Imagination Paves a Way 209
    We Are Our Stories 210
    Enhancing Our Mission Story 211
Finale 213
Our January Six 214

About the Authors 215

Preface to the American Society of Missiology Series

The purpose of the American Society of Missiology Series is to publish—without regard for disciplinary, national, or denominational boundaries—scholarly works of high quality and wide interest on missiological themes from the entire spectrum of scholarly pursuits relevant to Christian mission, which is always the focus of books in the Series.

By mission is meant the effort to effect passage over the boundary between faith in Jesus Christ and its absence. In this understanding of mission, the basic functions of Christian proclamation, dialogue, witness, service, worship, liberation, and nurture are of special concern. And in that context questions arise, including how the transition from one cultural context to another influences the shape and interaction between these dynamic functions, especially in regard to the cultural and religious plurality that comprises the global context of Christian life and mission.

The promotion of scholarly dialogue among missiologists, and among missiologists and scholars in other fields of inquiry, may involve the publication of views that some missiologists cannot accept, and with which members of the Editorial Committee themselves do not agree. Manuscripts published in the Series, accordingly, reflect the opinions of their authors and are not understood to represent the position of the American Society of Missiology or of the Editorial Committee. Selection is guided by such criteria as intrinsic worth, readability, coherence, and accessibility to a range of interested persons and not merely to experts or specialists.

The ASM Series, in collaboration with Orbis Books, seeks to publish scholarly works of high merit and wide interest on numerous aspects of missiology—the scholarly study of mission. Able presentations on new and creative approaches to the practice and understanding of mission will receive close attention.

ASM Series Committee Chair: Dr. Robert Hunt
ASM Publisher: Dr. Darrel Whiteman

Foreword

Paul W. Lewis

The development of this volume took place over a period of several years. Sarita Gallagher (now Edwards), Robert (Rob) L. Gallagher, DeLonn L. Rance, and I (Paul W. Lewis) have known each other for many years. While DeLonn and I taught together at the same school, Assemblies of God Theological Seminary in Springfield, Missouri, Rob was at Wheaton College Graduate School, in Wheaton, Illinois, and Sarita was at George Fox University in Newberg, Oregon. Yet we all connected in several of the same missions conferences: American Society of Missiology (ASM), Association of Professors of Mission, Evangelical Missiological Society, and the missions interest group of the Society for Pentecostal Studies.

Over the years, our friendships grew, and frequently our conversations would move into discussions about what we thought was missing in missions studies, contemporary missiology, and missions textbooks. Several years back, specific lacunae caught our attention from the lens of an introduction to missions themes through a narrative approach. Early on, Sarita became the ongoing champion of this project, and talked to Robert Hunt, the ASM series committee chair, about a book proposal with Orbis Books, the ASM series publisher.

Once the direction of the project was set, we finalized the structure of the volume, and refined the components that we wanted in each chapter. Then, we all settled on which chapters we would individually write. All along the way, we communicated together (including at conferences and through email or Zoom), assisted each other, and made suggestions. Toward the end of the project as the manuscript was coming together, Rob stepped up to assist in the final editing process, and worked tirelessly with our editor at Orbis, Jill Brennan O'Brien, PhD, to bring the manuscript to its current place. It has been quite the journey, yet an enjoyable one as well.

The volume serves as an introduction to key themes of missions and missiology through a narrative format. Structurally, the volume focuses on Christ, through four major lenses: Christ Our Savior, Christ Our Empowerer, Christ Our Healer, and Christ Our Hope. Each unit includes an introductory chapter, and then three narrative chapters: biblical, historical, and contemporary. Each narrative chapter has three to four stories that represent transformational aspects of global missions within the broader lens and are reflective of the diversity of the Christian family. The end of each chapter contains questions for group discussion.

While the vehicle of narrative demonstrates missiology and missions, we also had the implicit goal of teaching and challenging readers to learn (more) about missions, and perhaps even expand and/or reconsider their missions thinking and practices. It is our hope and prayer that the exemplars found in this volume will guide and inspire the next generation of missionaries, missiologists, and missions statesmen/stateswomen.

We are appreciative of many who had their hands in various parts of this project. First, we would like to express our indebtedness to the institutions in which we have worked that supported (with funds and/or time allotments) our participation at the conferences and missions societies: Assemblies of God Theological Seminary, George Fox University, and Wheaton College Graduate School. We also are very thankful for the conferences and societies that have provided the space and opportunity to talk about missions and missiology with peers: American Society of Missiology,

Association of Professors of Mission, Evangelical Missiological Society, and Society for Pentecostal Studies.

In addition, we would be remiss if we did not also declare our gratitude to and for the many missionaries, missiologists, and missionary statesmen/stateswomen, both past and present, who were interlocutors for this whole project (there are too many to mention, but all heavily influenced our thinking). Finally, for each of the authors, we also want to highlight our deepest appreciation to our spouses who were supportive during this project: Sarita's husband, Thomas; Rob's wife, Jayna; Paul's wife, Eveline; and DeLonn's wife, Valerie; as well as all of our children and grandchildren. Without them life would be drudgery, and with them and their support we were able to bring this volume to fruition. Ultimately, we want to express our deepest thankfulness to Jesus Christ, our Lord and Savior, for whom missions is not just an act of obedience but also an act of worship, joy, and privilege. To God be the Glory!

Introduction

DeLonn L. Rance

Disillusioned with life, Francisco worked as a tailor in rural El Salvador. As a young man, he made marriage plans with the girl who lived next door. When her family discovered their plans, they forbade the marriage, crushing Francisco's dreams. Francisco's poverty made him unworthy in their eyes. In time, he married another, but his lost love and despair led to a life of debauchery. One day in a drunken depression, he sought to borrow a gun from a neighbor to kill himself. The neighbor refused. He went to the kitchen, took out a large butcher's knife, and placed the point on his stomach, but the image of his own blood spilling out unnerved him. He then searched unsuccessfully for a rope to hang himself.

In desperation, he took off his leather belt and headed to the outhouse. He wrapped one end of the belt over the bamboo support beam and the other around his neck. After placing his feet on either side of the toilet's opening, he pulled them together and dropped. Incredibly, the thick leather belt snapped in two, and he fell, wedging himself in the opening. His banging to free himself alerted the neighbors who came and rescued him.

The following day in the yard he watched his six-year-old son take a rope, the one he had not been able to find, and wrap it around his two-year-old daughter's neck. His son threw one end of the rope over the branch of a tree, and began to pull while screaming, "I'm going to hang you like my daddy was going to hang himself!" Francisco rescued his daughter but felt the crush of his actions. Two days later a Bible school student came and preached the full gospel in Francisco's community. In the meeting that night, Francisco and his wife accepted Christ. The transformation in Francisco's life was immediate. He began to share his testimony and newfound faith with others, leading him to a life as an evangelist, church planter, and missionary, proclaiming Jesus Christ as Our Savior, Empowerer, Healer, and Hope: Christ among the nations.[1]

God's missionary story, recorded authoritatively in the Bible, reveals a God who in great love seeks those who are lost, women and men alienated from their Creator and from each other. God chose to communicate his good news of salvation and reconciliation through his church, his missionary or apostolic (i.e., "sent ones") people. From the very beginning, God sought human participation in his work. "Be fruitful and increase in number; fill the earth and subdue it" (Gen 1:28).[2] This "dominion mandate" finds its fullest expression in the verses, "Therefore go and make disciples of all nations, baptizing them in the name of the Father and of the Son and of the Holy Spirit, and teaching them to obey everything I have commanded you. And surely, I am with you always, to the very end of the age" (Mt 28:19–20).

Similar to Adam, Abram and the people of Israel participate in God's story as a missionary people, a kingdom of priests called to give light to the nations (Gen 12:1–3; Ex 19:5–6; Is 42:6). At his ascension, Jesus commissioned his apostolic/missionary people to continue his ministry of revelation and reconciliation. At Pentecost, he empowered his people with the anointing of the Holy Spirit to testify in holiness and service, giving witness to Christ (Acts 1:8; Acts 2).[3] "But you are a chosen people, a royal

---

[1] The narrative emerged from a personal interview with the author. For security purposes, the author used a pseudonym.

[2] Scriptural quotations throughout *Christ among the Nations* are from the New International Version.

[3] See Roger Stronstad, *The Charismatic Theology of St. Luke* (Peabody, MA: Hendrickson Publishers, 1984).

priesthood, a holy nation, God's special possession, that you may declare the praises of him who called you out of darkness into his wonderful light" (1 Pet 2:9). Guided by the principles revealed in God's word and empowered by the Holy Spirit, the Lord charges the church with making disciples of people from all nations.

The apostolic people of God communicate the full gospel message, proclaiming Jesus Christ as Savior, responding to humankind's spiritual needs; Empowerer, meeting their emotional and volitional needs; Healer, supplying people's physical needs; and our Hope and soon-coming King, providing both hope and reason for being. When proclaimed in word, deed, and sign in the power of the Spirit, this good news transforms lives. Men and women are reconciled to God and each other. Biblical, historical, and contemporary narratives bear witness to the love, truth, and power of this full gospel.

This narrative introduction to Pentecostal missions seeks to connect God's missionary story with the church's story in missions. The transformative missionary narratives in the following chapters serve as both an invitation and a challenge to participate in the missionary narrative. Research reveals a direct correlation between missional engagement and exposure to missionary stories. That is, the more an individual encounters missionary stories, the more likely that the individual's story will be committed to the missionary enterprise.[4]

Through biblical, historical, and contemporary narratives, this volume will challenge the reader to engage the God of mission, the God of the Bible, the God of history, the God active in contemporary mission, and the God who will culminate history by returning and bringing the fullness of the kingdom. This introductory chapter describes the transformative power of the "full gospel," underlines the importance of narrative in Pentecostal missions, highlights foundational aspects of missiology that emerge in the Pentecostal missions' narrative, and provides an overview of the book's design.

---

[4] See DeLonn L. Rance, *The Empowered Call: The Activity of the Holy Spirit in Salvadoran Assemblies of God Missionaries* (PhD diss., Fuller Theological Seminary, 2004), 253.

THE TRANSFORMATIVE POWER OF THE FULL GOSPEL

According to Donald W. Dayton, the pattern of the full or four-square gospel provides the basis of the historical and theological roots of Pentecostalism.[5] Influenced by A. B. Simpson's theology of the "fourfold" gospel—salvation, sanctification, healing, and the second coming of Christ—Pentecostal missionaries linked their experience of the baptism of the Holy Spirit to a supernatural empowerment to give witness of Christ among the nations in holiness and service. Communicating Christ as Savior, Empowerer, Healer, and Hope as the soon-coming King prioritized the Pentecostal missionary activities.

This fourfold framing of the message continues to be relevant in a constantly changing world because of the Christocentric focus of the message linking the power of Christ's life, death, and resurrection to human need. The proclamation of the full gospel bridges the gap between word and deed, and reaches both individuals and communities creating a sense of purpose and belonging. The gospel responds to the West's guilt, the South's fear, and the East's shame for Jesus is the way, the truth, and the life (Jn 14:6). When embraced, this gospel, grounded in a personal relationship to Jesus Christ, transforms individuals and communities, providing reconciliation with God and each other.

Jesus Christ, proclaimed as the only Savior, responds to each individual's spiritual need to be in fellowship with the Creator. Scripture states, "All have sinned and fall short of the glory of God" (Rom 3:23), and "There is none righteous, not even one" (Rom 3:10). In every person, there exists the desire to know the righteousness of God, a spiritual void that only the efficacious grace of Christ can fill provided by his life, death, and resurrection. Jesus the Savior fills humanity's deepest spiritual hunger. See chapters 1–4 in this volume.

---

[5] Donald W. Dayton, *The Roots of Pentecostalism* (Grand Rapids, MI: Baker Academic, 1987), 21. See also Wolfgang Vondey, *Pentecostal Theology: Living the Full Gospel* (New York: T&T Clark, 2017).

Jesus Christ responds to an individual's emotional and volitional needs as the Empowerer (Mt 3:11). In the experience of the baptism of the Holy Spirit, Jesus through the agency of his Spirit elevates a person to a higher emotional plane, a sphere of ecstasy in the presence of the Almighty, a plane where one is overwhelmed by God's presence, resulting in an endowment of power for holiness and service. Where one's own will and strength fall short, God provides the capacity to fulfill God's purposes (Is 40:28–31). Jesus Christ the Empowerer offers the individual an experience that surpasses all human emotional standards while providing the fortitude (empowerment) for service and holiness. See chapters 5–8.

The gospel of Jesus Christ also proclaims him as Healer (Is 53:4–5; Mt 8:17). Jesus Christ as healer responds to a person's physical needs. Jesus expressed his concern for immediate needs by miraculously breaking into the present with healing and relief. If Pentecostals have a physical need, they appeal to the healer. If sick, they call upon the great physician. If bound by the demonic, liberation comes in the name of Jesus. If financially destitute, they pray for his provision. If unemployed, they rely upon his employment service. Any physical need that we might have, we can take before the throne of grace. His people have his assurance that he will provide, he will intervene, and he will heal (Jas 5:15). See chapters 9–12.

Jesus as our hope is the soon-coming King (Mt 24:27–30; Rev 19:16, 22:12). The sovereign title reflects two aspects. First, he is the King (1 Tim 6:15). His subjects live with purpose, recognizing that every present action and thought falls under the scrutiny of their Lord and King (Titus 2:12–14; 2 Pet 3:11–12). If people truly encounter the gospel of Jesus Christ and accept Jesus as Lord, they must radically alter their life and lifestyle to one of obedience. Pentecostals maintain that a new way of life must accompany the new birth, a way of life that reflects the coming age and Jesus Christ himself.

Having established that Jesus's Lordship dramatically alters the present, Pentecostals rejoice and celebrate the second aspect of this title. Not only is he King, but the King promises to return to establish his kingdom in its fullness (Rev 21, 22). The believer's hope is not limited to this life or age, or to what humankind can accomplish in it. This hope abides in Jesus Christ who will personally usher in the fullness of the kingdom. See chapters 13–16. The communication of this full gospel narrative, the fourfold gospel of Jesus Christ, releases the transformative power of Christ in a lost and dying world.

THE TRANSFORMATIVE POWER OF NARRATIVE

God's narrative expresses the divine mission. "God is a storytelling God. Deeper than this, God is the creator of story, and it is in the context of story that God calls us into mission."[6] Mission is a continuation of the narrative that began with the calling of Abraham, and continues through the people of God under the leadership of the Holy Spirit.[7]

Historically, Pentecostals communicate truth, values, and priorities—and build faith—through story. These narratives testify to the acts and faithfulness of the Holy Spirit in the lives of those who encounter and communicate the full gospel of Christ among the nations. A story creates space inviting encounter, dialogue, and mutual sharing. In that space, God communicates, giving vision and guidance.[8] Stories allow the Spirit to communicate uniquely and contextually to each individual and each community of faith that seeks to walk in obedience to divine direction and surrender to the Spirit's empowerment. Globally, stories particularly empower people who think in terms of concrete situations and relationships to communicate both theology and missional practice.

Much of Pentecostal missions theology emerges from story, through the testimonies of those engaged in the word and in missions. In general, the acceptance of narrative theology will have a profound effect on missiology, and in particular, facilitate the

---

[6] Nancy Thomas, "Following the Footprints of God: The Contribution of Narrative to Mission Theology," in *Footprints of God: A Narrative Theology of Mission*, ed. Charles E. Van Engen, Nancy Thomas, and Robert L. Gallagher (Monrovia, CA: MARC, 1999), 225.

[7] Wilbert R. Shenk, ed., *The Transfiguration of Mission: Biblical, Theological, and Historical Foundations*, Institute of Mennonite Studies, vol. 12 (Scottdale, PA: Herald Press, 1993), 12.

[8] Henri J. M. Nouwen, *The Living Reminder: Service and Prayer in Memory of Jesus Christ* (New York: Harper Collins Publishers, 1977), 65–67.

articulation of Pentecostal missions theologies. Nancy Thomas explains, "Narrative theology has been called 'discourse about God in the setting of story.' It combines form (narrative) with content (theology) in a creative way that seeks to understand God, and God's dealings with the human race in terms of events that have happened, conflicts that have been resolved, people who have been transformed—in short, in terms of stories."[9]

The biblical narrative is more than story because it grounds itself in history, and "seeks to convey a deeper meaning, a deep-level revelation of the nature and purposes of God who breaks into human history."[10] Narrative theology contributes to mission theology by providing understanding that Scripture is the story of God's Trinitarian mission; bridging and integrating being, knowing, and doing in real life; facilitating contextualization; bringing together text, context, and faith community; and providing "the images, pictures, metaphors, and stories that are necessary for rounding out the propositional, textual, and historical aspects of today's global theological conversations in missiology."[11]

Narratives must be subject to the word,[12] however, and be presented with humility in view of the finite nature of the human perspective. Personal testimony is an important tool to understand the work of the Spirit in missions because the Spirit works through people. Nevertheless, people and their stories have inherent weaknesses, and only God sees the complete tapestry of God's work. "No one person can claim to have the whole story and every person must be willing to participate within the Spirit-led community's perception."[13]

Charles Van Engen notes that the community of faith continues to participate in mission because God's story and the story of

---

[9] Thomas, "Following the Footprints of God," 225–26.

[10] Charles Van Engen, *Mission on the Way: Issues in Mission Theology* (Grand Rapids, MI: Baker Books, 1996), 52.

[11] Ibid., 65–67.

[12] John H. Orme, "Identificational Repentance and Strategic Spiritual Warfare: A Hermeneutical Case Study," in *The Holy Spirit and Mission Dynamics*, ed. C. Douglas McConnell (Pasadena, CA: William Carey Library, 1997), 154.

[13] A. Scott Moreau, "Broadening the Issues: Historiography, Advocacy, and Hermeneutics," in McConnell, *The Holy Spirit and Mission Dynamics*, 124.

humankind have yet to finish. The acts of the Holy Spirit through the church in witness to the world will continue until the return of Christ.[14] Pentecostals participate in the transformative story of Christ among the nations, and compelled by the Spirit, they continue to participate in God's missionary narrative.

MISSIOLOGICAL FOUNDATIONS IN THE MISSIONARY NARRATIVE

The inspired, divinely authorized story of God's dealings with humankind and all of creation finds its articulation in the canon of Scripture, the Bible. God reveals Godself through words, acts, and Jesus the Son of God creating the possibility of reconciliation with women and men and to each other. While God continues to speak and engage in history today, God's revelation recorded in the Bible sets the agenda for the missionary people of God "determining the nature and scope of the church's mission."[15]

The Word of God

The word of God is the final authority for God's people in mission. The word declares that all humans are objects of God's wrath, lost and separated from God and each other because of sin (Eph 2; Rom 3:23; Lk 10). Human perspectives on justice are limited and flawed. Only God judges justly (Ps 50:6; Is 30:18; Acts 17:31). Despite their best efforts, human beings are incapable of saving themselves. Only the good news of Jesus's life, death on the cross, and resurrection from the grave creates the possibility of salvation and restored relationship with God and others. Jesus Christ alone is the Son of God, and the Savior of the world. "Salvation is found in no one else, for there is no other name under heaven given to humankind by which we must be saved" (Acts 4:12).

This good news of salvation is available for every person if he/she repents of his/her sin, believes that Jesus rose from the grave,

---

[14] Van Engen, Thomas, and Gallagher, *Footprints of God*, xxv.
[15] Melvin L. Hodges, *A Theology of the Church and Its Mission: A Pentecostal Perspective* (Springfield, MO: Gospel Publishing House, 1977), 19.

and surrenders his/her life to the Lordship of Christ (Mk 1:15, 16:6; Acts 2:38; Rom 10:9). For "everyone who calls on the name of the Lord will be saved" (Acts 2:21; Rom 10:13).

Missionary People of God

Those who believe and surrender to live under the rule of Christ, the kingdom of God, compose the church, God's treasured possession, and the missionary people of God. A people redeemed by the blood of the Lamb (1 Pet 1:18–19) becomes a redeeming community through the communication of the full gospel to every person and people (1 Pet 2:9–10).

The Spirit dwells in the church and empowers it to give witness to Christ in love, holiness, and service to make disciples of all nations (Mt 28:18–20; Jn 13:34–35; Acts 1:8; 2 Cor 5:14; Eph 2:19–22, 4:12; 1 Pet 1:15; 2 Tim 1:7). As William J. Seymour, leader of the Azusa Street Revival, asserted, "The Pentecostal power, when you sum it all up, is just more of God's love. If it does not bring more love, it is simply a counterfeit."[16] Tongue speech (*glossolalia*) demonstrates God's love for all peoples and every language to worship God for all eternity (Acts 2:4–6; Rev 5:9, 7:9).

Planting Communities of Faith

As local communities of faith live in obedience to the direction of the Holy Spirit, they give witness in word, deed, and sign to the presence and rule of Christ. The making of disciples occurs only when people are living together in communities. Therefore, central to the missionary enterprise is the planting and nurturing of local churches or communities of faith. As Van Engen states, "As the missionary people of God, local congregations are branch offices of the kingdom, the principal instrument, anticipatory sign, and primary locus of the coming kingdom."[17]

---

[16] William J. Seymour, *The Apostolic Faith* (Los Angeles), II:13, 3.

[17] Charles E. Van Engen, *God's Missionary People: Rethinking the Purpose of the Local Church* (Grand Rapids, MI: Baker Book House, 1991), 101.

These communities of faith live in hope and expectation of the return of Christ when the Lord will manifest the rule or kingdom of God in its fullness. His return remains the ultimate answer to this world's pain, division, and injustice—when all the powers of this world will be subject to him, and he will reign for all eternity (Lk 1:33; 1 Cor 15:23–25). "The kingdom of the world has become the kingdom of our Lord and of his Messiah, and he will reign for ever and ever" (Rev 11:15). L. Grant McClung asserts,

> At the heart of early Pentecostals' missiology was their personal experience with the Holy Spirit found around an altar of prayer with fellow seekers. This profound experience was integrated with an eschatological urgency and a passion for souls. Apparently, their earliest understanding of the experience that came to be known as the "Baptism in the Holy Spirit" was that it produced a missiological fervor and ministry, and it provided the empowerment for the same.[18]

Songs of Pentecost

Hymnody constitutes an important aspect of the Pentecostal missional narrative. Gary B. McGee affirms, "The songs of the Pentecostal Movement early in the [twentieth] century resonate with the fervor of evangelizing the world through the power of the Holy Spirit."[19] Songs such as "The Latter Rain" express the belief that Pentecost had come in fulfillment of biblical prophecy like rain "on parched ground, till it reaches all the earth around."[20] The hymn "Preach the Word," written by Aimee Semple McPherson (foundress of the International Church of the Foursquare Gospel) declared, "Preach the Foursquare Gospel with a certain sound.... Preach

---

[18] L. Grant McClung, "'Try to Get People Saved': Revisiting the Paradigm of an Urgent Pentecostal Missiology," in *The Globalization of Pentecostalism: A Religion Made to Travel*, ed. Murray W. Dempster, Byron D. Klaus, and Douglas Petersen (Irvine, CA: Regnum Books International, 1999), 36.

[19] Gary B. McGee, "Pentecostal Missionaries in Situations of Conflict and Violence, Part 1," in *Assemblies of God Heritage* 12, no. 2 (1992): 20.

[20] Ibid.

the word, Preach the word, till the nations all have heard."[21] Pentecostalism "sparked a vigorous new missionary diaspora beginning in 1906."[22] However, by midcentury "the romanticized missionary songs of the earlier generation gave place to more restrained lyrics of commitment to Christ, and reflections on the unreached millions who had not yet heard the gospel message."[23] In 1940, Melvin L. Hodges wrote the following words to a Central American tune: "Harvest is passing, night draweth nigh, millions are dying, oh, here their cry! Then haste, my brother, their souls to save, Christ to redeem them, his life-blood gave."[24] McGee confirms, "Fervent concern to evangelize before the closure of human history, motivated by love for Christ and obedience to the great commission, still remains at the heart of the movement."[25]

Pentecostal Experience

Pentecostals came to understand the Pentecostal experience as an endowment of power for witness or service and for an overcoming life: in other words, the necessity for Christians to live a holy life of total surrender to the Lordship of Christ. As individuals experience a direct encounter with the Spirit of Jesus who is the "same yesterday, today, and forever," they perceive themselves as participating in the advent of the "latter rain" and eschatological fulfillment. This encounter is both a crisis moment and a process, both individual and communal, demanding total surrender and resulting in a holy life of witness with a passion for the lost both near and far. The subjectivity of the experience maintains a balance of reverence and adherence to the written word. A significant aspect of the experience of Pentecost was people perceiving it as a return to the faith and experience of the New Testament. Believers discovered the "how to" of the missionary enterprise in the Bible, in the patterns found in the New Testament, especially the Book of Acts.

---

[21] Ibid.
[22] Ibid.
[23] Gary B. McGee, "Pentecostal Missionaries in Situations of Conflict and Violence, Part 2," in *Assemblies of God Heritage* 12, no. 3 (1992): 25.
[24] Ibid.
[25] Ibid.

For Pentecostals, they must not only believe the Bible but also experience the Scripture through the work of the Holy Spirit. This unique Pentecostal hermeneutic affirms, "The Holy Spirit enables a believer to translate creed into conduct, faith into practice, and doctrine into daily living," and the biblical text into personal experience and empowerment.[26] This Pentecostal hermeneutic also functions as a missiological hermeneutic. John V. York states,

> Since God has always had a mission, the Bible should be read missiologically. That is, all of Scripture should be read with a view toward its development of the theme of God's promise to bless the nations through the promised seed. It is as Christian believers recognize God's mission that they may purpose to participate in fulfilling that mission.[27]

A. B. Simpson's Missiology

The following five elements of the missiology championed by A. B. Simpson shaped Pentecostal missions: (1) the formation of missionary societies for the mobilization of the church to foreign missions, which allowed a significant role to laity, both men and women; (2) the organization of Bible institutes for the training of missionaries and ministers; (3) Simpson's theology of the "fourfold" gospel: salvation, sanctification, healing, and the second coming of Christ;[28] (4) Simpson's adherence to the missiology of the indigenous church with the purpose of planting churches in foreign lands after the New Testament pattern, which were self-supporting,

---

[26] Douglas Petersen, *Not by Might nor By Power: A Pentecostal Theology of Social Concern in Latin America* (Oxford: Regnum Books International, 1996), 81, 227.

[27] John V. York, *Missions in the Age of the Spirit* (Springfield, MO: Logion Press, 2000), 20.

[28] Simpson's view of sanctification included the perspective that the baptism in the Holy Spirit was a separate experience from regeneration to empower the believer for witness. He understood the second coming of Christ as premillennial, believing that Christ would not return until the church reached all nations, according to Matthew 24:14.

self-governing, and self-propagating; and (5) the development of missions conventions to raise missions awareness in the churches, and to mobilize believers to prayer and financial support of missionaries and missionary endeavors.[29]

Indigenous Church Principles

The indigenous church proponents never intended the three-self formula[30] to create a "self"-ish church, as critics contend. Rather, it marked the fact that churches, properly planted on the mission field, should be independent of the missions that planted them, and of the missions stations that sought to control and fashion them in the image of the mission culture.[31] The principles of the indigenous church are

> An indigenous church is a community of believers birthed in a specific context who are Spirit-driven (Spirit-led and Spirit-empowered) to accomplish God's purposes for and through that community. Like the various churches described in the New Testament, particularly in Acts, these local and national communities of faith are to be Spirit-governed, Spirit-supported, and Spirit-propagated. God, by his Spirit, calls and equips local leaders to disciple and mobilize believers in the faith, and guides them in discerning and fulfilling the will of God for their community. As a responsible community, the indigenous church turns to the unlimited resources of the Spirit for its sustenance so as not to depend on the missionary institutions, ministries, or agencies. As a community of faith, indigenous

---

[29] Gary B. McGee, *This Gospel Shall Be Preached: A History and Theology of the Assemblies of God Foreign Missions to 1959*, vol. 1 (Springfield, MO: Gospel Publishing House, 1986), 57–67.

[30] A missiological strategy for establishing indigenous churches, containing the principles of self-governance, self-support, and self-propagation.

[31] DeLonn L. Rance, "Fulfilling the Apostolic Mandate in Apostolic Power: Seeking a Spirit-Driven Missiology and Praxis," presented as the 2008–2009 J. Philip Hogan Professor of World Missions inaugural address on October 15, 2008, at the Assemblies of God Theological Seminary, Springfield, MO.

church members are impassioned and empowered by the Spirit to reach their neighbors, their nation, and their world with the gospel.[32]

From Pentecostal missionary narratives, the following core values of a Spirit-driven missiology emerge: (1) the Lord fulfills mission through his church by the direction and power of the Holy Spirit (Spirit-priesthood and Spirit-prophethood of all believers); (2) all members of the church are responsible for the apostolic mandate to reach all peoples with the good news of the kingdom (Spirit-propagated); (3) leadership equips the church by creating space for a supernatural encounter that holds to the standard of the word in contextually appropriate ways (Spirit-governed); (4) to be effective in missional praxis, the church must paradoxically exert great effort while relying fully on the power of the Spirit (Spirit-supported); and (5) reliance on the Spirit requires a commitment to prayer (Spirit-directed).[33]

God invites the apostolic people to collaborate with God in making Christ known among the nations. Prayer drives that divine/human cooperation with God. Prayer is Jesus's answer to the challenge of the harvest (Mt 9:37–38). Prayer releases the glory of Christ among the nations.

OVERVIEW OF THE BOOK

The authors have organized *Christ among the Nations* around the fourfold themes of the full gospel. Part I addresses Christ Our Savior (Redeemer); Part II, Christ Our Empowerer (Baptizer/Sanctifier); Part III, Christ Our Healer; and Part IV, Christ Our Hope (the soon-coming King). Each section includes an introductory chapter to identify key motifs, followed by chapters that address the Christological theme through biblical, historical, and contemporary narratives. These stories allow the reader to enter the narrative to hear God's voice. Each narrative chapter

---

[32] Ibid.
[33] Ibid.

concludes with reflection questions to stimulate interaction with the stories. No section is comprehensive or exhaustive, but rather is designed to open hearts and minds to God's plan as revealed in Scripture, as lived out in history, and as experienced in contemporary contexts.

CONCLUSION

This introduction described the good news of Christ among the nations and the transformative power of the "full gospel," addressed the critical role of narrative in Pentecostal missiology and practice, and highlighted critical components of Pentecostal missiology that emerge in Pentecostal missions. My prayer in writing this introduction is that it will create space in the heart, mind, and will of the reader, allowing the missionary Spirit of the Trinity to impassion, educate, and empower. Thus, this will let the reader participate as a member of God's missionary/apostolic people in missions, and discover the ways in which his or her stories find meaning and purpose in God's story. As God's people, let us continue telling the full gospel story of Jesus Christ our Savior, Empowerer, Healer, and Hope.

As you read the biblical, historical, and contemporary stories of mission, enter God's emboldening presence prayerfully, and intentionally listen for and yield to the promptings of the Spirit. Then step out in faith and obey in the power of the Spirit. When the missionary people of God live in obedience to the rule of Christ both individually and corporately, they communicate the full gospel of Jesus Christ to individuals and nations, and heaven swells with worshippers—"persons from every tribe and language and people and nation"—glorifying God (Rev 5:9).

PART I

CHRIST OUR SAVIOR

1

Centrality of the Cross: God's Historic Plan of Salvation in Lukan Perspective

Robert L. Gallagher

In this introduction to Part I, I will explore Luke's unique way of declaring God's great truth of salvation for humankind in the Gospel of Luke and the Book of Acts. Furthermore, at the end of the chapter I will provide an overview of Part I that deals with Christ our Savior in the form of biblical, historical, and contemporary narratives.

In the hermeneutical journey, I will seek to contribute toward a mission theology in two issues that have relevance in my context and the global arena. First, even though the Roman and Jewish leaders nailed Jesus to a cross and killed him, it was according to God's predetermined plan and foreknowledge. The early church witnessed God's predestined hand and purpose, and through the death and resurrection of the Christ, God manifested God's great purpose in the world.

Second, it was Luke's conviction that God implanted the divine plan of salvation within human history. The other Synoptic

Gospels do not have this concept that what God did through the Messiah was a part of a larger historic backdrop. Hence, scattered throughout Luke-Acts are historic references of both empire and local significance.

My hope is that in this study of Lukan theology, the Savior's connection with the nations will assist God's people. God desires all nations to know God's will, which came about through sending Jesus the Son of God, and continues to establish itself through the church today. The church needs the Spirit's insights concerning the Lord's salvation as it works out the implications of faith and practice in mission for a pluralistic and multicultural world.[1]

NOT MY WILL, BUT THINE BE DONE[2]

The cross of Jesus did not surprise God. Jesus declared, "The Son of Man will go [to die] as it has been decreed" (Lk 22:22). At the foothills of the Mount of Olives he prayed, "Father, if you are willing, take this cup from me; yet not my will, but yours be done" (Lk 22:42). Peter recognized this truth and declared to the audience at Pentecost that even though they nailed Jesus to a cross and killed him, it was according to "God's set purpose and foreknowledge" (Acts 2:23). Again, he says in his second sermon, "But this is how God fulfilled what he had foretold through all the prophets, saying that his Messiah would suffer" (Acts 3:18).[3]

The early church witnessed God's predestined hand and purpose that caused Herod, Pontius Pilate along with the Gentiles,

---

[1] For further understanding of Christ's salvation in the Gospel of Luke, see Robert L. Gallagher, "Good News for All People: Engaging Luke's Narrative Soteriology of the Nations," in *Contemporary Mission Theology: Engaging the Nations*, ed. Robert L. Gallagher and Paul Hertig, American Society of Missiology Series, no. 53 (Maryknoll, NY: Orbis Books, 2017), 193–202; and Robert L. Gallagher, "Salvation: Narrow Way but Broad Mission: A Response to Christopher J. H. Wright's *Salvation Belongs to Our God*," *Evangelical Interfaith Dialogue* 1, no. 4 (2010): 10–11.

[2] Lk 22:42.

[3] See Hans Conzelmann, *The Theology of St. Luke* (New York: Harper & Row), 90–91.

and the people of Israel to gather against God's holy Servant Jesus. "They did what your power and will had decided beforehand should happen" (Acts 4:28; see Ps 2:1–2). Unbeknown to these groups, God accomplished his purposes despite their defiance toward the Messiah. Luke underscores that God's plan was inevitable, no matter how powerful the opposition of human agencies. Gamaliel recognized this fact before the Sanhedrin Council, asserting that human plans can be overthrown, yet the plans of God can never be thwarted (Acts 5:38–39). The purpose of God reached its culmination at the death of Jesus, although it had operated throughout the First Testament (Acts 13:22), and continued to do so in the early church (Acts 20:27), especially via the apostle Paul (Acts 21:14; 22:14).

Use of the Verb Dei

Luke's point is that through the death and resurrection of the Christ, God manifested God's great purpose in the world. God desires all nations to know God's will, which came about through sending the Son, and continues to establish itself through the church. To reinforce this idea of God's will in the world, Luke uses the verb *dei*, which is translated as the English word "must" (or "ought" or "should") over twenty times in both his gospel and the Book of Acts, compared to Matthew (four times), Mark (seven times), and John (ten times). The meaning of *dei* here is a "binding necessity," which the Gentile writer employs to reinforce that God's plan of sending Jesus was essential for God's purpose. It was God's will declared.

Luke's gospel uses *dei* to describe Jesus's ministry in doing God's will (Lk 2:49). Jesus says, "I must (*dei*) proclaim the good news of the kingdom of God to the other towns also, because that is why I was sent" (Lk 4:43). In Luke's account, however, the most frequent binding necessity of God was for God's Son to suffer and die (Lk 9:22; 17:25; 22:7, 37; 24:7, 26, 44). In the synagogue at Thessalonica, Paul explained, "The Christ had to (*dei*) suffer and rise from the dead. This Jesus I am proclaiming to you is the Christ" (Acts 17:3). The death of Jesus was central to God's plan of salvation, and Luke emphasizes the fulfillment of Scripture in his death (e.g., Lk 4:21; 18:31–33; 21:22; 22:37; Acts 3:18; 13:27, 29; 26:22–23).

Salvation toward the Parousia

This intention was foretold repeatedly throughout the Hebrew Scriptures (Acts 1:16; cf. Lk 24:44–47), and did not stop with Christ's ascension. God's design of salvation for the world progresses toward the *Parousia*. Peter declared that God would send Jesus back to earth if the Jewish people would repent, and return to him to wipe away their sins, and subsequently receive the presence of the Lord. This Jesus is none other than "the Christ [or Anointed One; i.e., Messiah] who has been appointed for you [Jewish people]—even Jesus. Heaven must (*dei*) receive him until the time comes for God to restore everything, as he promised long ago through his holy prophets" (Acts 3:20–21). The time between the ascension and the messianic second coming is also in the divine necessity of God, whereby people might receive his salvation through Jesus Christ the Nazarene. As Peter announced before the Jewish Council, "Salvation is found in no one else, for there is no other name under heaven given to mankind by which we must (*dei*) be saved" (Acts 4:12). In particular, Luke sees Paul as an anointed messenger of God's way of salvation continuing beyond Christ's ascension (see Acts 9:6, 16; 14:22; 19:21; 22:14; 23:11; 26:16; 27:24).

Luke has a unique way of telling about God's absolute truth of salvation for undeserving humanity. Unlike the other Evangelists, he does this by using his second volume, the Book of Acts, to share the events after the ascension to show that God's plan is well defined. The path of God's salvation lies in following the risen Lord Jesus. We should not miss Luke's opinion that there is no other way of salvation. It has already come through Jesus. The words of Paul to the Philippian jailer confirm this route. He asked Paul and Silas, "'Sirs, what must (*dei*) I do to be saved?' They replied, 'Believe in the Lord Jesus, and you will be saved—you and your household'" (Acts 16:30–31).

Furthermore, Luke sees a necessary obligation within God's plan for Christians to obey. Even when standing before antagonistic leaders, Jesus promised that his followers would be given Spirit-inspired words that "you should (*dei*) say" (Lk 12:12; cf. Acts 5:32). It is God's purpose to give words to God's people to proclaim "the full message of this new life" (Acts 5:20). Peter and the apostles knew of this divine necessity as they boldly answered the high priest's accusation of insubordination, "We must (*dei*) obey God rather than men" (Acts 5:29; cf. 4:8f.). They were witnesses of the Messiah's death, resurrection, ascension, and dispensing of salvation, having received the Holy Spirit through obedience (see Acts 5:30–32).

NOW IT CAME ABOUT IN THOSE DAYS[4]

In Acts 5:31 when Peter professed that Jesus was the "Savior that he might give repentance and forgiveness of sins to Israel," it was Luke's conviction that God implanted the divine plan of salvation within human history. Scholars use the German term *heilsgeschichte* to describe this phenomenon in Luke-Acts, often translated as "redemptive history" or the "history of salvation." As noted earlier, the other Evangelists do not have this concept that what God did through the Messiah was a part of a greater historic canvas. The gospel writers only mention secular history when it directly involves the events of Christ such as his trial before Caiaphas (the high priest) and the Sanhedrin Council (Mt 26:57f.; Mk 14:53f.; Jn 18:12f.).

Only Luke draws attention to both Roman and Palestinian history as the background to the intention of God in Christ Jesus. He moves from census decrees sent forth by Caesar Augustus and the subsequent records taken by Quirinius, governor of Syria (Lk 2:1–2) to road trips in Palestine. For instance, Mary and "Joseph also went up from the town of Nazareth in Galilee [to register for the census] to Judea, to Bethlehem the town of David, because he belonged to the house and line of David" (Lk 2:4–5). Our gospel

---

[4] Lk 2:1.

writer sets the messianic birth narrative firmly in the context of Roman secular history. In Luke 3:1–2, the author again thrusts his theological purpose securely into human history, stressing that even the most powerful figures are significant only because of God's plan through Jesus. This passage highlights Luke's breadth of historic understanding from imperial Rome (Tiberius Caesar) to political Jerusalem (Pontius Pilate, Herod, Philip, and Lysanias), including Jewish religious leaders (Annas and Caiaphas).

Secular History of Acts

This same embedding of God's work into secular history via Jesus the Messiah continues into the Book of Acts. The first persecution of the people of the Way[5] occurred under the auspices of the Sadducees, and Luke names the high priests implicated: Annas, Caiaphas, John, and Alexander (4:6). During the reign of Emperor Claudius, Luke mentions a great famine (11:28), and the expulsion of the Jewish people from Rome (18:2). The Gentile author notes the names of Roman proconsuls such as Sergius Paulus of Cyprus, "an intelligent man" (Lk 13:7, 8, 12), and Gallio of Achaia (Lk 18:12); Asiarchs, political officials of the province of Asia who were friends of Paul (Lk 19:31); and Roman governors such as Felix (Lk 23:24) and Porcius Festus (Lk 24:27) with King Agrippa and Bernice (Lk 25:13). In addition, Luke speaks of Roman centurions, for example, Cornelius of the Italian cohort or battalion (10:1), and Julius of the Augustan cohort (27:1), together with Claudius Lysias, the Roman commander in Jerusalem (23:26).

Peppered throughout Acts are historic references of both imperial and local significance, from the Roman officials of the paragraph above to church leaders and antagonizers. Luke records the names of the Hellenistic servers of Acts 6:5 (Stephen, Philip, Prochorus, Nicanor, Timon, Parmenas, and Nicolas); the ministry team in Antioch of Syria: Barnabas, Simeon, Lucius, Manaen, and Saul (13:1); and Paul's traveling companions: Timothy and Erastus (19:22), Gaius and Aristarchus (19:29), and Sopater, Aristarchus, Secundus, Gaius, Timothy, Tychicus, and Trophimus (20:4). More-

---

[5] See Acts 9:2; 16:17; 18:25–26; 19:9, 23; 22:4; 24:14, 22.

over, together with the early church leadership, Luke cites the opposition of the silversmith Demetrius who instigated the Ephesian riot (19:24, 38), and Ananias, the high priest, with Tertullus the lawyer (23:2; 24:1), who before Felix, accused Paul of causing a riot in Jerusalem. God's salvation story in Luke-Acts is set firmly in the real history of everyday life and people.

Summary of the Argument

For Luke, the central pivot of human history is the death and resurrection of the Lord Jesus. There was history before and after Jesus, yet the sovereign plan of God's salvation hinges on the central figure of Christ: his life set in secular history, the cross, and subsequent ascension to the Father (Lk 9:51). Leon L. Morris states, "History is the stage on which God works out his salvation plan, and for Luke, Jesus is right at the center."[6] For Luke, Christ empowers the new era of salvation through the Holy Spirit by continuing his ministry in the early church and in subsequent generations through the present day.

OVERVIEW OF CHRIST OUR SAVIOR

After the introduction to Part I, Chapter 2 examines a biblical narrative in the Gospel of Luke that deals with the author's concept of salvation through *sōzō*, the Greek root of the term. Chapter 3 is a reflection on the historical account of Bartholomäus Ziegenbalg, a German Pietist missionary bringing Christ our Savior to India in the early eighteenth century. The last chapter considers a contemporary salvation story set in the Oro region of Papua New Guinea.

Love that Saves a Harlot

The Lukan study not only reinforces the importance of Christ as the source of God's salvation but also provides an opportunity to consider the Lord's all-inclusive provision of deliverance from

---

[6] Leon L. Morris, *New Testament Theology* (Grand Rapids, MI: Zondervan, 1986), 177.

sickness and sin through Jesus Messiah.[7] Luke's gospel records nineteen occasions where the author uses the word *sōzō* (meaning safe, save, deliver, or protect).[8] The focus of the study, however, will consider only one such episode that involves the idea of *sōzō*. The following is a brief description of the story found in Luke 7.

Luke 7:36–50 records the narrative of Jesus meeting a woman in the town of Capernaum who was a prostitute. At a luncheon organized by Simon the Pharisee, the host rejects Jesus as a prophet for allowing the woman to touch him. Kissing Jesus's feet, the party-crasher anoints them with her tears and an expensive perfume, mopping up her shame with her hair. Jesus then says to the woman, "Your faith has saved (*sōzō*) you; go in peace" (Lk 7:50). During the all-male exclusive luncheon, Jesus recognizes faith through the woman's actions, and accordingly she receives salvation or deliverance of her many sins, and the peace of God.

Ziegenbalg and the Salvation of Souls

Ziegenbalg developed a missional strategy of education, translation, mutual respect, discipleship, and indigenous leadership that was revolutionary for his time. His work in translation, collection of indigenous religious writings, and correspondence with fellow missionaries sent shockwaves through and beyond the European courts of ecclesiastical and political power.

The consequences of his missionary ventures not only provide a valuable insight into the Pietist missions' movement, but his mission strategy also offered an example and source of inspiration for early Western Protestant missions. Chapter 3 is the salvation

---

[7] This essay will not observe the Lukan narrative of Jesus healing the demoniac Legion (8:36), the woman hemorrhaging for twelve years (8:48), Jairus's dead daughter (8:50), the ten lepers (17:19), and a blind beggar (18:42) because of its limited scope. In a number of these instances, the Lord recognizes that the person's faith had healed [*sōzō*] them, and made them whole.

[8] The Greek word, *sōzō* ("salvation"), occurs thirty-two times in Luke-Acts (Lk 6:9; 7:50; 8:12, 36, 48, 50; 9:24 [twice], 56; 13:23; 17:19 ["made well"], 33; 18:26; 42; 19:10; 23:35 [2x], 37; 39; and Acts 2:21, 40, 47; 4:9 ["made well"], 12; 11:14; 14:9 ["made well"]; 15:1, 11; 16:30, 31; 27:20, 31).

account of the first Protestant missionary to India complete with unexpected twists, ironic turns, and surprising pathways. It is a story that still models the way for holistic missions today.

Salvation's Call in Papua New Guinea

Bruce and Joan Cartwright, Australian missionaries with the CRC Churches International, left the comforts of Adelaide, South Australia, in the 1970s to bring Christ to the Melanesian people in Papua New Guinea (PNG). It was during a gospel outreach among university students in the PNG capital of Port Moresby that the Cartwrights experienced a powerful manifestation of God whereby many attendees received Christ as their Savior and Empowerer in the Holy Spirit.

After this occurrence, Vele Wari invited the Australians to his northern village where there occurred a number of outstanding miracles of God's salvation. This phenomenon resulted in the spread of the gospel to surrounding animistic villages that subsequently changed their allegiance over to Jesus Christ. Eventually, the regional elders declared their desire that the entire people group should receive water baptism since their communities were now following Jesus. Hence, the Cartwrights and Wari were in a quandary. What should they do? In this story, the dilemma before them was the gospel validity of mass salvations.

2

Holy Tears of a Weeping Harlot: Love that Saves

Robert L. Gallagher

One of the Pharisees in the town of Capernaum repeatedly invited Jesus to eat with him, begging him to come to his home. Jesus finally went into the Pharisee's house, and, taking his place, reclined at the table. Now there was an immoral woman in that village who lived a notorious life.[1]

A NOTORIOUS LIFE

The woman was the town harlot. Everyone knew that fact, and the pious residents shunned her. My Capernaum was a comfortable and restful small town. She brought shame to our citizens. Townsfolk held her in low esteem. When she walked along the street, people moved to the other side of the road or turned their back on her when she passed by. At other times, some of the more opinionated inhabitants hurled obscenities at her such as "whore,"

---

[1] In this chapter, I imaginatively expand the biblical pericope of Luke 7:36–50; the italicized sections signify my paraphrased translation.

"contemptuous dog," "disgraceful waste," "devilish evil," "infidel," and "playing the Corinthian." No decent person wanted to associate with her. It was embarrassing to have her in our community. Yet she was still selling her body for the sexual gratification of men lurking in the shadows of the night who were willing to pay the price. She was no sacred prostitute,[2] however. She was merely a common public prostitute, playing the harlot and opportunist; dripping with *pornē* in the urban center; stealing husbands from wives by shattering the exclusive covenant relationship; exploiting infidelity with fiancés and their betrothed; and seducing sons and brothers—who were looking to her for sustenance and comfort—into pits of desolation. Some say that she provided a community service by offering a deterrent to adultery. Although people stigmatized her, our Jewish town tolerated her continued presence. In our province, the inhabitants knew her as the patron of prostitutes: Mary of Capernaum. She was not outlawed but regulated: one who wore distinctive clothing, registered with the local magistrate, and paid Roman taxes.

Sleeping with the Enemy

What was even more intolerable to our Jewish community than her paying taxes to the Roman enemy, via an avenue of sin, was her fraternizing with the conquerors of our land. She slept with the enemy. This notorious woman sold her body for pagans' sexual pleasure. There was minimal prostitution in our Jewish towns before the invasion of these pagans. The district capital of Tiberias was the center of such disgrace, with its mixture of ethnic groups and demoralizing societal standards.

Situated on the northern political frontier of Palestine, Capernaum is important for the strategic security of the empire. We are located on the *Via Maris*, the leading international trade route from Syria and Damascus that runs south along the coast to Egypt. The town serves as a trading hub for transnational dealers, as well as a center of buying and selling produce from nearby villages.

---

[2] That is, a prostitute connected to temple prostitution, which was acceptable by non-Jewish standards.

Thus, Herod Antipas, tetrarch of Galilee, stationed a Roman *auxilia* in our little town: a royal army composed of provincial thugs from Sebaste and Caesarea Maritima, mostly ethnic Syrians who speak our local language. At full strength there are eighty soldiers trained to ruthlessly eliminate banditry and rebellion, as well as collect taxes, while protecting tax collectors and provincial administrators. It is understandable that a place of whoredom would be expedient to these hooligans commissioned hundreds of miles from their women with military authority and plenty of money. This is the business area where the town's notorious harlot lived and worked.

Abandonment in Poverty

There was some talk about this woman's husband abandoning her. You understand that I am not one to tell pernicious tales. I am only basing my judgment on what others have told me. He was an extremely unpleasant man. Nobody liked him in the township. He created a great deal of ill will among the shopkeepers with his miserly and petty ways. He was such a worthless man that no one could speak to him. Her family betrothed the virgin to the brute when she had lived barely thirteen years. He was so much older than she was, and ugly. During one market day, right in the center of our town before a crowd of buyers and traders, he suddenly turned and yelled at the poor girl three times, shouting at the top of his voice, "I divorce you!" The marriage was over. That was all the fool had to do to get rid of her, and it was legal. The villagers felt sorry for the child, but they could not go against the customs of our people. Her parents had already died, and she had no siblings or relatives to support her. She was homeless, without any financial security. What could she do to get money, even just for food?

When I next heard about her situation, she was living in the basement of our local inn working as a barmaid and server. At the beginning, I do not think she realized that the inn doubled as a brothel. Because of her poverty, the proprietor treated her as a slave, forcing her to provide him income for her room and food by exploiting her body. The innkeeper was her master. For a small fee, those staying upstairs in the hostel could send for the downstairs maid. It must have been especially difficult for her to face those first few slobbering and drunken men bellowing that she come to their room upstairs and entertain them.

The rumors soon spread among the village hangouts that the teenager was desperate and available, causing some of the uncouth of our town to slink to the hotel, have a drink, and pay their respects. It seemed that she quickly got into the swill of things. In fact, the girl became so popular with her clientele that she was able to steal away some money and eventually break away from the clutches of the inn. The owner was furious, and tried to discredit her before the judicial authorities. Higher echelons, however, had already appreciated her unique expertise, and the judge promptly dismissed the case.

By selling her licentious product, it took only a short time for her to accumulate a small fortune. She was always such an attractive little girl, with youth and sexual prowess as her strengths. The once grassy paths to her harlotry scuffed to dirt by the increasing flow of unscrupulous Gentiles. Her decision to play immoral tunes for venal men sounded loud in her soul, suppressing the rumbles of spiritual hunger in her belly. How else could she afford the expensive clothes and perfumes, and the beautiful house on the edge of town hidden from wandering tongues? Anyhow, enough of that tale since I am not a busybody who talks about other people's anecdotes. Let me get back to the real story.

SHAMELESS ENTRY

News rippled quickly through the streets that Jesus was in town. Somehow, the shameless woman learned that he was in Simon the Pharisee's house, reclining and eating as his guest.

Perhaps she leaned into the ubiquitous gossip of the streets. Certainly, there were plenty of willing mouths to tell the story. What made her even want to go and see the renowned rabbi? What was going through her mind that she was willing to endure more embarrassment by sneaking into the male-exclusive luncheon of the rich and famous? Was it something she had heard about Jesus from other despised women of the night? Business had certainly decreased since the rabbi had come to town. Perhaps one of her clients had changed his ways because of the man from Nazareth. Or was the motivation an act of compassion that she saw Jesus do, which inspired her that day to scuttle though the back lanes to appear before the Pharisee's stately mansion? She may have heard about some of his miracles: a fisherman's mother-in-law healed of a fever, or the healing words of Jesus at Cana— "Your son lives," given to the dying son of one of Herod Antipas's royal officials—declared some seventeen miles from Capernaum on the road to Tiberias. Following the miracle, the father and his whole household at Capernaum believed.

In the end, what finally convinced the woman to believe in Jesus, the messianic hope, was what she saw one evening at sunset after a Capernaum Shabbat. She was a part of a huge crowd of people from all over the town who had gathered outside a fisherman's hovel to listen and watch. The town's people had brought to Jesus the sick and demon possessed, and he healed them of many kinds of diseases and expelled demons from them. He had an amazing authority and power, unlike any other rabbi. What the woman saw that evening stunned her toward a holy realization. Jesus of Nazareth was like no other man she had ever known.

Invading the Party

She came by herself and stealthily invaded the party. Surely, none of the guests had invited her to come. She snuck past the servants in the courtyard, carrying a special sealed alabaster jar of perfume—a flask of fragrant myrrh, which was a very expensive perfume.

The cost of the ointment was equivalent to a full year's wage for a farm laborer. Everyone in the closed community would know how she got the money to pay for such a prized ointment reserved for royalty. The infamous woman knew what she was doing, however. You do not creep through the streets of our town with a flask of extremely expensive perfume under your gown without knowing what you are going to do with it. This is especially so when you arrive at a stranger's home (or was he a stranger?).

When she left her home, she knew where she was heading, and what she was going to do when she arrived. Before that day, I wonder if she had visited the Pharisee's house. They are such hypocrites! They love to spout pious platitudes while performing evil deeds with self-righteous promotion. She was determined to pour out her illicit savings over the sacred Jesus—to waste her fortune on this man. Why would she do such an action? Why such unadulterated adoration? What was her motivation? Was it adoration or allurement? What was the message in her method of splashing forth the ointment? Was it a message to the whole town, the houseguests, Simon the Pharisee, or only to the one whom she revered? What was she thinking in this desperate act?

At first, the guests at the gathering did not see her. There was a lot of bustle and noise as the servants weaved about the room delivering platters of delicious morsels to tempt the appetite of the special guests. It was as if she suddenly appeared before their eyes like a cool mist.

She stood behind the Teacher suspended in time; looking down at his feet, weeping. She placed herself at the back of him, near his feet, and continued weeping; wetting his feet with her tears, bathing, and weeping.

Why was she crying? Was this tragic figure grieving over dashed expectations that could never be? Perhaps she was sorrowful of hopeful dreams ruined. Maybe her emotions overcame her as impurity saw purity, infidelity faced fidelity, sin confronted sinlessness, humanity witnessed the divine. Living the temporal lie, she stood center-stage before eternal truth, her lewd life unfolding like dirty linen before the table of the holy Son of God.

There were rumors. You know how people talk in small towns such as Capernaum. We had just over a thousand people living in our community before the Romans came. The weeping harlot's house was away from the main arena of urban activity, but it was close to the Roman army encampment, a Sabbath day's journey away. There were occasional whispers telling of muffled noises late at night behind the house of ill repute. What I am about to divulge I received from some of the women twisted within this pagan tragedy. With guilt and shame, I relate this dark shadow of Gentile sin that fell upon our Jewish purity.

The Roman world considers a child not a proper human being until they are two years old. Because of this belief, children are not ready for burial at such a young age. If an infant dies and is not right for interment, then the Romans do not conduct a burial in a cemetery, but hide the little body in a garden or under the floor of a house.[3] The harlot's brothel had a small garden in the back. If a prostitute became pregnant, upon birth after forty weeks of gestation, the whorehouse would deliberately kill the child because of the dishonoring burden and the disgrace of treachery. They would wrap the little bundle and dispose of the infant surreptitiously after dark in an unmarked grave within the small garden area. Our notorious woman had instigated and conducted scores of such burials.

Questioning Looks

At the Pharisee's dinner, men turned to each other with furrowed brows. Why were her tears falling so heavily on the rabbi's dust-encrusted feet? She lifted her head and saw every eye upon her tears. Conscious of their disdainful gaze, she continued in gentle loving strokes to wipe away her shame.

She wiped his feet with her hair, lovingly kissing them, and breaking the vial, poured forth pure myrrh over them, anointing them with the ointment for a future sadness yet to be unveiled.

The house filled with the sweet fragrance of the perfume, engulfing the languid stench of bodies pressed together in the scorching heat of summer sun. She washed his feet with the drops of her eyes. With her smooth hair, she made them dry. She cleansed her soul. Her lips, for once in holy affection, kissed the soiled flesh and earth. Standing behind him raining tears on his feet, she never saw his eyes. Letting down her hair, she wiped his toes with the hairs of her head. So many village men, so many foreign soldiers, had seen her hair before but in a lewd scene of seduction.

---

[3] In 1912, the British archaeologist Alfred Cocks discovered ninety-seven infant bones/burials at Yewden Roman villa near Hambleden in Buckinghamshire (he published the report in 1921). Dr. Simon Mays of Heritage England offers the best explanation as infanticide at forty weeks gestation as a result of a brothel near a Roman army encampment.

The audience was in shock. It is a disgrace! What shame! Such dishonor to the village name! Wicked infamy against our holy God that such a woman should reveal her sacred honor before all. And, in such humiliation and indignity. Why has she not stopped crying? Why is she still kissing away the dirt and drying his feet—over and over, and over again? Why carry on so?

Feelings of Devastation

The Pharisee who had invited Jesus felt devastated when he saw this degradation. It was an embarrassment in his home before all his important family and friends. The entire town would know about this fiasco within the hour. In a day, the surrounding region would be laughing about the debacle. For years to come, village folk would be smirking and clowning about the day the whore became the entertainment of the Pharisee's religious party. Shame on you, woman of harlotry who invaded the sacred place! Shame on you, religious leader who allowed such a wicked turn of events!

That afternoon, she tainted Simon and his family, one tear at a time. The Pharisee could count the number of tears that brought forth the dishonor. The stench of his soiled reputation hung above the banquet hall like foul air in the market place, the stain on his civic status seeping through his religious piety.

What a Waste!

While I am thinking about this distressing situation, I am also questioning the huge monetary waste of such an expensive ointment. Why this misuse of a precious commodity? The woman is lavishly squandering the perfume! What is the purpose? If we sold it at the markets, we could get a high price, at least equal to a worker's yearly income. How many hungry children could we feed with such a sum of money? How many village poor could benefit from the sale of the alabaster flask? This is another blatant example of the poor getting poorer and the rich getting richer. This wealthy harlot is wasting God's precious resources. Jesus's followers could have sold the perfume, and used the return for a godly cause, all for the sake of the Lord's kingdom. What a waste!

IF ONLY HE KNEW

With these thoughts churning in the host's head as he saw what was happening, he concluded to himself, "If this man were a prophet, he would know who is touching him, and what kind of immoral woman she is—that she is a sinner. This impure woman who is falling all over him is putting her polluted hands on him who is supposedly a chaste prophet of our pure God."

Jesus turned and looked at the member of the Jewish sect. "Simon, I have something to tell you. Are you listening to me in trust, or obeying the fears and prejudices in your head?"

"Oh?" Simon responded. "Really? To me? Then go ahead. Tell me, teacher. Say on. I am listening to you." The room filled with silence.

A Story in Silence

"Two people owed money to a certain moneylender; a creditor. The debt to the banker for one person was $5,000 (eighteen months of salary), and for the other debtor it was only $50 (six weeks of salary). Neither of the debtors had any money to pay him back. They were broke. Yet he was so kind to them that he graciously forgave the debts of both of them. He released them from any financial obligation to him from that day on. He cancelled their debts as if they had never owed him any money. Simon, I have a question for you. Which of the two debtors will love the banker the most? In other words, of the two men, who do you think would be the most grateful?"

Simon reluctantly replied, "I suppose the one who had the bigger debt forgiven."

"Your judgement is correct. You hit the center of the target," Jesus replied.

Then he turned his gaze away from Simon the Pharisee, toward the woman, while still continuing his lesson.

Do You See This Woman?

Jesus said, "Simon, do you see this woman? Why do you bother her? For she has done a good deed toward me. You insisted that

I come to your home to eat a meal with you and your friends. I listened to you and your persistence, and I came into your dwelling. Yet you did not give me any water for my feet."

Jesus continued speaking to the banquet audience. "From the rhyme of little children we recognize the Israelite tradition of every hospitable home. 'Your feet you wash before you eat.' Otherwise, as you know Simon, you execute a grave sin by allowing an unholy and impure act: permitting people to eat with feet coated with the garbage and animal excrement of our streets. You identify with that unbreakable custom. Equally, so does every other guest in your home who is listening to my voice."

"In contrast," he said, *"this woman has not stopped wetting my feet with the drops from her eyes, however; raining tears on my feet, bathing, and wiping them with her hair."*

"Simon, did you instruct your servants to wash the feet of your other guests when they came to your home? Were they eating with feet washed clean while I ate with grime and filth upon mine? Simon, did you purposely ignore our Jewish rules of hospitality to humiliate me before the leaders of this community?"

Where Is My Kiss?

"You did not even give me a kiss of greeting as you gave everyone else as the men came to your celebration."

"You kissed everyone but me. And yet the woman whom you hypocritically despise, from the time I entered your banquet room has not stopped tenderly kissing my feet."

"You did not even have the courtesy to anoint my head with a cheap every-day olive oil from your kitchen. She has poured an expensive myrrh, however, on my toes and the soles of my feet."

"The sweet perfume that has soothed my feet now floods this room, as well as your entire home, where once there was decayed and rotten air. Long after I leave your property, you will smell the fragrance of her act of devotion as a clinging witness to her sanctity and righteousness towards our holy God."

BEHOLD THE WOMAN!

Then Jesus, turning his gaze from the man looking with scathing reproach at the woman kneeling in holy adoration, spoke to the assembled self-righteous proclaiming: "I declare before all of you this day as a glorious testament for all time that this woman, whom you and the town unceasingly scorned, will from this day be admired wherever God's kingdom is established among the nations of this world. In her memory, generations will speak about what this woman has done. Is it not impressive? I am going to tell you another crucial truth."

"God has forgiven her sins, her many sins—as her great love towards me has shown. She is very, very grateful. That is why this woman since the time I came into this house has not stopped kissing my feet. Someone whom the Lord forgives only a little, loves only a little. If the forgiveness is small, then the gratitude is small."

Then Jesus spoke to the crumpled woman, "Your sins are taken away. It is as if you had never defiled or degraded your body by having sexual intercourse with so many men for money. No longer are you to wallow in promiscuity and adultery. Gone is the evil of harlotry as idolatry before your heavenly Father. This day, your sins are cleansed."

That set the dinner guests reclining with him to talk among themselves behind his back: "Who does he think he is, forgiving sins! How can he take away her shameful sexual behavior of whoredom?"

Jesus ignored them, and turning to the woman declared, "Because you believed, your faith has healed you. Go in peace with the Lord's shalom. As you go, receive God's salvation through your faith. You are clean and pure. Your sins in judgement no longer come before your heavenly Father."

Her many sins forgiven, the audience continued responding indignantly, "Who is this who even forgives sins?" And what was the answer for all to hear? Only God, since only the Lord can forgive sin.

JESUS ENDS THE STORY

"The harlot will get into the kingdom of God before you if you do not likewise repent and believe. You think that you have the exclusive right to be God's children because you have some special religious privilege or birthright. I tell you, unless you humble yourself like this woman, you will not see the kingdom of my Father in heaven. I come to you in the way of righteousness, and you do not believe me. Yet this despised prostitute did believe me; and you seeing all this happen before you, still do not even feel remorse afterward so as to believe me.

"Is this scenario true of you? Then allow the Holy Spirit to change you! The actions of the prostitute confirm the rescuing power of God's salvation. I say to you, do not be afraid; only believe, and you will be made well (*sōzō*). For the Son of Man came to seek and to save (*sōzō*) the lost."

CONCLUSION

Let me finish my narrative of Mary, the notorious woman of Capernaum. You might ask what happened to the weeping harlot after this salvation miracle. I must confess that my story now takes a dramatic twist, which lays shame upon my previous sordid account. The infamous woman remained in the town of Capernaum, joining the followers of Jesus the Messiah meeting at the home of Peter the fisherman. There she encountered many other believers of the Way, both peasant and powerful, including Marcus Antoninus Pius (the resident Roman commander), and the wealthy Matthew Levi (son of Alphaeus), the former tax collector. After meeting Christ, the redeemed woman became a stellar example of enduring faith and righteous conduct among the entire Capernaum community. The messianic revolution that came from within her—a transformation of attitude and behavior—brought great strength and courage to those who were obedient to the mission of God, the Lord who desires to bless all the families of the earth.

REFLECTION QUESTIONS

1. In the narrative of Luke 7 told in this chapter, how would you describe the life of the notorious woman of Capernaum before she encountered Christ as her Savior?
2. What do you observe about Jesus's reaction to and engagement with the infamous woman?
3. What influence do you think that Jesus's interaction with the prostitute had on her as an individual, on her business colleagues, and on the larger community?
4. How have you witnessed Christ's holistic salvation in your own life, family, church, and/or ministry?
5. What role should Christ our Savior play in our lives and ministries today?

3

Seeking Nothing but the Salvation of Souls: The Story of Bartholomäus Ziegenbalg in Southern India

Robert L. Gallagher

My name is Bartholomäus Ziegenbalg, and I want to tell you my story of God's salvation in and through my life.[1] I was born to pious Lutheran parents in 1682 in the Saxon farm village of Pulsnitz near Dresden in Germany. In the years leading up to and just after my birth, the Thirty Years War had ravaged the countryside, and my village had suffered a plague. Then when I was five, a severe fire swept through my birthplace and altered the landscape. While still a child, I lost both parents and two sisters. No wonder I gave so much thought to death, heaven, and hell.[2]

---

[1] The author composed this version of the narrative by drawing from historical facts and his own research.

[2] For an overview of Pietistic missions, see Robert L. Gallagher, "Encountering Pietist Missions," in John Mark Terry and Robert L. Gallagher, *Encountering*

CONSECRATION TO CHRIST

At the age of ten, I left home to attend Latin school at Kamenz, Saxony, and sought answers to my theological questions. Two years later, I moved to the Gymnasium (high school) in Görlitz, Saxony, where the rector of the school remarked that I was weak in body and mind. At eighteen, in the midst of nine months of wrestling with questions of God's purpose for my life, I found comfort in Christ's saving grace. From this moment of my salvation, God became to me the greatest, loveliest, best, sweetest, wisest, and noblest of all treasures.

Following this spiritual liberation, I wrote to August Hermann Francke at Halle University, Saxony, seeking new direction for my Christ-committed life. The respected scholar advised me to enroll at the Friedrich Werderschen Gymnasium near Berlin in 1702, under the tutelage of Joachim Lange, a controversial Pietist educator. I was most thankful that Philipp Jakob Spener, the venerated theologian of Pietism and provost of St. Nicholas Church in Berlin, provided a letter of recommendation, together with Baron von Canstein, founder of the Canstein Bible Society, supplying a financial scholarship. Reoccurring anxiety and academic overload, however, caused periods of chronic stomach disorders, forcing me to interrupt my studies and making me unable to complete my final examinations.

One year later, at the invitation of Francke, I enrolled at the University of Halle, and thrived in its academically rigorous program, which included Latin, Hebrew, and Greek. My studies in pietistic convictions and values confirmed my beliefs in personal conversion, faith, study, and witness. At the tertiary institute, I joined a group of students who met daily for scriptural exegesis, prayer, and singing, and whose members were pledged to the pietistic ideal of religious devotion and Christian service. At this time, I declared in my journal my life's direction: "For this reason we are made Christians, that we should be more bent upon the life to come, than upon the present. This is my daily memorandum,

---

the History of Missions: From the Early Church to Today, Encountering Missions Series (Grand Rapids, MI: Baker Academic, 2017), 173–97.

lest I should perhaps forget, entirely to consecrate my life and actions to an invisible eternity, minding little the world either in its glory and smiles, or in its frowns and afflictions." Yet I continued to battle physical ailments and depression. After one semester at Halle, I temporarily withdrew to become a family tutor in Merseburg, and later in Erfurt. In both locations, I organized pietistic meetings, and witnessed about Christ. Despite my own doubts and feelings of inadequacy, I retained my interest in missions through the influence of Pietist leaders, including Joachim Justus Breithaupt, a friend of both Spener and Francke. At Merseburg, I made a promise with a friend that foreshadowed my future vocation in southeast India. I vowed, "We two will seek nothing in this world but the glorification of the name of God, the extension of his kingdom, the spread of the divine truth, the salvation of our fellow-men, and the continued sanctification of our souls, in whatever part of the world we may be, and no matter what amount of cross and affliction may befall us on account of it." Before I continue my story of God's work in my life, let me give you some historic background of southern India, the place that the Lord Jesus eventually sent me to be a witness of his great salvation.

MISSIONS TO TRANQUEBAR

At the beginning of the eighteenth century, Muslim overlords governed the southern peninsula of India, who in turn appointed local Hindu kings as their regional governors, each with their own monetary organization and army. Under this oppressive system, the impoverished lower castes suffered immense social injustices. The major groups were Armenians, Jews, Muslims, Portuguese, Tamils, and Thomas-Christians, and the main languages included Gujarathi, Marathi, Portuguese, Sanskrit, Tamil, and Telugu. This was a time of rapid social change within Hindu society in South India, and the scattered Portuguese, French, Dutch, English, and Danish trading settlements added to the turbulent socioeconomic situation.

In 1620, Denmark obtained the town and surrounding territory of Tarangambâdi, or Tranquebar, on the east coast of southern India, from Rakunaāta Nāyak, the Rajah of Tanjore. Eighty-five years later, the king of Denmark, Frederick IV, under the influence of his Pietist wife, Louise of Mecklenburg-Güstrow, commissioned Franz Julius Lütkens, his German Pietist court chaplain, to find missionaries for his colonies. Lütkens, through Pietist friends in Berlin, contacted my mentor Lange, who suggested as worthy candidates his theological students Heinrich Plütschau of Mecklenburg, Germany (five years my senior), and myself.

I received the invitation with reservation. I had not completed my university studies or my ordination process, and I knew I lacked ministry experience, as well as still suffering from poor health. Lange forwarded our names to Lütkens in Copenhagen, nevertheless, even though neither Heinrich nor I had formally accepted. The Danish king approved the choice, allocated the finances, and commanded us to report to the capital for ordination and final instructions. Evidently, Lütkens first proposed that our objective be the Danish West Indies, then suggested the West African "slave coast" of Guinea. Ultimately, the king altered our destination to southern India.

After a dangerous seven-month voyage on the *Princessa Sophia Hedwiga*, my companion Heinrich and I arrived on July 9, 1706, at the Danish Crown Colony of Tranquebar on the Coromandel Coast. At that time, Tranquebar comprised 15 square miles, 20 small villages, and between 18,000 and 30,000 inhabitants. We were the first Protestant missionaries to India for the express purpose of evangelizing the indigenous people. Drawing on the principles and teachings learned at Berlin and Halle, we sought to share the Scripture with cultural awareness. Our message was a blend of Lutheran theology and pietistic relevance, believing that the Word of God was efficacious and powerful for personal conversion and holiness.

Immediately on arriving, we met opposition from Johann Hassel (the Tranquebar Danish chaplain), local Hindu leaders and Brahmins, the Danish East India Company, and the hostile Danish governor, Johan Sigismund Hassius. Despite my success in Christian outreach to the governor's household, Hassius later imprisoned me for four months between 1708 and 1709 for rebellion against his authority. I believe that my imprisonment, however, was associated not with political issues but with my speaking against the local Catholic practice of separate churches for high and low caste, and accusing the Catholics of a limited knowledge of the Christian faith. Even though we were German Lutheran missionaries receiving salaries from the Danish crown and working in a Danish colony, we did not have any interest in gaining a political or territorial advantage over the local people. As Pietists, we tried to minister the gospel without racism or imperialism, which aggravated the European colonialists. Certainly, our work in southern India challenges the popular view that all missionaries in India participated in colonialism.

ROYAL DANISH MISSION

By God's grace, the Royal Danish Mission grew through our vision and skill, heavily supported by intensive prayer and extensive correspondence. At point after point, with hardly any precedent to guide us except the blessed Holy Spirit, Plütschau and I made the right decisions, modeling a way that I hope other Protestant missions will follow. Below, I will expand the five missional principles that we recognized as characteristic of the Tranquebar Mission in South India.

Church and School Together

Church and school are to go together. Missionaries need to link the propagation of the Christian faith with education since they need to train children to read the Word of God. To this end, we began day schools for the Portuguese and Danish co-workers a year after we arrived. Following the Francke Foundation's model, we made a revolutionary innovation in 1707 when we started a day school for girls, India's first. As Halle missionaries we adapted Francke's pedagogical principles (e.g., children divided by age), and taught in the vernacular with the Bible and the Lutheran catechism as our core texts. We believed it was critical to teach children the Scriptures before they grew hardened to spiritual truth. Furthermore, our curriculum included astronomy, cooking, geography, mathematics, medicine, poetry, reading, rhetoric, and writing using European clocks, globes, and world maps.

Later I wrote a letter to Halle concerning the connection between church and school. I asserted, "It is a thing known to all persons of understanding that the general good of any country or nation depends upon a Christian and careful training of children in schools, exercising due care and diligence, and thereby producing wise governors in the state, faithful ministers of the gospel in the church, and good members of the commonwealth in families."

Although the Tamil society had a rich history in the arts and sciences—astronomy, cosmology, mathematics, medicine, moral teaching, music, physics, poetry, surgery, and writing—education was restricted to the high-caste Brahmins. In 1715, Plütschau and I founded a Tamil free-charity boarding school, and an orphanage where indigenous communities entrusted poor children to the care of house parents. The start of a seminary one year later—with eight senior Tamil students—to train teachers, catechists, and pastors, looked forward to a time when the indigenous church would no longer need missionaries. As Europeans, we were against Westernizing the Indian Christians; we taught the Tamil schoolchildren their own language and customs using free-Tamil church members. Some of the Tamils involved in the teaching were Andreas (my former cook, originally named Cepprumāl), Johann Almede, and Rāyappan (alias Petrus). In addition, teachers, such as Otto Friedrich, Ole Ollussen Thoren, and Manuel de Coste (the Portuguese catechist), also taught the children a European curriculum.

Bible in the Vernacular

If Christians are to read the Word of God, then that word must be available to them in their own language. Scripture needs to be available in the vernacular to build a native church, and facilitate a noncolonialist approach to mission.

During the voyage to India, Heinrich Plütschau and I studied Danish, not realizing that the trade language of Tranquebar was Portuguese. Upon arriving, I studied the Tamil language, while Plütschau learned Portuguese. Thanks be to God who has gifted me in learning languages, so that I quickly mastered colloquial and written Tamil.

In learning the language, I built upon the Tamil dictionaries of the Jesuit missionaries Henrique Henriques, Roberto de Nobili, and Constantino Giuseppe Beschi. In addition, I devoted myself to the study of Tamil literature. I explained the process in my journal as follows: "I chose such books as I should wish to imitate, both in speaking and writing, and had such authors read to me a hundred times that there might not be a word or expression which I did not know, or could not imitate." In Tranquebar, there were two dialects of Tamil—Shen and Kodun—so I learned both by hiring indigenous tutors such as Ellappar, a high-caste Hindu. Although Shen was the dialect of the Brahmins, as well as sacred literature and scholarship, it had ceased to be intelligible to the common people. Thus, Plütschau and I chose the ordinary dialect of Kodun for our pamphlets, books, and translations. Within eight months, I preached my first sermon, recording my thoughts: "With God's grace I was able to read, write, and speak in this very difficult language, and even understand the conversation of others."

By 1708, I had compiled a 40,000-word Malabar (Tamil) dictionary, *Grammatica Damulica* (published at Halle eight years later), and a dictionary of poetical terms of some 17,000 words (*Lexicon Poeticum*). This enabled me to write, print, and promote Tamil literature. With the help of Johann Ernst Gründler (a former schoolteacher at the Francke Foundations), I translated the entire New Testament into Tamil in less than five years after my arrival in Tranquebar. This was the first translation of the Bible in any Indian language. Following this accomplishment was a Tamil translation of *Luther's Small Catechism* (printed in 1713). In that same year, Plütschau returned to Germany, due to ill health, and became a Lutheran country pastor at Beyenflieth in Holstein in northern Germany. Accompanying my missionary friend to Europe was Timothy, a Tamil Christian from Tranquebar, who provoked missionary interest at Halle, and remained there to teach the Tamil language at the Collegium Orientale Theologicum.

An English printing press and paper arrived at Madras in 1712, but the printer, Jonas Fink, fell overboard and drowned on the voyage. I subsequently recruited a German soldier, Johann Heinrich Schloricke, who printed the first book in India in the Portuguese language. By 1715, a printer named Johann Gottlieb Adler, using Halle-manufactured Tamil typefaces, printed the first Tamil New Testament. The Tranquebar Tamil press was now in business to print studies of the Tamil language and culture. The outcomes of this breakthrough were the spread of the gospel, a uniformity of script for the Tamil writing system, and an increased desire to read by the indigenous people.

Contextualized Gospel

Missionaries need to base the preaching of the gospel on an accurate knowledge of the mind of the people. That is, they need to understand the worldview of the indigenous inhabitants in order to share the gospel with them. I was aware of the importance of understanding the Hindu customs of the people of southern India with whom I was sharing the gospel. I set out to study the belief systems and lifestyle of the Bhakti religion, analyzing the social and religious thought in order to present a meaningful message. I reflected in my journal, "Hardly an hour passes that I do not have an opportunity to speak with the heathens on the way," as I visited villages and towns. For instance, I asked Kanabadi, a Tamil poet, to translate some Christian literature, and upon his subsequent conversion, the local artist wrote poems using Christian themes in place of Hindu legends, which the Tamil school teachers then used to teach the children.

As a Halle missionary, I wrote about my cultural discoveries of the Tamil society in a number of monographs. My two significant publications were the 1711 *Malabarian Gods* (which quoted 176 passages from Tamil literature to introduce Europe to the Tamil worldview), and the 1713 *Genealogy of the Malabar (South-Indian) Gods*—a detailed study of Savaite and Vaishnavite beliefs using 145 letters written by Tamil scholars, allowing the people to speak for themselves. On receiving this material, Francke wrote critically to me. My mentor concluded that such studies were "not to be thought of, inasmuch as the missionaries were sent to extirpate heathenism, and not to spread heathenish nonsense in Europe." Consequently—I found out on my only return trip to Europe—the Halle director deliberately hid my ethnographies in the archives of the university so that his students could not have access to my materials.

Personal Conversion Is Paramount

The aim must be definite and personal conversion. The spread of Christianity should focus on individuals rather than on mass movements, unlike the Catholic missionaries in Asia. In southern India, we avoid mass conversions, and pray instead for individual salvation. Within the first few months of our arrival, we assembled the Malabar slaves of the settlement two hours every day for religious instruction in the fundamentals of the Christian faith. One year after arrival, we baptized multiple slaves after we publicly examined them on the Lutheran Articles of the Christian Faith, and in 1707 we erected the "Jerusalem Church" to conduct Tamil services. Church membership gradually grew.

I recorded on May 12, 1707, that the first church members—Friedrich, Christian, and Conrad—were Governor Hassius's servants. Then on September 5 of the same year, Francisca, the widow of the president of the Catholic Church in Tranquebar, together with her mother and two daughters, became Protestants. Later, the two slave women of Johann Hassel became members of our church: Martha (October 16, 1707) and Hagar (February 7, 1708). Eleven years after constructing the first church building, it became too small, and the members built an expanded "New Jerusalem Church."

As the Indian Christians moved away from the Danish protectorate in search of work, most bore faithful witness, which resulted in church growth in South India. In contrast, we Europeans were mainly restricted to the Tranquebar colony. Plütschau and I endeavored to work not only with the indigenous people, but also with the German and Portuguese inhabitants employed by the Danish monarchy, so we started a church service especially for them in the local Danish church.

In addition to these accomplishments of Plütschau and myself as bearers of the gospel of Christ, we held interreligious dialogues with Hindu priests, doctors, and poets. From these meetings I wrote three collections of conversations in which I argued the truth of Christianity. In 1719, my friend Mr. Phillip made an English translation of Gründler's and my *Thirty-Four Conferences between the Danish Missionaries and the Malabarian Bramans (or Heathen Priests) in the East Indies, Concerning the Truth of the Christian Religion*, which was published in London—an account of our religious discussions in Tranquebar with Hindus.

Thanks be to God, we also founded stations in Srirangam, Tanjore, Madura, Kanchi, Chidambram, and Tirupathi, and upon traveling through the region, we established contacts with Brahmins, and held fifty-four conversations with them. From 1715 onward, the administration of Halle published the recorded dialogues that I sent to Saxony. Moreover, I sent a large number of letters with different questions to a selection of Hindu Brahmins and non-Brahmins. I then translated the answers to these questions into German, and forwarded the results to Halle. In these evangelistic conversations, I attempted to meet the Hindus on their own level. Yet I was determined to proclaim an uncompromising gospel of the free-saving grace of God in Jesus Christ as the heart and center of my evangelism.

Indigenous Leadership and Church

The dissemination of Christianity must result in an indigenous church with indigenous leadership. Hence, I insisted on developing a Tamil church of Lutheran faith and worship with Indian characteristics. Rather than follow a Danish or German pattern of church life and administration, I adopted aspects of the Malabar culture. For example, men and women sat together on the floor (emphasizing the equality of women), and wedding and funeral services, along with music and meals, followed Tamil customs. Further, because I realized that Christian theological concepts needed to be clothed in Hindu thought, I used indigenous metaphors and parables in my preaching. I also arranged hymns using German chorales and Tamilian melodies and lyrics for corporate worship, instructed children in the catechism, and introduced the singing of Psalms. We published our first hymnal in 1715, which contained forty-eight hymns. The converts were encouraged simultaneously to be faithful Tamils and sincere Christians.

I am pleased to report that the Society for Promoting Christian Knowledge in England supports the Christian education of indigenous children from Madras to Calcutta. A number of the young men in our Tranquebar congregation became followers of Christ through these schools, and developed as valuable teachers and preachers. Below is part of a letter I wrote regarding the relationship between the mission church and school:

> We try to deeply plant in these young minds the true Christian doctrine. We pay special attention in the daily instruction to catechization. We have several catechists who go from house-to-house and catechize our people. We are not satisfied merely with an outer appearance of the Christian religion, but press for a real change of heart and an implicit obedience of faith, and we look not so much for large numbers, but that all who accept our religion should attain a living knowledge of the truth unto godliness and the true way of salvation.

Three years after my arrival I petitioned the Danish authorities to ordain a native believer so that the clerical ministry would not be dominated by Europeans. Only partly realized were my convictions of a fully indigenous church. Aaron, an Indian catechist of some years, who is pastorally responsible for several congregations in the Māyāvaram area, is still waiting to become the first Protestant Indian pastor. His assistance has greatly helped me in easing cultural awkwardness in my administering the Holy Sacrament and the feast days of Easter, Pentecost, and Christmas.[3]

We are certainly careful in choosing our indigenous pastors, and there are few failures. Extreme caution still prevails. Yet I

---

[3] The Christian beliefs were so different from Hinduism that there was a need for an insider to help navigate the cultural and religious differences.

cannot help but feel that our European racial prejudice and superiority influences our strong reluctance to accept the notion of equality between a German Lutheran missionary and an Indian pastor. Irony heightens this prejudice when I compare the Tamil's intense dislike of the European's evil lifestyle to that of the Tamil views of cultural piety and simple living.

DRAWING TO A CLOSE

I feel very tired after working night and day for the last twelve years in Tranquebar. I am not at all well. My body is wearing out although I am only thirty-five years on this earth. Perhaps this is taking place because of my poor diet, which causes me much stomach discomfort often resulting in constipation, besides sleepless nights wrestling over the constant Malabar pressures of conflict from within and without: the Danish governor and chaplain, Danish East India Company, Catholic hierarchy, and Hindu Brahmins. There is much still to be done for Christ's kingdom here in southern India, yet it feels that there is so little time remaining.

Aggravating my stresses are the policy disputes with Christopher Wendt, the secretary of the Copenhagen Mission Society, which weigh heavily upon me. My relationship with the secretary is fragile. From my point of view, Wendt lives in Copenhagen, and does not have any idea of the stresses involved in personally engaging in missionary work. His unrealistic opinions are so insensitive and hurtful that he has thrust upon me great psychological wounds. Wendt emphatically wants a self-supporting Indian church where the missionaries only preach and are not involved in social action. He criticizes me for financially sustaining the poor Christians. I follow the Francke pattern at Halle, however. I want to speak words of love but also desire to demonstrate that the service of souls and the service of the body are connected—salvation ministry cannot be truly effective without social action.

In a recent letter to Wendt, I wrote,

> As the body is bound to the soul, so precisely is the service of the body connected with the service of the soul, and we cannot separate them from each other. This work at the Tran-

quebar Mission demands the service of the whole person. If I deny such service, I deny that in which the Scripture places the proper manner of faith and love. The more one devotes to the service of neighbors, and gladly helps in bodily and spiritual needs, the stronger one must be in Christianity.

If I die tomorrow and see my Savior face-to-face, I will say to my Lord Jesus that I tried to be faithful to his calling on my life. This has resulted in the following: over 250 Christians saved and worshipping in the New Jerusalem Church, the completion of studies in the Hindu religion and culture, two church buildings and a seminary for the training of national leaders, and the New Testament and Genesis to Ruth translated into the Tamil language.

I would conclude that, even though I endured feelings of inadequacy, depression, and physical maladies throughout my life, God has allowed me to pioneer the Western study of South Indian culture, society, and religion. In the process, I have modeled a ministry philosophy to generations of Pietist missionaries who will surely follow in my path. By God's grace, I have demonstrated how to bring an uncompromised gospel to an Asian society by confirming Christian care and concern of the indigenous people as well as bringing an awareness of the importance of world missions to Protestant Europe and Asia.

As a Protestant missionary, I live in an age where colonialization and prejudice are normal. With God's help, however, I have a respect and empathy for the indigenous culture that focuses on the people over the missionary program. I love the Indian people, and share God's salvation message wherever I can at festivals, work, and play. I believe that I have gained commendable respect from many Hindus. This has happened even though I have publicly criticized some members of the Brahmin caste for their disregard of the lower divisions in Hindu society such as the outcaste Pariahs. I believe that this was so because as I presented Christianity, I demonstrated a high regard for Hindus as human beings. This I did through my knowledge of Hinduism, my desire to preserve the integrity of the Tamil language and culture, and my lack of superior attitudes, coupled with my repudiation of the racism of other Europeans toward Indians.

In closing my story, I want to reiterate my deep desire—until my very last breath on earth—to take hold of the principles of enculturation with the help of the Lord Jesus. This I will do by continuing to develop an indigenous church with Indian characteristics in architecture, music, and customs so that the southern Indian people will come to know Christ as Savior.

REFLECTION QUESTIONS

1. How would you describe Bartholomäus Ziegenbalg's life before he went to India?
2. What were the influences that shaped Ziegenbalg's commitment to seek nothing but the salvation of souls for Christ's kingdom?
3. What were the missionary challenges and successes of Ziegenbalg and Heinrich Plütschau in the Tranquebar Mission in south India?
4. Choose one of the five missional principles of the Royal Danish Mission and describe how the missionaries influenced the Tamil people through their cross-cultural ministry.
5. Which of the five missional practices of the Pietists in southern India are applicable in your ministry context? How would you apply those ministry philosophies as your missional model?

4

Salvation's Call in Papua New Guinea: How Can We Baptize All These People?

Robert L. Gallagher

It seemed that all the people from up and down the entire Oro valley in the Northern Province of Papua New Guinea (PNG) had come to the central village to await the decision. There were hundreds of men, women, and children milling about, talking in low tones. The tribal chiefs and elders of the various villages had already presented their request. Looking over the crowd, Bruce Cartwright turned to his friend Vele Wari and said, "How can we baptize all these people? How can we say that they have all individually received Christ as their Lord and Savior? We can't baptize them in water if they haven't personally confessed Christ. Can we?"[1]

---

[1] The author has changed the names of the people and places involved in this historical narrative for the purposes of security. The story comes from the author's understanding of the happenings in PNG. For an understanding of the ministry of CRC Churches International in PNG and Oceania, see Sarita D. Gallagher, *Abrahamic Blessing: A Missiological Narrative of Revival in Papua New Guinea*, American Society of Missiology Series, vol. 21 (Eugene, OR: Pickwick Publications, 2014), 187–217.

SPIRITUAL BACKGROUND

Bruce and Joan Cartwright had come to Papua New Guinea under the auspices of the CRC Churches International (CRC) to start missions work in the highlands. Pastor Leo Harris, their spiritual father, had founded the organization in 1945. Harris had received a vision of God's Spirit lighting revival fires across Australia and was inspired to start the first indigenous Pentecostal movement in the country. Harris also had a heart for missions, and sent the first CRC missionaries to PNG in 1963. Harris had declared, "C. T. Studd buried himself in the heart of Africa, but it brought multitudes of Africans to Christ. CRC missionaries need to bury themselves in New Guinea that thousands of nationals might rejoice in eternal life." Inspired by this challenge, the leaders of CRC Australia sent the Cartwrights as their first missionaries to PNG.

Bruce and Joan both had radical conversions to Christ during the early days of the Jesus movement. In the mid-1960s, the hippie movement from southern California swept across the Pacific to Australia, and influenced their worldview. They met while attending the University of New South Wales in Sydney, fell in love, and became involved with the hippie counterculture. To escape army conscription for the Vietnam War, Bruce persuaded Joan to drop out of university. She eventually came with him to live at a commune in the subtropical rainforests near Cairns, Queensland. Against both their parents' wishes, they entered the surf, sex, and drug community.

Some months after their arrival, a Pentecostal witnessing team came to the commune from a nearby town. Their lifestyle of care and concern challenged the couple with the truth of the gospel of Christ. Though at first highly skeptical and suspicious of the radical Christians, the couple slowly softened in their attitude, and began to listen with interest to the salvation story of Christ and the early church. During one of these gatherings with the Christian young people, Bruce and Joan asked for prayer. They were then led in the sinner's prayer, confessed their sins, asked for forgiveness through the blood of Jesus, and received a powerful infilling of the Holy Spirit whereby they immediately spoke in tongues as recorded in the Book of Acts. After this experience, the couple committed their lives to serve Jesus as Lord. There was only one way to God, and that was through confessing Christ as their Savior.

SALVATION'S CALL IN PAPUA NEW GUINEA

A few months after their change of allegiance to Christ, Bruce and Joan went back home to New South Wales, got married, and moved to Adelaide, South Australia, to attend a small CRC Bible College. While in their second year of college, they received what they believed was a salvation call of God to be missionaries in PNG. Under the instruction of Leo Harris, they spent the next three years in a small established church at Stirling in the Adelaide Hills until they could raise enough financial support from a number of the churches in the CRC movement. Those years were emotionally draining for the young Cartwrights.

In the midst of the Charismatic renewal of the early 1970s, the Cartwrights experienced strong opposition from the mainline Protestant denominations in the Stirling region that brought much discouragement. They felt ostracized in the small town by the local churches because of their Pentecostal message. Newspaper articles even branded them as an American religious cult. These feelings against their church were so vehement that some of the residents came by their meeting hall, and threw stones at the windows and on the galvanized steel roof while they were conducting Sunday services. Through all these trials, the couple held to their original vision of being missionaries to PNG.

New Beginnings in Port Moresby

On arriving in the PNG capital of Port Moresby, they rented a small apartment with their two children. While Joan home-schooled their eldest child, Bruce purchased a small motor bike and traveled each morning to the national university some fifteen minutes away. There he would spend most of the morning walking the grounds, praying for opportunities to make friends with some of the English-speaking students. After lunch, Bruce would then return home to his family, and spend the rest of the afternoon in language study. As Joan continued looking after their children, Bruce had a neighbor come to the house and teach him Pidgin English, the national trade language.

At the end of the first year, Bruce's grasp of the language enabled him to begin to form friendships with a number of the male students. Each month he was in regular postal communication with the movement's mission headquarters in Adelaide, reporting his mission activities. Financial support was at first consistent, yet there was a tone in the mission director's letters that implied the need for some quantifiable evidence of their progress.

Pressure of Missions Reports

With the correspondence from headquarters, there were always attached CRC mission reports from other parts of PNG such as the coastal province of Moro. The end-of-the-year report from this area declared, "There were 950 conversions, over 400 baptized in water, and 20 filled with the Holy Spirit." By the beginning of the next year, CRC had commenced the first English Bible School with ten young men at Goroka who began preaching in the surrounding villages and learning "how to be led by the Holy Spirit in the field." The reports of other CRC missionaries' endeavors in PNG kept coming on a regular basis filled with details of missionary activities, monthly statistics, and testimonies of people saved, baptized in water, filled with the Holy Spirit, and healed. Bruce and Joan tried to rejoice in the revival statistics from their fellow missionaries but felt uncomfortable with the sweeping advancement in other parts of PNG while in the midst of their own struggles to make any inroads in the capital city.

During the second year, Bruce decided to start a lunchtime Bible study, sitting under the trees within the university grounds. Most of the students were respectful, yet only a few showed any real interest in establishing a friendship. Vele Wari was different from the other students, however. Bruce had met him when he first came to the campus, and they had started a relationship almost straightway. He was an undergraduate studying education who hoped to establish a primary school back in his highland village of Tokarara, where his father was the tribal leader. Vele was one of the few in his valley that had taken the opportunity to learn to read and write Pidgin English from the German missionaries. His family then reluctantly allowed him to continue his studies at the boarding school in Popendetta. A government scholarship allowed Vele further tertiary education to attend the University of Papua New Guinea in Port Moresby. This young Melanesian had shown some interest when Bruce told him his personal testimony. On subsequent visits to the Cartwrights' home, he developed a close friendship with the children.

LIGHTING OF REVIVAL FIRES

Toward the end of the second year, Bruce invited Vele to a prayer meeting at his home. A number of local Christians and unsaved neighbors were also going to join them for the evening. Vele was reluctant at first, yet with some warm coaxing, he agreed to come. It was while the small group was praying that the young man began crying and shaking under the power of the Holy Spirit. Bruce was amazed at what God did that night. In the presence of the whole group, Vele began confessing his sins to God with deep sobbing, after which he began praising the Lord. He then spoke in tongues. That night Vele had a glorious and joyous salvation experience. Others in the meeting followed Vele's experience and received Christ as Savior. The group also heard a man who spoke only Pidgin, suddenly speak in English, "The Bible is the Word of God."

Further, the Holy Spirit filled a village woman from the Sepik region, and she began to speak in Pidgin English, a language she could not normally speak. She was saying, "You come and partake of God's words, and live by them." This was a powerful manifestation of the Spirit. In the days and weeks following that prayer meeting, Vele devoured the Bible from cover to cover, asking Bruce all sorts of questions about the Christian faith. Eventually the church leaders baptized him in water in the name of the Lord

Jesus. He grew quickly in prayer and word, and with great boldness began sharing about his newfound faith. It was an exciting time for Bruce and Joan as they watched their first national convert enjoy such a personal conversion experience.

Historic Christianity

At the end of the academic year, Vele was returning to his village for the holidays, and he invited Bruce to travel with him in a few days' time. The Australian missionary was hesitant about going with his new friend. He believed that God had brought him and his wife to PNG to plant churches in the highlands. Yet this was a difficult decision for a number of reasons. The village was in the Northern Province among the Oro people, one of the 851 indigenous language groups among the Melanesian population of nearly five million people in PNG (at that time). The late nineteenth century saw the first missionaries in the valley come from Halle in Germany, and they slowly established a small number of Gutnius Bethel churches. In the one hundred years since that time, Christianity had made little evangelistic progress. The national government had aggressively restricted Christian access to the region because of the practice of comity; the European Christendom model only allowed Gutnius missionaries into the region.

In the early years, Christian witness had persuaded a number of key tribal leaders in the Oro valley to align themselves with the missionaries. In turn, these chiefs had gradually brought their entire tribes under the pastoral oversight of the Bethel denomination. A mass movement of people seemed to have occurred. Yet Bruce Cartwright was extremely critical of the legitimacy of their conversion process. Even though he was aware of a number of similar instances in the early church, he maintained that a personal conversion experience, similar to Vele's and his own, must always accompany a genuine change of allegiance from animism to Christianity.

The Bethel churches that still existed were now strongly influenced by the liberal German theology of the early twentieth century, especially that of Adolf Harnack. Hence, over the years, the few rotating European missionaries had neither selected nor trained national leaders, nor translated the Scriptures into the vernacular language. In fact, they had not effectively penetrated the culture with the full gospel. The form of Christianity that had evolved over the many years was a highly syncretistic blend of European liturgy with ancient animistic practices.

The Spirit's Open Door

In talking with Vele over the months, Bruce was convinced that in the Oro valley there was no current Christian witness. The majority of the people were illiterate, shamans commonly practiced sorcery, tribal wars were frequent, and there were rumors that the people were still practicing headhunting with cannibalism. Should he go with Vele to visit his *wontuks* (an ethnic group that speaks the same language), and risk the regional authorities discovering and deporting him from the country? In addition, what could he possibly achieve among the unpredictably savage people, who already had a sort of Christianized folk religion? Bruce shared his concerns with his wife. After a day of prayer and fasting, he felt that God wanted him to go. Joan was not entirely convinced. Yet after further discussion and prayer, she finally felt at peace with her husband's decision. There was now no time for Bruce to contact his mission director in Australia for approval. Therefore, he simply packed an overnight bag, paid for an afternoon flight for himself and Vele, and caught a local put-put (a shuttle service operated by a local contractor) to Jacksons International Airport, Port Moresby. He was unsure when he would return.

MESSAGE OF SALVATION

The two men flew to the city of Popendetta, and from there caught a ride on a truck to the outskirts of the Oro region near Tara. They then walked for three days toward the valley where Vele's village was located, being careful not to be seen by the government officials or the Gutnius missionaries. The terrain was especially mountainous, and after hours on unmarked trails in the tropical rain, wading through rivers and skirting Oro villages, they finally arrived at Tokarara just before dark on the third day. The people at first were suspicious of the white man, but Vele assured them that he was a friend who had come a long way to speak a special message from the spirit world.

During those first days in the village, Bruce spent most of his time in his hut asking for God's wisdom, and gaining physical strength after the long hike. After a few days when the people had exchanged small gifts and the hospitality ceremonies had ended, Vele invited the village elders to come to the men's long-house to listen to Bruce's message, which Vele would translate. In the long-house, Vele's father asked Bruce to tell them the words he had carried from far beyond the mountain range. For over two hours, Bruce told the elders about the Way of salvation and answered their questions.

Toward the end of that time, Bruce had a strong impression from the Holy Spirit. Later he told Joan that in his mind he saw a picture of a young village woman, and somehow immediately knew that she was both deaf and dumb. He shared this insight with the elders, and said he believed that his God wanted to heal the woman. This declaration at first brought stunned silence, followed by a scurrying about as two elders quickly departed from the long-house. Bruce continued telling them about Jesus for about fifteen more minutes until the men brought to the assembly a young woman called Gabi. Through Vele, the Australian discovered that the young woman was both deaf and dumb. Bruce then quietly prayed—without laying hands on her—that God would extend his hand to heal this person through God's servant, Jesus Christ. Then a miracle happened. While he was praying, the woman began to cry out with joy, jumping up and down. She could now speak and hear.

Good News Spreading

Word of the miracle quickly spread throughout the valley. When the villagers heard the news, they came to see the woman for themselves. Nobody could deny this supernatural event. Everyone in that region knew of Gabi's physical challenges. Some years earlier, the village sorcerer had placed a curse on her at the request of her older husband who was suspicious that she had committed adultery. The husband never proved his accusation, but the village elders had condoned the punishment, and the woman had been unable to hear or speak from that time on. People traveled for many days to Tokarara to see the healed woman and the Australian wonder-worker. Bruce and Vele were excited. Never did they dream that such a thing would happen.

During the days that followed the miracle, the two missionaries were busy speaking about the one true living God to the men of the Oro valley, and praying for the sick. Early each morning Bruce would record the events of the previous day. He wrote the following description in one of his journal entries:

> Yesterday during the meeting, it was a great joy to see so many of the village people moved by the Holy Spirit, and so receptive to the word of God. As well, we saw some spectacular healings. Many deaf people received their hearing. A man who had been shaking for two years (with what I guess was Parkinson's disease), stopped shaking immediately after prayer; and a huge growth on the side of a man's foot just disappeared under my hands.
>
> Perhaps one of the most remarkable miracles I have ever seen was praying for a young man from a neighboring village who was about 18 years of age. He had never spoken in his life. As I prayed, he fell to the ground, and a huge growth appeared in his throat. This was obviously a demonic power. I prayed for him, and cast out a mute spirit, after which he lay limp for a number of minutes. Then I stood him up on his feet, and prayed for him. God gloriously filled him with the Holy Spirit, and he began speaking, for the first time in his life, with a heavenly language. How wonderful to see him utter his first words as praise to God. These and other miracles of the Holy Spirit, made yesterday the most outstanding time in God I have ever experienced.

Surprised by the Spirit

In the midst of this time of revival, there was also an air of uncertainty. Most of the people wanted to know more about this new God. However, others were declaring that it was best to stay with the spirits of their ancestors who cared for them in the spirit world and with the ancient tribal gods who had been victorious over their enemies in the many previous tribal wars. There seemed to be more and more loud and long debates among the men of the villages as they argued for and against following this new God. Then one day the arguments stopped, and the village chiefs called a meeting, inviting Bruce and Vele. At the gathering in the longhouse, Vele's father came to the missionaries and said in broken English, "In valley we want to follow way of Jesus. We want what Vele is talking. We want baptism."

Although it was late and Bruce and Vele were tired, they could not sleep after the meeting. Not only had the movement of God caught them by surprise but also the decision of the chiefs. Vele had told the CRC missionary that his tribal people often made important decisions—such as moving the village, or making tribal war—through group discussion-making and consensus. Up until now, they never thought that the Oro people would so quickly choose a new god by this method. Long into the night, Bruce and Vele talked and prayed together. All their theological training and study of the Bible had taught them that to become a follower of Christ was a personal decision. In this PNG highland valley, the leaders of the various villages had decided for everyone. What were they to do? Was it a legitimate decision before God, especially since there had been so much aggressive debate right up to the final declaration? Obviously, even some of the key leaders had opposed the decision. Now the elders were asking them to baptize whole villages when surely not everyone was born again of the Holy Spirit.

For hours, both men pored over their pocket New Testaments searching for clues that could bring some resolution to this delicate situation. Bruce even tried to recall if there were similar instances in church history that would provide some helpful insights. Further, if they did not agree to the demand of the chiefs, the villages might return to their ancestral gods. The chiefs and elders of the tribes had already performed a number of ceremonies in the Tokarara long-house, calling on their pantheon of tribal spirits to leave the Oro valley since they now served a new God. In addition, the leaders might consider Vele's involvement as a betrayal to his father and clan if the missionaries did not comply with their decision. This could even provoke the villagers into some form of physical retaliation against the two men. Moreover, how would the Northern Province government and the Gutnius Bethel missionaries react when they heard what had happened?

As Bruce and Vele finally fell asleep, emotionally and physically exhausted after the week of excitement and apprehension, they were still uncertain as to what to do—and they knew that the chiefs expected an answer in the morning.

REFLECTION QUESTIONS

1. How would you describe the lifestyle of Bruce and Joan Cartwright before and after they found Christ as their Savior?
2. In the spiritual background of the Cartwrights, how did they prepare for their cross-cultural ministry in PNG?
3. Compare and contrast Vele Wari's recent experience of Christ with the historic Christianity of his people in the Oro valley of the Northern Province.
4. How were the revival fires of the Lord's presence and power manifested to Wari's Melanesian village and its surroundings? What were the consequences of the message of Christ's salvation?
5. Portray the spiritual dilemma of Bruce Cartwright and Vele Wari the night before their meeting with the Oro valley leaders. If you were in a similar situation, how would you respond to the village elders, knowing that they "expected an answer in the morning"?

PART II

CHRIST OUR EMPOWERER

5

Biblical, Historical, and Contemporary Components of Empowerment

Paul W. Lewis

The importance of Christ as our Empowerer is self-evident, yet also heavily nuanced. Christ's empowerment through the Holy Spirit directly enables the missionary or proclaimer to pronounce or "evangelize." Scripture constantly reminds us that Jesus is the Savior of humanity, yet it is a common situation that missionaries or ministers can act or assume a part of that role. I am reminded of a professor that I had at Baylor University in Waco, Texas, who would say that the greatest temptation of ministers is to "ride the coattails" of Jesus to our own self-aggrandizement. Lord, forgive us! Christ is the Empowerer.

The role of empowerment has two key elements. First, there is the empowerment to be a witness, to proclaim, to evangelize. Second, there is the empowerment to live a Christ-like existence. While the two are connected, they are both equally necessary in the life of every believer, especially to those called to the ministerial or missionary vocation.

BIBLICAL COMPONENTS[1]

While there are multiple passages in the New Testament that highlight Christ as our Empowerer, I will focus on Acts 1:8 to unpack what "empowerer" means. The immediate context of the first chapter of Acts is instructive to the meaning of the passage, and the book as a whole. The passage in question, Acts 1:2–11, is the introduction to the Book of Acts, which highlights the addressee of the volume and the connection to the Gospel of Luke (v. 1), as well as being bookended by the forty days of miraculous signs (vv. 2–3), and the ascension of Jesus with the angelic commentary (vv. 9–11). The pattern of these verses follows:[2]

> Vv. 2–3: Jesus demonstrates "many convincing proofs" of his resurrection from the dead.
>
>> V. 4: Jesus commands the disciples, "Do not leave Jerusalem."
>>
>>> V. 5: Jesus promises the disciples, "You will be baptized with the Holy Spirit."
>>>
>>>> V. 6: The disciples ask, "Lord, are you at this time going to restore the kingdom to Israel?"[3]
>>>>
>>>>> V. 7: Jesus replies, "It is not for you to know the times or dates."[4]

---

[1] See an expanded consideration of this topic in Paul W. Lewis, "Reconsidering Certain Popular Interpretations of Acts 1:8," *The Spirit & the Church* 8 (2016): 3–16.

[2] I will summarize the pattern with direct quotes from the New International Version. All subsequent biblical citations are from the Book of Acts unless otherwise stated.

[3] While it seems out of context for the disciples to ask this question at this time, the prophetic literature (e.g., Is 32:15; 44:3; Ezek 36:25–28; 37:14; 39:29, and notably Joel 2:28–3:1, which Peter cites in Acts 2) had tied the outpouring Spirit with the restoration of Israel. See Craig S. Keener, *Acts: An Exegetical Commentary*, vol. 1 (Grand Rapids, MI: Baker Academic, 2012), 682–84; and Craig S. Keener, *The IVP Bible Background Commentary: New Testament,* 2nd ed. (Downers Grove, IL: IVP Academic, 2014), 319.

[4] F. F. Bruce combines verses 6 and 7 together in his treatment in *Com-

V. 8a: Jesus asserts that the Holy Spirit will empower them to "be my witnesses."[5]

V. 8b: The Spirit-filled disciples will be witnesses "in Jerusalem, and in all Judea and Samaria, and to the ends of the earth."

Vv. 9–11: Jesus's ascension and the witness of the angels.

In verse 12, Luke highlights that the disciples returned to Jerusalem—they followed Jesus's command. There is an *inclusio* of the miraculous when in verse 3 Jesus appeared to the disciples for forty days, showing them "many convincing proofs" of his resurrection; and verses 9 to 11 with Jesus's ascension and the angelic proclamation. Jesus in verse 4 mandates that the disciples stay in Jerusalem, and God shall baptize them in the Holy Spirit. Not surprisingly, the disciples still perceived the kingdom as a political realm that the Messiah would restore.[6] Jesus responds but highlights the role of the Holy Spirit. Thereby he reformulates what the kingdom of God will look like in this present age. As such, verses 2 to 3 and 9 to 11 function as couplets relating to the miraculous signs of Jesus (and the angels). In addition, verses 4 and 8b are a couplet emphasizing Jerusalem (and beyond in 8b); and verses

---

mentary on the Book of the Acts, New International Commentary on the New Testament (Grand Rapids, MI: Eerdmans, 1981), 60.

[5] Hans Conzelmann notes the couplet of verses 5 and 8a in *Acts of the Apostles*, trans. James Limburg, A. Thomas Kraabel, and Donald H. Juel, Hermeneia (Philadelphia: Fortress Press, 1987), 7.

[6] See Bruce, *Book of Acts*, 38; I. Howard Marshall, *The Acts of the Apostles: An Introduction and Commentary*, Tyndale New Testament Commentaries (Grand Rapids, MI: Eerdmans, 1980), 60; and Eckhard J. Schnabel, *Acts*, Exegetical Commentary on the New Testament, General ed. Clinton E. Arnold (Grand Rapids, MI: Zondervan, 2012), 76. Simon J. Kistemaker notes that while the political concern may be true, the focus of the question was about the timing, not about whether it would happen. Jesus's response does not limit the kingdom to Israel but also includes the "ends of the earth." See *Exposition of the Acts of the Apostles*, New Testament Commentary (Grand Rapids, MI, 1990), 52. Ernst Haenchen agrees with this perspective in *The Acts of the Apostles: A Commentary* (Philadelphia: Westminster Press, 1971), 142–43. Also see Keener, *Acts*, vol. 1, 682–84.

5 and 8a are a couplet about the promise of receiving the Holy Spirit. Finally, verses 6 to 7 are a couplet of the disciples' question about restoring the kingdom, together with the kind response of Jesus that it is not for them to know when that will take place. Jesus is redefining what the kingdom means in the age of the Spirit. This leads us to Acts 1:8. "But you will receive power when the Holy Spirit comes on you; and you will be my witnesses in Jerusalem, and in all Judea and Samaria, and to the ends of the earth." In the first part of the verse, the focal point of Jesus was the empowerment of the disciples. While the focus was on receiving power (*dynamis*), the Spirit ties his presence directly to the disciples. Throughout Acts the author stresses the accompanying elements of signs and wonders, exorcisms, healings, and prophetic speech, all demonstrating the Spirit's enablement.[7] The same Spirit who was upon Jesus in the Gospel of Luke is now on the recipients in the Book of Acts. Further, *glossolalia,* prophecy, guidance, and especially witness, show the power of the Spirit of Jesus.[8] Luke's usage of Joel's prophecy in Acts 2:17–21 emphasizes that the supernatural dynamics of the Spirit's empowerment were to be transgenerational and inclusive of both genders, all social status levels, and nature itself, all of which were to be transformational and declarative of the divine power.

Empowerment of the Holy Spirit

The issue of "power" is prominent in contemporary thought.[9] From this biblical context, however, it is clear that this verse is not talking about political power, since Jesus had just clarified

---

[7] See William W. Menzies and Robert P. Menzies, *Spirit and Power* (Grand Rapids, MI: Zondervan, 2000), 145–58. While outside the purview of this chapter, there is a vast amount of literature on power confrontations in the spiritual realm, especially in missionary contexts. For example, Opal L. Reddin, ed., *Power Encounter: A Pentecostal Perspective*, rev. ed. (Springfield, MO: Central Bible College Press, 1999).

[8] Leander E. Keck, "Listening to and Listening for: From Text to Sermon (Acts 1:8)," *Interpretation* 27, no. 2 (1973): 189.

[9] On the broader definition of power with a pneumatological engagement of such power, see Bernard Cooke, *Power and the Spirit of God* (Oxford: Oxford University Press, 2004).

that it is not for his disciples to know the "times or dates" for the establishment of God's kingdom.[10] Jesus is clearly dissuading the disciples from the potential establishment of a political kingdom at that time,[11] and from "all expectation of an imminent end."[12]

"Power" was to be a Spiritual power.[13] It was a power provided and defined by the Holy Spirit through Christ (the Word who became flesh).[14] Further, in the last century theologians have emphasized the charismatic aspects of the Spirit.[15] This Holy Spirit is likewise the "Holy" Spirit, which embeds the moral aspects of God within the body of Christ, and within the believer.[16] This

---

[10] The theme of the kingdom of God is important in the Book of Acts but with the emphasis on Jesus's kingship and what it means for the disciples. See Schnabel, *Acts*, 73.

[11] This does not mean that there are no political ramifications of the Spirit's infilling. Rather there will be implications from Spirit's presences in all aspects of one's life such as in political and social interaction and engagement. See Cooke, *Power and the Spirit of God*.

[12] Haenchen, *Acts*, 143.

[13] Keck, "Listening to and Listening for," 194. Frequently, theologians use "spiritual power" to clarify that what the Bible highlights is not political or other forms of physical power. In Stanley Horton's noted work, *What the Bible Says about the Holy Spirit*, within the book itself, he uses the term "power," but he indexes it under "spiritual power" (Springfield, MO: Gospel Publishing House, 1976), 301.

[14] I will not expand on the role of Christ and the Spirit in creation and salvation because of the limited scope of this chapter.

[15] For example, Menzies and Menzies, *Spirit and Power*; and J. Rodman Williams, *Renewal Theology 2: Salvation, The Holy Spirit and Christian Living* (Grand Rapids, MI: Zondervan, 1990).

[16] On the Holy Spirit in the moral life, see Henlee H. Barnette, *Introducing Christian Ethics* (Nashville, TN: Broadman Press, 1961), 87–97; Leon O. Hynson, "The Church and Social Transformation: An Ethics of the Spirit," *Wesleyan Theological Journal* 11 (1976): 49–61; L. Gregory Jones, *Transformed Judgment: Toward a Trinitarian Account of the Moral Life* (Notre Dame, IN: University of Notre Dame Press, 1990); and Paul W. Lewis, "A Pneumatological Approach to Virtue Ethics," *Asian Journal of Pentecostal Studies* 1, no. 1 (1998): 42–61. For the Spirit's role in social ethics, see Samuel Solivan, *Spirit, Pathos, and Liberation: Toward a Hispanic Pentecostal Theology*, Journal of Pentecostal Theology Supplemental Series 14 (Sheffield, UK: Sheffield Academic Press, 2000); Eldin Villafañe, *The Liberating Spirit: Toward an Hispanic American Pentecostal Social Ethic*, 2nd ed. (Grand Rapids, MI: Eerdmans, 1993); and Matthias Wenk, *Community-Forming Power: The Socio-Ethical Role of the Spirit in Luke-Acts*, Journal of

spiritual power then should include moral power as well. It is clear that we cannot equate a believer's abilities and role with that of the Spirit, and that Christ's role is unique in human history. Yet the Acts 1:8 empowerment includes the creative, salvific, charismatic, and moral aspects derived from the Lord. Thus, the Holy Spirit's empowerment of the believing recipient should include the Spirit's creative, salvific, charismatic, and moral enablement.[17]

Empowerment to Be Witnesses

One of the key components of this verse is the emphasis on Jesus's declaration that the disciples, upon receiving the Holy Spirit, would "be my witnesses." They were eyewitnesses of the events of Jesus's death, burial, and resurrection, and of salvation through Jesus.[18] The disciples were not purely to reiterate the teachings of Jesus. Rather they were to "proclaim Jesus himself in the resurrection."[19] The disciples (and later believers) were to "be witnesses," not to just "do witnessing."[20] Their proclamation and witnessing activity was to flow from their "being." That is, to spring from their character: formed, informed, and transformed by the

---

Pentecostal Theology Supplemental Series 19 (Sheffield, UK: Sheffield Academic Press, 2000).

[17] This is one reason why the baptism of the Spirit and gifts of the Spirit cannot be distant from the fruit of the Spirit.

[18] This is a key theme in Acts. See Acts 2:32, 3:15, 5:32, 10:39, 13:31, 22:15; cf. Lk 24:48. For a detailed discussion of the contextual understanding of "witness," see Keener, *Acts*, vol. 1, 691–97, and H. Strathmann, "μάρτυς, . . ," in *Theological Dictionary of the New Testament*, vol. 4, ed. Gerhard Friedrich, trans. and ed. Geoffrey W. Bromiley (Grand Rapids, MI: Eerdmans, 1967), 474–514, esp. 489–94. Strathmann states, "The witness to facts and the witness to truth are one and the same. . . ." (492). Also see T. W. Manson, "Martyrs and Martyrdom," *Bulletin of the John Rylands Library* 39, no. 2 (1957): 463–84.

[19] James D. G. Dunn, *The Acts of the Apostles*. See the foreword by Scot McKnight (Grand Rapids, MI: Eerdmans, 1996), 11. Matthew 28:18-20, the Great Commission, also notes that the disciples were not to teach the nations what Jesus taught. Rather they were to teach others to *obey/observe* what Jesus taught.

[20] Highlighted by David A. Dorman, "The Purpose of Empowerment in the Christian Life," *Pneuma* 7, no. 2 (1985): 150–51. Also see Simon Chan, *Pentecostal Theology and the Christian Spiritual Tradition*, Journal of Pentecostal Theology Supplemental Series 21 (Sheffield, UK: Sheffield Academic Press, 2000), 54–55.

Holy Spirit into the image of Christ.[21] The disciples were "first and foremost about *being* witnesses, about lives being transformed."[22] For the disciples, it is an affirmation of who they were to be as Spirit-empowered witnesses. As a state of "being" witnesses, it was to be a twenty-four-hours-a-day and a seven-days-a-week situation—a lifestyle empowered by Christ.

This lifestyle did not preclude witnessing. Indeed, their witnessing activity was to be an expression of who they were: disciples of Jesus the Christ. As has often been noted, the disciples were to be witnesses to the Good News, which is the death and resurrection of the Lord Jesus. They had witnessed his resurrection with "many convincing proofs" for over forty days and had witnessed his forgiveness.[23] They were also to be a witness to his salvation, and the need for repentance—a belief necessary for a believer to be in Jesus. Apart from the content of their witness, the disciples participated in two types of being a witness. First, they were to witness the things that they saw in reference to the Lord Jesus Christ. Second, they witnessed to the Good News—the salvation that they could prove through their own testimony.[24] While the disciples were to be the initial "witnesses" as original observers, it becomes clear that Acts 1:8 was for all believers.[25] All believers are to be witnesses to Jesus Christ—his salvation and forgiveness. Later believers would bear witness to Jesus's life, death, and resurrection, not as personal eyewitnesses, but as those who could testify that Jesus resides in their lives.

Empowerment of Creativity and Charismata

Creativity is part of this empowerment. Believers are not to be innovative in their own abilities. The vastness of God's creativity enables believers to be truly creative, in the same vein as C. S.

---

[21] Dorman, "The Purpose of Empowerment in the Christian Life," 151. On the role of the Holy Spirit in character, especially in ethics, see Jones, *Transformed Judgment*; and Lewis, "A Pneumatological Approach to Virtue Ethics," 42–61.

[22] Chan, *Pentecostal Theology,* 55 (italics original).

[23] For example, Schnabel, *Acts,* 78. This witness was to include the divine Christology; Keener, *Acts,* vol. 1, 696–97.

[24] Kistemaker, *Acts,* 54.

[25] Ibid.

Lewis stating upon reading George MacDonald: "My imagination was . . . baptized."[26] Creativity and the imagination can be tainted by sin (and the Fall), but the supernatural empowerment of the Spirit can endow the believer with divine creativity. We can use the baptized imagination to its fullness in witness. With this broader sense of witness, this allows the Spirit's enablement to be in the creative arts, music, and literary endeavors, all aspects that demonstrate God's grace, love, forgiveness, and goodness.[27]

The charismatic aspects of the Holy Spirit accompany the empowerment for witness.[28] In one sense, the signs and wonders (healings and miracles) are a "sign" of the trustworthiness of the message being witnessed (see Part III: Christ Our Healer). These miraculous deeds, including the gifts of the Spirit in 1 Corinthians 12, speak to the reality of the divine presence and power with the presentation of the gospel. Further, in many cases these miraculous occurrences are the divine in-breaking of the future kingdom into our present day. It is the eschatological healing (when we will be in heaven) meeting our present time—the *now* hits the *not yet*. The prophetic, miraculous, and immediate aspects of the Spirit are part of the witness—both in what we proclaim and in the way that the witness takes place.

As expressed in Acts 1:8, the witness was with proclamation: word accompanies the deed. The disciples were to proclaim the death, burial, and resurrection of the Lord Jesus Christ, and his salvation. This proclamation can be to large groups, for instance, Peter's speech at Pentecost (Acts 2:14–41) and at the Temple (Acts 3:11–26); house-to-house, such as in Jerusalem (Acts 2:42–47); to families, for example, with Cornelius in Caesarea (Acts 10:24–48)

---

[26] C. S. Lewis, *Surprised by Joy* (New York: Harcourt, Brace, Jovanovich, 1966), 181.

[27] For example, see Steven Felix-Jäger, "Inspiration and Discernment in Pentecostal Aesthetics," *Journal of Pentecostal Theology* 23 (2014): 85–104; Steven Felix-Jäger, *Pentecostal Aesthetics: Theological Reflections in a Pentecostal Philosophy of Art and Aesthetics*, Global Pentecostal and Charismatic Studies 16 (Leiden, the Netherlands: Brill, 2015); and Patrick Sherry, *Spirit and Beauty* (Oxford: Oxford University Press, 1992).

[28] See Robert P. Menzies, *Empowered for Witness: The Spirit in Luke-Acts* (New York: T & T Clark, 2004); and Roger Stronstad, *The Charismatic Theology of St. Luke* (Peabody, MA: Hendrickson Publishers, 1984).

or the jailer in Philippi (Acts 16:22–34); and one-on-one with Philip and the Ethiopian eunuch (Acts 8:26–39). This part of the witness is through the proclamation of the reality of Jesus's resurrection together with the effect on the lives of believers.

Empowerment of Ethical Dimensions

Christians often neglect, however, another aspect of being a witness: the role of the moral nature of the Spirit in the ethical dimensions of empowerment. The witness of Acts demonstrates moral components of God and being his witnesses to holiness (see 1 Pet 1:15–16). For example, the interaction between Peter and Ananias and Sapphira in Acts 5:1–11 demonstrates the Lord's holiness. In this case, the witness of the Spirit-empowered Peter clearly rejected the lies. Holiness as a moral code became a noted part of being a witness. "Being a witness" is an element of character. Living and talking morally is an expression of the Spirit's presence, and a witness to Jesus's salvific (sanctifying) power. Being witnesses filled with the Spirit embeds the believer with a moral sense within the prophetic community, which has both personal and communal components.[29] Therefore, the empowerment is to be both empowered to "be my witnesses" and to be "set apart" or to be holy.

We see Christ our Empowerer through the life changes of people who met him and followed him, and whom the Spirit transforms. For example, Luke narrates the story of the Roman centurion that met Jesus in Luke 7 to show what Christ the Empowerer can do in one's life journey (see chapter 6).

HISTORICAL COMPONENTS

Throughout church history, especially including missionary enterprises, we readily see the empowerment of Christ. We have seen that Christ's empowerment is "for witness," and to be "set apart." The church knew those "set apart" as "saints." While we under-

---

[29] See Roger Stronstad, *The Prophethood of All Believers*, Journal of Pentecostal Theology Supplemental Series 16 (Sheffield, UK: Sheffield Academic Press, 1999); Wenk, *Community-Forming Power*; and Amos Yong, *The Spirit Poured Out on All Flesh* (Grand Rapids, MI: Baker Academic, 2006), 140–41.

stand that biblically a saint was anyone sanctified by Christ (e.g., Rom 1:7; 1 Cor 1:2), believers later used the term to designate those who lived exemplary holy lives. Over the centuries, however, Christians have interpreted being "set apart" differently.

Empowerment to Proclaim the Gospel

For many throughout church history, divine empowerment meant to separate oneself from the familiar to proclaim the Good News outside of one's own cultural and/or geographic comfort zone (e.g., Acts 1:8; "Samaria, and even to the ends of the earth"). History is full of those who left family, friends, and the familiar to proclaim the gospel under God's empowerment.[30] The Book of Acts highlights some of these people such as the labors of outreach by Paul, Silas, Philip, and others. In the first couple of centuries, Thomas (one of the twelve) pioneered the church in India; Mark, according to tradition, established the church in Alexandria; and Addai, who traditionally was one of the seventy sent out by Jesus in Luke 10, established the church in Edessa of Syria on the Silk Road.

Some of the other notables who were "set apart" through the remainder of the first millennium include Bishop Alopen who in 635 CE met the emperor of the Tang Dynasty in China, and proclaimed the Christian message. In addition, Patriarch Timothy I (eighth to ninth centuries) of the Church of the East sent missionaries throughout central, east, and south Asia with the gospel. The two brothers Cyril and Methodius in the ninth century evangelized the Slavs, devising the Slavic alphabet.

Many also in the second millennium, likewise, went to unreached areas under the empowerment of Christ. Some renowned proclaimers include Francis of Assisi and Raymond

---

[30] Significant works looking at missions history biographically are Gerald H. Anderson, ed., *Biographical Dictionary of Christian Missions* (New York: Macmillan Reference, 1998); Ruth A. Tucker, *From Jerusalem to Irian Jaya: A Biographical History of Christian Missions*, 2nd ed. (Grand Rapids, MI: Zondervan, 2004); and John Mark Terry and Robert L. Gallagher, *Encountering the History of Missions: From the Early Church to Today*, Encountering Missions Series (Grand Rapids, MI: Baker Academic, 2017).

Llull, who reached out to Muslim populations when most of Christendom was actively focusing on the Crusades. In the sixteenth century, Matteo Ricci, who worked in the Qing Dynasty, China, and Francis Xavier, a missionary to India, the East Indies, and Japan, were other famous missionary pioneers.

In the later part of the second millennium, numerous others went under divine empowerment to the ends of the earth. For instance, William Carey to India; Adoniram Judson to Burma; Robert Morrison to China; and later the Cambridge Seven together with C. T. Studd to China; and, famously, Studd to Africa where he founded the Heart of Africa Mission. While these are some distinguished "missionaries," the vast majority of those who went to proclaim the gospel under Christ's empowerment (and, at times, were martyred), did so without being known in history—unsung heroes of the faith. Distinguished church historian Kenneth Scott Latourette highlighted and modeled that genuine documenting of the church's history is through the lens of outreach, not primarily as an institution. Where the church reaches out, the church grows, is vibrant, and is the expression of Christ.[31]

Empowerment to Be Not of This World

A key component of being "set apart" is to be "in the world, but not of it" (Jn 17:16–18). Definitions vary in many ways, however. For some believers, especially in the early centuries of Christianity, they saw themselves as needing to be set apart personally for prayer and to be untainted by the world. Historians call these followers of Christ "anchorites." Anthony (the Great), a hermit of the Egyptian desert during the late third and early fourth centuries—whose biography was written by his contemporary Athanasius Patriarch of Alexandria—lived in this fashion. Another noteworthy anchorite

---

[31] See Kenneth Scott Latourette, *A History of the Expansion of Christianity*, 7 vols. (New York: Harper & Brothers, 1937–45); and *A History of Christianity*, rev. ed. 2 vols. (New York: Harper & Row, 1975). Also see Kenneth Scott Latourette, "The Christian Understanding of History," *American Historical Review* 54, no. 2 (1949): 259–76, and "New Perspectives in Church History," *Journal of Religion* 21, no. 4 (1941): 432–43.

was Simeon Stylites, who sat on a pillar (called a style) in the Syrian Desert near Aleppo for thirty-seven years. In both cases, the faithful saw the dedication to prayer and God by these anchorites as a clear demonstration of holiness because so many pilgrims came to them seeking advice, prayer, and miracles.

Others defined "in the world, but not of it" in a communal fashion. Living in a cloistered community, they prayed, read Scripture, and labored together. They incorporated spiritual life and growth with spiritual leadership. Known as cenobites, they lived in monasteries. An early founder was Pachomius (the Great) of the early fourth century in Egypt. He focused on the corporate aspects of the "set apart" communal life and was a contemporary of the aforementioned Anthony. In Western Christianity in the sixth century, St. Benedict of Nursia established a cenobite monastic movement called the Benedictines. Benedict set down the "Rule of St. Benedict" that established the rules by which monks were to live in community. While not cenobitic monasticism, contemporary groups such as the Amish still follow the communal aspects of being separated from the world.

Empowerment for Diversity of Proclamation

Not only was empowerment important, but there was also a diversity of ways to proclaim or demonstrate the "witness" and being "set apart." Proclamation was important and included proclaiming and engaging in the local language. Frequently, "signs and wonders" and healings accompanied the proclamation to support the gospel that Christians preached (see Part III: Christ Our Healer). For some, the empowerment to "be my witnesses" and to be "set apart" was not only an aspect of preaching but necessarily included action, such as that of St. Francis and St. Clare of Assisi, and expressed through John Wesley (see chapter 7).

In a different way, songs and poems transmit empowering theological aspects such as those produced by Ephrem the Syrian (see chapter 7) and Charles Wesley, among others. Through song, Christians today still extol the empowerment of God, and the meaning of being "set apart." Yet while proclaiming and acting accordingly, some also expressed themselves in theological works, with heavy practicality, which a broader audience read. These publications delineated and clarified who Christ the Empowerer is, and what this means for believers. Dietrich Bonhoeffer and John Wesley also convey this notion. Yet for both these communicators, there is an intertwining of their theology and lives, as they showed personally who Christ our Empowerer is.

CONTEMPORARY COMPONENTS

The importance of the contemporary aspect of Christ the Empowerer is that the empowerment seen biblically and historically is equally available today. People from around the world, historically and globally, can be empowered by Christ through the Holy Spirit as they avail themselves of his presence and empowerment. This empowerment we see in the testimonies of enablement, holiness, service, and call to missionary work in word and deed such as seen in the stories of Dan, Katy, Ana, and Ray in chapter 8. Each story is their own journey, yet we readily see Christ the Empowerer through the enabling and embodying work of the Holy Spirit.

OVERVIEW OF CHRIST OUR EMPOWERER

Christ our Empowerer, through the work of the Holy Spirit, is the reason the missional task can go forth. Not only is Christ the "author and perfecter of our faith" (Heb 12:2), he is also the guide, enabler, and empowerer for our journey. The empowerment of Christ means that we are his "witnesses" by the power of his Holy Spirit, which includes proclamation by word and deed, through mighty signs and healings, and in the twenty-four-hours-a-day/seven-days-a-week life lived as "set apart" lives. In one sense, every believer is to be a witness since Acts 1:8 is for all who follow Christ. Acts 13:1–3, however, highlights that God separates some for focused ministry. The Lord calls all to be "witnesses," but God calls only some personally to cross-cultural gospel engagement. All are called to "make disciples of all nations" (Mt 28:19) and have their "witness" felt to the "ends of the earth" (Acts 1:8). Nevertheless, only some the Lord calls to go. In either case, however, to be a witness, to be "set apart" in holiness and service, and to go outside the comfort zone is only possible through the empowerment of Christ through the Holy Spirit.

In this introductory chapter, I have emphasized the role of Christ our Empowerer, which involves being a witness to the resurrection of the Lord Jesus, together with living a Christ-like existence. The Lord intertwines these equally important elements of the Christian life, especially for those in ministerial or missionary vocation. The following chapters of Part II, Christ Our Empowerer, demonstrate these truths.

A Beloved Servant at Death's Door: Faith that Empowers

Chapter 6 deals with the narrative in Luke 7 regarding Christ empowering the Roman centurion through the healing of his beloved servant. Through this imaginative story, the author approaches a number of questions concerning the cultural background of the Roman captain, along with insights as to why his imperial administration sent him to the fishing town of Capernaum. In addition, the centurion explains the confrontation of Palestine's sociocultural barriers, how he first encountered Jesus of Nazareth, and Christ's subsequent influence on his life.

St. Ephrem, St. Francis, St. Clare, Wesley, and Bonhoeffer

It is through Christ and the indwelling of his Spirit that the Christian is empowered for witness. Christ also empowers believers to be "set apart." Some have interpreted being set apart as being physically separated as hermits, communities, or living in the world, but separate in actions.

While being empowered can have two different aspects—enabled or set apart—it is also true that biographies narrate different ways by which the saints expressed the empowerment of Christ. In chapter 7, the author considers St. Ephrem, St. Francis, and St. Clare, as well as John Wesley and Dietrich Bonhoeffer, all of whom demonstrate different ways that Christ was their Empowerer.

Empowerment to Holiness, Service, and Witness

In chapter 8, the writer tells the contemporary stories of believers who have experienced Christ as their Empowerer. Christ empowered Dan of North Dakota to live in holiness and witness. Empowered by Christ, Katy of El Salvador sacrificed her final year of industrial engineering to serve as a missionary with her husband in Africa.

The Lord Jesus also empowered Ana to cross-cultural ministry by moving her to Puerto Lempira, Honduras, where she lived among the Miskito people learning their language, leading them to Christ, and planting churches and a Bible school. Later Ana witnessed to Christ among the tribal peoples of India.

Finally, God called Ray to preach the gospel while wandering aimlessly around the world. On returning to El Salvador, Christ empowered Ray to start churches in Paraguay, Ecuador, and Colombia by holding evangelistic tent campaigns characterized by the miraculous.

6

A Beloved Servant at Death's Door: Faith that Empowers

Robert L. Gallagher

Jesus entered the town of Capernaum after he had imparted all he had to say to the people who were listening to him. A captain of the conquering Roman military living in the vicinity had a beloved servant on his deathbed. Death was at the door of this highly valued man. The soldier did not want to lose to the sickness that was ravaging his friend's body. He heard that Jesus had come back to town, and sent leaders of the Jewish community to ask the Teacher a huge favor.[1]

The beginning of the narrative journey regarding the empowerment of the centurion and the healing of his servant presents a number of initial questions. What was the background of the Roman captain? Why did the imperial administration send him to Capernaum? What sociocultural barriers did he confront to live there? How did the centurion first encounter Jesus of Naza-

---

[1] In this chapter, I imaginatively expand the biblical pericope of Luke 7:2–10; the italicized sections signify my paraphrased translation.

reth? What were the consequences of interacting with the Jewish Messiah? To answer these and other questions, let me allow the Roman soldier to tell the story in his own words.

MAGNIFICENCE OF ROME

My name is Marcus Antoninus Pius. The city of Rome is my beloved home. I thought that my adoration of the metropolis would last for an eternity. Seven hills corral the ancient city, which hugs the east bank of the Tiber some ten miles up the river from the port of Ostia. In the first 750 years of the city, the Roman people conquered Italy and the Mediterranean world. We accomplished the mission by establishing the dominance of our naval power together with the conquest of Rome's powerful army into Asia, Cilicia, and Bithynia, followed by Syria, Macedonia, Egypt, Greece, and much of central Europe. By incorporating the indigenous people into our military might, we continued this triumph by expanding possessions in Africa and completing the conquest of Hispania and Britain. The world has never witnessed the splendor of such a victorious military empire as that of Rome.

The cosmopolitan inhabitants of Rome mirror the magnificence of the realm through the grandeur of their building projects. The conurbation boasts some of the most impressive architectural structures in the Mediterranean world. The city possesses the palaces of Augustus, Caligula, and Tiberius; the temples of Claudius, Concord, Diana, and Jupiter; the forums of Augustus and Julius; and the theaters of Balbus and Pompey (which hold 40,000 people) as well as the circuses of Nero and Maximus (which hold 150,000 people).

I was born and raised in Rome in the midst of a municipality flourishing with growth in economic, social, and political arenas. Multistoried housing catered to a crowded population of over one million people drawn from the entire Mediterranean. A river of migrants had flowed into the city from Africa, Asia Minor, Egypt, Spain, Syria, and later Gaul and Germany. The international aristocracy manifested their wealth through suburban villas and country estates as the Caesars gave the city lavish public buildings together with economic benefits and entertainment for the masses. The city attracted goods, foods, and diplomatic connections on top of literary and artistic expressions from every region and state of the empire.

In addition, Rome possesses urban infrastructures like no other metropolis in the history of humanity. The Appian Way to Puteoli dissects the densely cloistered arrangement of buildings from north to south; the Flaminian Way dissects it from east to west to Ariminum on the coast of the Adriatic Sea. Two main aqueducts, the Aqua Claudia and Virgo, sustain our city's burgeoning population, along with agricultural produce supplied by the villas and gardens straddling the west bank of the River Tiber. Rome is the greatest city of all time.

COMING TO CAPERNAUM

It was not an easy transition moving from Rome to Tiberias, the capital of Palestine, and then to Capernaum (both towns on the western shore of the Sea of Gennesaret). Rome, the magnificent! Rome, the center of the empire! Rome, my city—admired as the greatest capital of the greatest empire of all time. Then there is Tiberias and Capernaum. Has anyone in Rome ever heard of these towns in Palestine? In fact, has anyone ever heard of Palestine? Has anybody of significance ever come out of this backwater Capernaum? I don't believe so. No, never!

At first, it was quite a setback to have my military commission transferred from the cosmopolitan metropolis of Rome to Tiberias and then to finish up in this little fishing town of Capernaum, which skirts Gennesaret on the eastern-most border of the Roman Empire. Capernaum is nestled within the northern region of Galilee, a fertile valley within limestone hills surrounded by an abundance of natural resources in the midst of a wilderness. Its lush soil, reliable rainfall, and temperate weather produce a diversity of fruits and vegetables the whole year round, like no other region I have witnessed in my travels. There is a luxurious abundance of vineyards, citrus orchards, and olive groves, along with date, fig, and walnut farms all lavishly watered by springs peppered across the district.

These pastoral scenes in Capernaum of Galilee slowly swallowed the drive and energy that I enjoyed while living in Rome. The sights, smells, and sounds of the rural town were so different to what I had embraced in Rome, with its noxious mayhem and toxic atmosphere of garbage and excrement. Here I encountered sheep bleating as they filed along ruts of dusty haze; tingling aromas of fresh manure mingled with the fodder of cut grass; and the strange guttural sounds of fishermen, farmers, and traders going about their daily drudgery. Compared with the exhilarating chaos of capital life, Capernaum was an invasion of alien senses that made me a stranger in my world and desperately cautious of change. Yet there was a provocation within my soul toward stillness and peace, which felt natural and beautiful—even spiritual.

Capernaum is a prosperous frontier town of about 1,200 people, mainly composed of Jewish families whose economic base is agriculture and the local fishing industry. The latter includes fresh-water fishing in the Sea of Gennesaret, building and repairing boats, and making and mending fishing nets. During the day, I would see the fishermen wading in the lake along the shore casting their nets in shallow waters, or washing their nets with their small boats and oars lying at the edge of the sea. They would work hard all night, with several men using large dragnets in deeper waters. Sometimes the men would empty the fish into the boat, but more often, they dragged the nets to the shore where they sorted the fish and placed the salable ones in baskets. Early in the morning, the women of the town would come to buy the fresh catch at the fish market on the beach. It is a strenuous life requiring a strong physique, and their language at times is rough and colorful.

When the elders finally found Jesus, they began beseeching him to come to the centurion's home and heal his slave. Pressing their petition, they earnestly pleaded with him to come to the home and give power to the life of the servant. They exclaimed, "He deserves a miracle. He loves the Jewish people. He is a good friend of our race, and at his own expense, he built our place of worship with black-basalt stone from the hills north of the town. He deserves this favor from you. Show him kindness at your hands."

RELIGIONS OF ROME

As a citizen of Rome, I was very religious in all respects. I followed the city's beliefs that merged the gods of human form (Jupiter, Mars, Minerva, and Juno) with the reinterpreted traditional practices of foreign cults brought by immigration such as Asclepius (Epidaurus, Peloponnese), Cybele (the Anatolian mother goddess), Dionysus (Campanian, Italy), Isis (Egypt), and Mithra (Persia). Religious exclusivism is unknown in Roman thinking.

I was devout in my allegiance to the Roman gods and regularly attended the temples. Dominating the city landscape is a large temple dedicated to Jupiter, Juno, and Minerva located on Capitolium Hill opposite the palaces of Augustus, Tiberius, and Caligula on Palatine Hill. There is also the Temple of Diana on Aventine Hill and the Temple of Claudius on Caelian Hill in the south and southwest of the city. My public worship parallels my private worship in my home, with shrines of *lares* (my dead family members), and *di penates* (gods of my family cupboard) acting as constant reminders of the connection between this temporal world and eternity.

Life in Rome is full of religious ritual, with membership in specific religious groups based on occupation or ethnic background. It is crucial that all the public and private religious rituals lie within the political laws of the city. As a resident of Rome, if I observe the correct ritualistic procedures of the city's legislature, then I will obtain the "peace of the gods." This is not necessarily establishing a personal relationship with the rational divine beings, however. The polytheistic religion of Rome is a concern of the state even though there is no ordered system of theology except a tolerance of all national deities, as long as they do not attack polytheism as a whole.

CHANGING ALLEGIANCE

I will now shift my story toward how I connected with the Jewish people of Rome and changed my spiritual allegiance from polytheism to monotheism. Emperor Pompey brought to Rome a large number of Jewish slaves so that when I was born, there were over 40,000 Jews in the city. They lived in seven communities, each with its own synagogue and council of elders, and were some of the poorest sections of the city across from the Tiber River near the Circus Maximus and outside the Porta Capena. As *peregrini* (foreign residents), they experienced racial discrimination, even though the authorities allowed them to meet in synagogues, observe the Sabbath, and travel to Jerusalem to represent their respective synagogues at the annual Jewish celebrations of Passover, Pentecost, and Tabernacles. When I was a boy, Tiberius issued an imperial decree, nevertheless, temporarily expelling a number of the Jewish leaders from Rome because of Jewish proselytizing.

Even so, it was through one of my devout slaves who were in constant attendance upon me that I heard about Judaism. He enthusiastically told me about the monotheistic faith of living a moral life. Thus, he persuaded me to attend a Jewish place of prayer and worship called the Synagogue of the Freedmen located within the Jewish enclave. The multicultural assembly included former slaves from Cyrene, Alexandria, Cilicia, and Asia whom the empire privileged with Roman citizenship.

It was sometime during the first few months of attending Sabbath worship at the place of meeting that I changed loyalty from polytheism to become a God-fearer or official sympathizer within the believing community. I now worship the one, true, and living God, having repented to faith and obedience according to the laws of Noah, together with social integration into the local Jewish community. I hesitated to become a proselyte through circumcision and baptism, however. Yet sitting at the back of the synagogue, I still appreciated the Sabbath ceremony: an interpreter paraphrasing the Hebraic reading of the Jewish Law and Prophets into the vernacular Greek, interspersed with prayers for the restoration of the Davidic dynasty, the temple in Jerusalem, and the nation of Israel. At first, the prayers caused an awkward conflict of imperial interest within me, as did the necessity of putting aside my Latin colloquial speech. Where should my true loyalties lie: with the Hebrew God, with the emperor of Rome, or with myself?

ENTERTAINING UNFIRED PASSIONS

In the eastern empire, Emperor Augustus ratified Herod the Great's bequest that Rome give the territory of Galilee and Peraea to Antipas, his youngest son. Upon Herod Antipas's appointment, the emperor sent a Roman legion to secure the royal selection. This is how I arrived in Herod's capital at Tiberias of Palestine. Then you might ask how the tetrarch of Galilee sent me—a senior centurion of the first cohort of a Roman legion—to serve in Capernaum, a remote northern Galilean fishing town. Although it is embarrassing, I will tell you the true story.

The stringent Roman military code forbade my rank to marry. Yet the grand empire expected me to conduct myself with a moral standard that adhered to a strictly monogamous marriage (*conubium*) between the honor of Rome and the centurion militia. My assignment in Capernaum provided an opportunity of discipline and political diversion for an imperial officer who had disturbed a marital harmony by expressing wanton indiscretion toward Joanna the wife of Cuza, the manager of Herod's household.

Claudius Lysias, the legate who commanded my legion in Tiberias, chastised me for this recklessness by stationing me in the remote backwoods of the eastern empire. Consequently, my carelessness brought much humiliation and dishonor upon my family in Rome. My father of the family (*paterfamilias*) felt disgraced. In the city of Rome, I had already exchanged my allegiance from the Roman gods to monotheistic Judaism. Yet upon arriving in the fishing village with distant accountability to Lucius Appius Caecus, my tribune in Tiberias, I felt distraught and overwhelmed with indignity, which distorted my thinking.

Instead of finding solace in the local synagogue, I sought relief of my discomfort by entertaining my unfired passions. I found myself walking in the night to the parlor of women frequented by my men. There I met the patron of the commerce, Mary of Capernaum, who over the months became a forbidden lover and later a close confidant. Afterward, upon learning that my mistress was expecting, we agreed for her to carry the infant until birth and then dispose of the child. After all, according to Roman custom, it was not human until two years of age. Yet during Mary's months of waiting, I became double-minded toward our decision and argued for restraint. My courtesan remained steadfast, and against my wishes, killed the child upon birth; then in the dark of the night she secretly buried the little bundle in the back garden. Broken in grief, I strangely found myself questioning why the innocent should suffer such evil in our world. In doing so, I surprisingly began searching for answers through the faith I left in Rome and once again started sitting in the back row of the local synagogue.

Persuaded by their petitions, Jesus followed the elders toward the home [of the centurion]. Walking through the streets of the town, not far from the house, Jewish friends of the powerful foreigner met the Master with a message. They had heard of their friend's severe concern for his adored slave, and had gathered in support, not knowing exactly what to do. Yet they listened. After sharing his concerns, the soldier commissioned them to repeat to Jesus what they had heard him implore. This is what they reiterated from the conversation: "Do not take any more trouble; don't go to any more bother. I am nobody. It is not right for you to come at my beckoning. It is embarrassing. I was even ashamed to come to you in person. I am not suitable for you to come to my home. I am not important enough for you to listen to my plea. I did not even presume to come to you. I know that I was not good enough to come to you in person."

Following this admission, on behalf of their Roman friend, the messengers continued recalling the captain's words before they left on their mission. He told us, "Tell the Teacher to only give the order for my servant to be healed. Tell Jesus to say the word. Then my servant will receive his healing. Jesus, just say the word, and heal my boy."

JESUS COMES TO TOWN

You might ask where my assurance of Jesus's supernatural ability comes from. Well, as I said before, Capernaum was a small town where my role as the head of imperial security meant that I needed to know the whereabouts and dealings of everyone in the region. This was easily manageable because of the small population, until the young rabbi from Nazareth came out of the wilderness and made the town his ministry headquarters. It was from Capernaum that he began his public declaration: "Repent, for the kingdom of heaven is near." This announcement ignited a flickering flame of messianic expectations. Sitting with the God-fearers in the back of the Capernaum synagogue, I had heard about the Holy and Righteous One coming to usher forth God's reign of peace, justice, and righteousness. I also knew that the assembly was careful in speaking about such controversial matters around me. Over the years though, I felt that there was a gradual fermenting of messianic anticipation. Then Jesus comes to town.

My first glimpse of the Nazarene was in the midst of a group of local fishermen walking along the shore of Gennesaret. I found out later that the men with Jesus that morning were the brothers Simon and Andrew who were business partners with James and John, the sons of Zebedee. The next time I saw Jesus was in the local synagogue, which I had helped to construct. Certainly, my love of the people, demonstrated by my recent support of their building program, had helped in attaining the confidence of the community. This occurred in spite of the obvious tension arising from the fact that I represented the emperor, the only king who demanded Jewish obedience and respect.

I was amazed at Jesus's teaching, which was so unlike the instructions of our local teachers of the law. He spoke with the authority of God about a wide range of topics, from such worldly matters as paying the temple taxes to the need of humility in community leaders. Standing at the back of a crowd near the shoreline I also heard him preach on subjects difficult to understand. One day he told the people that he was the bread of life—the living bread come down from heaven—to bring eternal life to whoever eats his flesh, which he will give for the life of the world. This topic was truly hard to understand—I could not grasp his meaning.

Jesus of Nazareth was so different compared to the local religious leaders. He had the ability to love people from all sorts of vocations and social hierarchies. Calling himself a doctor of sinners, he enjoyed the hospitality of spiritually unclean people whom most of the community despised, such as tax collectors and prostitutes. I often saw him in fishermen's lodgings with an overflow audience. On one occasion, town officials called me to investigate a civil disturbance caused by a group of men destroying a roof to lower their sick friend into a home for Jesus to heal. Some of the scribes were extremely displeased with Jesus. When I came with my soldiers, the healed man was walking around for all to see; and the privileged were complaining about a blasphemy law that Jesus had broken. I had never seen anything like it and dismissed their petty droning by pointing to the sick man made well. Despite witnessing the miracles of Jesus, there were many in the town who rejected him because of their jealousy and unbelief.

GOOD NEWS SPREADING

The news about the rabbi Jesus went out into every locality of the surrounding district, resulting in crowds inundating Capernaum from all over Galilee, bringing their sick and demon possessed. And Jesus healed them, cast out demons, and performed many signs and wonders in the town. In fact, I was present in the Shabbat synagogue when Jesus expelled an unclean spirit from a regular attendee. I shall never forget what the demon shouted out: "Go away! What do you want with us, Jesus of Nazareth? Have you come to destroy us? I know who you are—the Holy One of God!" Jesus rebuked the demon, which cried out loudly as it emerged from the tortured man. What amazing authority and power this man Jesus has, that even the unclean spirits obey him.

Following this demonic deliverance, Jesus began to travel from Capernaum throughout Galilee—even though the Jewish elite despised the area because of its religious and ethnic diversity—teaching in their synagogues, proclaiming the Good News of God's kingdom, and healing every sickness among the people. Consequently, the Good News about Jesus spread among the Jewish communities of Bethsaida, Caesarea Philippi, Judea, and Jerusalem, on top of the Gentile territories of Dalmanutha, Decapolis, Idumea, Sidon, Syria, Tyre, and beyond the Jordan with great multitudes following him; and he healed the demoniacs, epileptics, paralytics, and diseased.

Thousands of people poured into our region from all these areas—such as Canaanites, Phoenicians, Samaritans, and Syrians—overturning the lethargic town of Capernaum. The townspeople erected makeshift dwellings propped against their fishing huts to accommodate the overcrowding; and merchants scrambled to supply the throngs with food and water. With Jesus in town, the population more than tripled. I have never heard so many different languages spoken in the streets alongside the trade language of Greek and the local Aramaic. Every day seemed like a market day as people with exotic clothing and unfamiliar appearances mingled with the residential Jews. My auxiliary soldiers were constantly on duty to prevent social unrest, especially any suggestion of political riots. It was an exacting time for the community as the man from Nazareth turned the languid rural town into a vigorous city of chaos. If there was any bedlam, then the manifestation of God's glory caused the turmoil, as hundreds of formerly sick and diseased men, women, and children danced in the streets in praise and adoration; and then they were reluctant to leave Capernaum because of the astonishing wonders that they were experiencing and seeing.

POWER FROM ABOVE

On behalf of their Roman friend, the messengers continued recalling the captain's words: "I know about such matters since I am in the army. I give orders and the soldiers and slaves under me have to obey. They don't have a choice. I am under orders, but I also give orders. I too am a man that obtains his power from above. I know what it is like to obey orders since my whole life is commanding and submitting to commands. But Jesus, you have such authority from God that you can command anything, and it will happen, even creative miracles."

As an imperial centurion, I know about the chain of command that summons the great authority and power of the Roman military. It starts with Emperor Augustus, the greatest leader of all time who rules the greatest empire of all time. Throughout the expanding Roman Empire, Augustus, my sovereign lord, established and maintains *pax Romana*, the peace that exists between ethnicities within the Roman Empire. He also orchestrated legal and financial reforms, besides promoting traditional Roman values and morality such as family life, the virtues of human dignity, and devotion to duty. He even introduced in Rome a city police force of three urban cohorts, and employs 600 to 1,000 former slaves to form seven fire brigades (with each brigade responsible for two of the fourteen districts) to bring order to the expanding city. I follow this mighty ruler with unwavering devotion and loyalty. It is not difficult to respect and obey a leader whose morality is evident in his orders.

After Herod Antipas's appointment as tetrarch of Galilee and Peraea by Emperor Augustus, Antipas converted his royal army into a Roman *auxilia* composed of recruits within the province from Sebaste and Caesarea Maritima (mainly ethnic Syrians) serving alongside Roman legionaries; all were bestowed with Roman citizenship. This formed a *cohors equitata*. As an experienced *primus pilus* under military discipline, Antipas stationed me at Capernaum in charge of a *centuria*. With the centuria's full strength of eighty soldiers (who spoke the local *lingua franca* and not Latin) and twenty auxiliary servants, our role is to repel any disorder of banditry, help protect provincial administrators and tax collectors, maintain the road network, and police any actions of insurgence that might arise in the territory. The royal force does not directly serve Rome but is under the authority of the client king who nevertheless has an alliance with the empire even if he maintains his own military. As a senior centurion in the Roman army, the legate, the senior tribune, the camp prefect, and five junior tribunes outrank me. Thus, as a Roman citizen who had to pay a big price for my citizenship,[2] I have some influence and importance in Capernaum's local affairs. I understand and regularly experience this chain of regal military authority as a centurion stationed at Capernaum.

---

[2] See Acts 22:28.

ROYAL ARMY OF CAPERNAUM

The selection of Capernaum as the major post of a royal army in the region might seem unusual. This is especially true since the town is encircled by numerous cities of prosperity and power such as Tiberias (the multicultural city on the southwestern shore of the sea named in honor of the second emperor), and Sepphoris (the largest city in Galilee, and the capital of government). The answer to this paradox lies in the realization that these Galileans had doggedly resisted the Roman army for years, more so than the Jews of Judea. Furthermore, not only is the town rich in nature's supplies, but it is also situated on the *Via Maris*, the leading international trade route from Anatolia, Syria, and Damascus that runs south to Egypt by way of the coast. Positioned on the northern political frontier of Palestine, the town is important for the strategic security of the empire. In addition to its tactical location, the site was only three miles from the border between the tetrarchies of Herod Antipas (east of the Jordan River) and Herod Philip (west of the Jordan), which provides a seaport for both regions.

Capernaum on the *Via Maris* serves as a trading hub for transnational dealers, in addition to a center for nearby villages interested in buying and selling goods. A customs station collects imperial taxes, which includes customs taxes of local and foreign trade, taxes on products moving between districts, toll fees on roads, and fishing contracts for mercantile fishermen. One of my main roles in the region is to secure the collection and delivery of taxes to Governor Herod Antipas of Galilee. I am aware of monitoring the reputation of my provincial soldiers whom the townspeople often accuse of taking money by force, falsely indicting village peasants, and not being content with their wages. It is also an unfortunate occurrence that whenever I employ Jewish men to gather our taxes, the local inhabitants treat them with great disdain, as if they were subhuman. I can understand the local perspective, however: tax collectors who work for the oppressive conquerors are traitors to Jewish independence and the law of God, and are stealing from their brothers through their exorbitant commissions. Indeed, there is a truth to those accusations.

In this regard, one of the chief Jewish tax collectors I work closely with is Matthew Levi, the son of Alphaeus, whom I regularly see sitting at his tax booth. The townspeople shun him as if he is someone who is beyond contempt. Their harsh treatment of Matthew disturbs me, since in my business dealings I have found him to be a most intelligent man. Still, I noticed a steady change in his disposition from a defensive arrogance to one that was more contrite and remorseful. Then suddenly he closed his office, sold many of his household possessions and gave the money to the poor, and informed me that he was now following the Teacher from Nazareth. I was alarmed that he would throw away his position of prestige, wealth, and power to be a disciple of a country rabbi. Putting these thoughts of the transformed Matthew Levi aside, let me not digress too far from my personal interactions with the Nazarene that also altered my life.

These words [from the Jewish friends of the centurion] amazed Jesus. He was staggered at the commander's declaration through his friends. "I have not found faith like this anywhere in Israel," Jesus acknowledged. "Not a single case have I found among the Jewish people. What faith this man shows. In my travels through Israel, I have never heard or seen such a simple and trust-filled understanding of God. You Israelites could do well to look at his faith, and imitate what you see. You are supposed to know God and his ways. Yet you do not. This Gentile does, however. Take note of this moment, and follow his example."

Turning to the messengers, Jesus spoke a creative and healing word of empowerment. "The servant is whole. Go back home to your friend." On returning to the centurion's barracks, the supporters found the domestic servant no longer lying down and dying, but walking and talking. In perfect health, he scuttled around the house organizing the staff, and serving his beloved master. God had given him empowering enablement to continue his work.

CONCLUSION

What happened to Marcus Antoninus Pius, the Roman centurion, after this powerful miracle is worth recalling. He remained in Capernaum following his retirement from the military, after which he could then legally marry. Similar to Naaman of old (the commander of the army of the king of Aram), the former soldier remained loyal to the One he knew as the King of kings and Lord of lords. Further, Marcus became a faithful believer and regular adherent—along with his devoted servants—at the fledgling congregation of the Way in the home of Peter the apostle.

It was in this assembly that he enjoyed the warm fellowship of many of the Galilean disciples of the risen Christ, including Matthew Levi, the former tax collector. In particular, Pius esteemed the presence of Mary of Capernaum and her loving ability to model her faith to the children of the flock. Committed to the leaders, he recalled the ancient story of Salmon and Rahab, and submitted to them his desire to raise a family on a small farm he bought, which ran down to the shoreline of the lake, some four miles southwest of Capernaum.

REFLECTION QUESTIONS

1. In the narrative of Luke 7 developed in this chapter, how would you describe the life of Marcus Antoninus Pius, the resident Roman commander of Capernaum, before he encountered Christ as his Empowerer?
2. In what ways did Christ empower the centurion to have faith to believe that he would physically heal his beloved servant?
3. How do you imagine that Christ's healing of the Roman's servant influenced the town of Capernaum and its surroundings?
4. How has Christ empowered you and/or your Christian community to have faith to believe in miracles of divine healing?
5. What is the relationship between Christ our Empowerer and global missions today?

7

Historical Narratives of St. Ephrem, St. Francis, St. Clare, Wesley, and Bonhoeffer

Paul W. Lewis

As noted in the introduction to Part II, the focus of Christ the Empowerer has two main aspects. First, Christ is the Enabler. It is through Christ, and the indwelling of his Spirit, that the Christian is empowered "for witness" (Acts 1:8). This is the evangelistic and missional thrust of Christians, personally, and collectively through the church. Second, Christ also empowers believers to be "set apart" or "made holy." Theologians identify this action of empowerment as sanctification. Historically, the church called those who lived recognizably holy lives "saints."[1] Over the centuries, the meaning of the term "set apart" has had varied responses by diverse Christian groups. Some have interpreted being set

---

[1] The authors of the New Testament use the term "saints" to describe all the faithful followers of the Lord Jesus Christ. However, church historians use the term to highlight those who lived notably holy lives. See John H. Corbett, "Saints," in *Encyclopedia of Early Christianity*, ed. Everett Ferguson (New York: Routledge, 1990), 821–23.

apart as being physically separated as individual hermits, called anchorites,[2] separated in communities such as the monastic orders, called cenobites;[3] or living in the world, but separate in actions—the mendicant orders—such as the Franciscans or Poor Clares.

Furthermore, while being empowered can have the two different aspects—enabled or set apart—as shown above, it is also true that biographies narrate different ways by which the saints expressed the empowerment of Christ. Worthy of note are St. Ephrem, St. Francis, St. Clare, John Wesley, and Dietrich Bonhoeffer, each of whom demonstrates different ways that Christ was their Empowerer.

ST. EPHREM (ca. 306–373)[4]

St. Ephrem was born in or near Nisibis (present-day eastern Turkey), and lived in the area of Syria. While he grew up in a Christian family, he did not have good character. Later, Ephrem committed himself to God. During his lifetime, Nisibis shifted

---

[2] Anchorites include such notables as St. Anthony of Egypt and St. Simeon Stylites of Syria.

[3] For Cenobites, see such saints as St. Pachomius the Great of Egypt, together with the monastics. For example, the Benedictines and Cistercians, and Protestant groups such as the Amish.

[4] Apart from the works of St. Ephrem in the *Nicene and Post-Nicene Fathers*, second series, volume 13, a few of the notable collections of his works are Ephrem the Syrian, *Ephrem the Syrian: Hymns*, Classics of Western Spirituality (Mahwah, NJ: Paulist Press, 1989); St. Ephrem the Syrian, *The Harp of the Spirit: Poems of Saint Ephrem the Syrian*, Publications of the Institute for Orthodox Christian Studies 1, intro. and trans. Sebastian Brock, 3rd ed. (Cambridge: Aquila, 2013); and St. Ephrem the Syrian, *Selected Prose Works*, ed. Kathleen McVey, Fathers of the Church Patristic Series (Washington, DC: Catholic University of America Press, 1994). Introductions of Ephrem's life and work are in Stanley M. Burgess, ed., *Christian Peoples of the Spirit: A Documentary History of Pentecostal Spirituality from the Early Church to the Present* (New York: New York University Press, 2011), 48–51; and Kathleen McVey, "Ephraem the Syrian," in *Encyclopedia of Early Christianity*, ed. Everett Ferguson (New York: Routledge, 1990), 304–305. See also Sebastian Brock, "Ephrem and the Syriac Tradition," in *Cambridge History of Early Christian Literature* (Cambridge: Cambridge University Press, 2004), 262–72; and Sebastian Brock, *The Luminous Eye: The Spiritual World Vision of Saint Ephrem the Syrian*, Cistercian Studies 124 (Kalamazoo, MI: Cistercian Publications, 1992).

between the Sasanian and Roman Empires. In 363, the Romans gave the city to the Sasanians. Ephrem with other Christians from Nisibis, moved to Edessa in Syria (in the Roman Empire) to flee the ensuing persecution of Christians, which was happening at that time in the Persian Empire.[5]

Ephrem exegeted biblical texts, both in writing commentaries and as a preacher—we have many of his homilies. However, he was and is most famous for his hymns and poems. Ephrem used hymns to express and perpetuate theology. These hymns not only articulated theology but also helped instruct average Christians about their faith. He used a vast array of symbols and imagery to engage the thinking of those who sang these songs or read his commentaries, homilies, and poems. The singing and poetic meter of his hymns, as well as his imagery, aided in comprehension and remembrance for the church masses. These hymns were very influential in the Syriac church; indeed, the church today still sings some of his songs. Due to his theological acumen, and hymnic or poetic ability, the church called him the "Harp of the Spirit."

Ephrem also represents an aspect of Syriac Christianity that highlighted the importance of asceticism. The Syriac Christians—including Ephrem—saw asceticism as a way to demonstrate one's devotion to God by taming the carnal aspects of life. Yet even more importantly, asceticism fostered a devotion of single-mindedness to the Lord. Ephrem expressed his "set-apartness" through his ascetism, and his hymns and poems perpetuated this theme centuries after his death. More than that, he highlighted Jesus as the "only-begotten Son." The Syriac language also uses this term to describe a single person or celibate.[6] Thus, Jesus became the model of ascetics who focused on a celibate, single, and holy

---

[5] In part, this persecution was due to the well-meaning, yet naïve, letter from Constantine to the Shah of the Sasanians on behalf of the Persian Christians. On this persecution, see Dale T. Irvin and Scott W. Sunquist, *History of the World Christian Movement: Volume 1: Earliest Christianity to 1453* (Maryknoll, NY: Orbis Books, 2001), 197–99; and Samuel Hugh Moffett, *History of Christianity in Asia: Vol. 1, Beginnings to 1500*, rev. ed. (San Francisco: HarperCollins, 1998), 136–47.

[6] See Brock, *The Luminous Eye*, 131–41; Thomas Kathanar Koonammakkal, "Ephrem's Ideas of Singleness," *Hugoye: Journal of Syriac Studies* 2, no. 1 (1999): 57–66; and Robert Murray, *Symbols of Church and Kingdom* (Cambridge: Cambridge University Press, 1975), 11–17, 154–58.

lifestyle. Several other ascetics, such as St. Anthony of the Desert (ca. 251–356) in Egypt—whose life was chronicled by St. Athanasius—and St. Simeon Stylites (ca. 390–459), who lived on a pillar near Aleppo in Syria for over thirty years, were also hermits devoted to focusing on the Lord Jesus through prayer, fasting, and meditation in solitude. Due to their devout lives, many people came to them seeking advice and/or prayer.

The following is an example of one of Ephrem's hymns, which highlights the ascetic aspects of his theology. *Hymns of Paradise,* Hymn 7, stanzas 15 and 18:[7]

Stanza 15

The Virgin who rejected
    the marriage crown that fades
now has the radiant marriage chamber
    that cherishes the children of light,
shining out because she rejected
    the works of darkness.
To her who was alone
    in a lonely house
the wedding feast now grants tranquility:
    here angels rejoice,
prophets delight,
    and apostles add splendor.

Stanza 18

The man who abstained
    with understanding, from wine,
will the vines of Paradise
    rush out to meet, all the more joyfully,
as each one stretches out and proffers him
    its clusters;

---

[7] St. Ephrem the Syrian, *Hymns of Paradise,* intro. and trans. Sebastian Brock (Crestwood, NY: St. Vladimir's Seminary Press, 1990). See hymn 7, 118–30.

or if any has lived
    a life of virginity,
him too they welcome into their bosom,
    for the solitary such as he
    has never lain in any bosom
    nor upon any marriage bed.

The choir and/or congregants were to sing this hymn, extolling the virtues of celibacy (even in marriage), and the simple life in order to see Paradise.

ST. FRANCIS (ca. 1181–1226) AND ST. CLARE (1194–1253) OF ASSISI[8]

One of the most influential people throughout Christian history is St. Francis of Assisi. Francis's merchant family raised him with means and great indulgence. When he was a youth, he ended up

---

[8] For further understanding of the works of St. Francis and St. Clare, see "Francis of Assisi and Clare of Assisi," in *Francis and Clare: The Complete Works*, The Classics of Western Spirituality, new ed. (Mahwah, NJ: Paulist Press, 1982). There are numerous works on Francis and Clare. For instance, a contemporary of Francis wrote a biography: St. Bonaventure, *The Life of St. Francis of Assisi*, Tan Classics (Charlotte, NC: Tan Books, 2010). A classic biography of Francis is G. K. Chesterton, *St. Francis of Assisi*, rev. ed. (1923/1951; repr., New York: Image Books, 1987); and a notable recent biography is Augustine Thompson, *Francis of Assisi: A New Biography*. (Ithaca, NY: Cornell University Press, 2012). Also see Viviana Díaz Balsera, "Sacrificial Labors of Colonization: Sixteenth-Century Franciscan Missions in Central Mexico and in La Florida," in *Sixteenth-Century Mission: Explorations in Protestant and Roman Catholic Theology and Practice*, ed. Robert L. Gallagher and Edward L. Smither, Studies in Historical and Systematic Theology (Bellingham, WA: Lexham Press, 2021), 322–46; Robert L. Gallagher, "Dying to Witness: Early Franciscan Mission to the Muslim World," in *Practicing Hope: Missions and Global Crisis*, ed. Jerry M. Ireland and Michelle L. K. Raven, Evangelical Missiological Society Series, no. 28 (Pasadena, CA: William Carey Publishing, 2020), 93–118; L. Hardick, "Francis of Assisi, St.," in *New Catholic Encyclopedia*, vol. 6 (New York: McGraw-Hill, 1967), 28–31; and Michael J. P. Robson, ed., *The Cambridge Companion to Francis of Assisi*, Cambridge Companions to Religion (Cambridge: Cambridge University Press, 2012). On Clare, see L. Hardick, "Clare of Assisi, St.," in *New Catholic Encyclopedia*, vol. 3 (New York: McGraw-Hill, 1967), 913; and Joan Mueller, *A Companion to Clare of Assisi*, Brill's Companions to the Christian Tradition (Leiden, the Netherlands: Brill, 2010).

going to war against Perugia, resulting in the enemy imprisoning him for a year. These experiences, and seeing beggars in the marketplace, brought about a conversion within him. He started a movement to live a life of simplicity, and demonstrate brotherly love to all.

Traditionally, monks (cenobites) would separate themselves into cloisters, which disconnected them from the world. The followers of Francis (Franciscans), called friars, however, would go and live among the people to exhort penance, peace, and love. One goal was to live the life of simplicity intentionally, following the teachings of Jesus Christ by walking in his footsteps. The Franciscans were to labor among the people exuding the holiness of God, their food provided to them as gifts from the people among whom they labored.

St. Clare of Assisi heard Francis speak in 1211, and God touched her through his message. Thus, she realized her own calling. The following year, she established the Order of Poor Ladies. This became the Second Franciscan Order, commonly called the Poor Clares. These women were to dedicate themselves to holiness and simplicity—they were to neither own property nor wealth, but live purely from the alms given to them. Clare served as the female head of the mendicant order of the male version started by Francis.

Two anecdotes about Francis will demonstrate aspects of his perspective on empowerment. First, Francis saw that all nature mirrored God. All creation (including the sun and moon—poetically calling them brother sun and sister moon), and animals (whom Francis called brothers and sisters), were worthy of recognition since they reflected God. In fact, Francis preached to the birds. Numerous artistic depictions show this aspect of Francis—not only was he called to preach to every person, but all creation was included in his audience. This is partially because Francis took seriously Mark 16:15, where Jesus tells the disciples to preach the gospel to "all creation" or "every creature."

As part of Francis's vision to be holy, yet interact with others in love, he opposed the crusades, and emphasized the importance of engaging the Muslims directly with the love of Christ. With this view, Francis had a dialogue with the Sultan of Egypt. In 1219, in the midst of the fifth crusade, Francis sought out and received an audience with the Sultan—Al-Kamil, the nephew of Saladin. During a cease-fire, he preached and discussed Jesus Christ with the Sultan. Although there was no apparent conversion, this did show the attitude of Francis. He returned to the crusader lines safely. For Francis, to be "set apart" meant that God connects us with his love.[9]

JOHN WESLEY (1703–1791)[10]

John Wesley grew up in an Anglican home with his father, a rector of Epworth in England. His mother, Susanna, an amazing woman on all accounts, taught John and his numerous siblings Latin, Greek, and the Bible, among other subjects. She was a woman of the Bible and of prayer.[11] As students at Oxford University, John and his brother, Charles, started a group that emphasized prayer,

---

[9] Several works note this meeting between Francis and Sultan Al-Kamil. This includes the biographies of Francis such as John Tolan, *Saint Francis and the Sultan: The Curious History of a Christian-Muslim Encounter* (Oxford: Oxford University Press, 2009); and Robert L. Gallagher, "Dying to Witness: Early Franciscan Mission to the Muslim World," in *Practicing Hope: Missions and Global Crisis*, ed. Jerry M. Ireland and Michelle L. K. Raven, Evangelical Missiological Society Series, no. 28 (Pasadena, CA: William Carey Publishing, 2020), 93–118.

[10] There are numerous works on John Wesley such as Kenneth H. Collins, *A Real Christian: The Life of John Wesley* (Nashville, TN: Abingdon Press, 1999); and Stephen Tomkins, *John Wesley: A Biography* (Grand Rapids, MI: Eerdmans, 2003). A current readable version is Henry H. Knight III, *John Wesley: Optimist of Grace* (Eugene, OR: Cascade, 2018); and on Wesley's theology, see Kenneth J. Collins, *The Theology of John Wesley: Holy Love and the Shape of Grace* (Nashville, TN: Abingdon Press, 2007); Thomas C. Oden, *John Wesley's Scriptural Christianity* (Grand Rapids, MI: Zondervan Academic, 1994); Thomas C. Oden, *John Wesley's Teaching*, 4 vols. (Grand Rapids, MI: Zondervan, 2012-14); and the readable William J. Abraham, *Wesley for Armchair Theologians* (Louisville, KY: Westminster John Knox Press, 2005). For an overview of John Wesley's influence in missions, see Robert L. Gallagher, "Encountering Methodist Missions," in John Mark Terry and Robert L. Gallagher, *Encountering the History of Missions: From the Early Church to Today*, Encountering Missions Series (Grand Rapids, MI: Baker Academic, 2017), 224–42.

[11] Scholars have a high regard for Susanna Wesley, John and Charles's mother. See Eric Metaxas, *Seven Women: And the Secret of Their Greatness* (Nashville, TN: Nelson Books, 2015), 31–58.

fasting, Bible study, and weekly communion. Initially called the "Holy Club," people eventually called them the "Oxford Methodists." Later, an incident happened on a ship bound for the Americas, in which he feared for his life. Yet he noted the staunch faith displayed by the Moravians onboard in the midst of a storm. After a stint as a pastor in the American colony of Georgia, John Wesley returned to England downcast. He attended a Moravian meeting at Aldersgate, whereupon hearing a reading from Martin Luther's preface to his work on the Epistle to the Romans, Christ's faith flooded and transformed him. As is commonly noted, "His heart was strangely warmed." While Wesley was highly influenced by the Moravians and their Lutheran Pietism, it is the interaction with them where Wesley's focus on empowerment is evident.

Wesley highly regarded the piety and spirituality of the Moravians. Yet the distinction between Luther's and Wesley's understandings of empowerment through sanctification is telling. John Wesley and the Moravian-Lutheran leader, Count Zinzendorf, interacted in a meeting in England on September 3, 1741, prior to Zinzendorf's trip to Pennsylvania.[12] Luther and Zinzendorf defined salvation as God looking to believers and seeing Christ. Consequently, Christ's righteousness becomes that of the believer in the sight of God. For Wesley, while this is true, God also does a work of empowerment within the Christian. There is a qualitative difference internally. It is not *just* that God sees the follower of Christ differently; there is *also* a transformative process of Christ the Empowerer within. For Wesley, this internal work is by God's grace and sanctification, and can have immediate and progressive elements. Wesley even proposed that a believer could live in such a way as to attain "sinless perfection," which is also called "Christian perfection." Wesley understood that this is a potential goal yet rarely achieved in this life. The basis of the internal work of separation was the internal empowering work of Christ within a person.

---

[12] On the interaction between John Wesley and Count Zinzendorf and its importance, see Jürgen Moltmann, *The Spirit of Life*, trans. Margaret Kohl (Minneapolis: Fortress Press, 1992), 163–71, esp. 167–71. Also see Robert L. Gallagher, "Encountering Moravian Missions," in Terry and Gallagher, *Encountering the History of Missions*, 216–17, 228–29.

DIETRICH BONHOEFFER (1906–1945)[13]

Dietrich Bonhoeffer was born into a highly educated family. Later he became a leading Lutheran pastor, theologian, and churchman in Germany. During the Nazi regime in Germany, Bonhoeffer was a founding member of the Confessing Church, which opposed the Third Reich and the state church that supported Adolf Hitler. His family became key members in the German resistance of the Nazis. Bonhoeffer was in a dilemma, however. He had become a pacifist, but the stark realities of Nazi Germany and the obligation to undertake ethical action brought him into a conspiracy plot against Hitler and the Nazis. In fact, the Nazis—in response to the July 20, 1944, plot to assassinate Adolf Hitler—executed several of Dietrich's siblings and in-laws, along with Dietrich himself. He was thirty-nine years old.

Bonhoeffer was devoutly Christ-centered. He birthed his theology from deep thought, contemplation, and prayer within his ministry context. He saw the practicality of theology lived out. This informed his understanding of the church—how one was to be "in the world, but not of it." As Bonhoeffer emphasized, preaching is to be side-by-side with political responsibility; and prayer is to be side-by-side with ethics. These were inseparable. For Bonhoeffer, a great enemy of the church was "cheap grace."

> Cheap grace is the preaching of forgiveness without requiring repentance, baptism without church discipline,

---

[13] The classic biography on Bonhoeffer is Eberhard Bethge, *Dietrich Bonhoeffer: A Biography*, rev. ed., ed. Victoria J. Barnett (Minneapolis: Fortress, 2000). An abridged version is in *Bonhoeffer: An Illustrated Biography*, Fount Classics (London: Fount, 1979). See the readable Eric Metaxas, *Bonhoeffer: Pastor, Martyr, Prophet, Spy* (Nashville, TN: Thomas Nash, 2010), or his abridged version in *Seven Men* (Nashville, TN: Thomas Nelson, 2013), 89–112. Also see the video *Dietrich Bonhoeffer: Memories and Perspectives*, dir. Bain Boehlke, 2003, with interviews of his friends and relatives. There are numerous works on Bonhoeffer's thought and ethics. For example, John W. de Gruchy, ed., *The Cambridge Companion to Dietrich Bonhoeffer* (Cambridge: Cambridge University Press, 1999); and James W. McClendon, Jr., *Systematic Theology: Ethics* (Nashville, TN: Abingdon Press, 1986), 188–208.

communion without confession, absolution without personal confession. Cheap grace is grace without discipleship, grace without the cross, grace without Jesus Christ, living and incarnate.[14]

The church is to be Christ incarnate in the world. Genuine theology is not divorced from day-to-day life existence. This took place in his own life, as he was part of the plot to overthrow Hitler. Empowered by Christ, Dietrich Bonhoeffer was in the world but not of it.

REFLECTION QUESTIONS

1. In what ways did St. Ephrem, St. Francis, St. Clare, Wesley, and Bonhoeffer demonstrate Christ the Empowerer to be a gospel witness?
2. How did Christ empower the saints of this chapter to express their "set apartness" as sanctified persons?
3. In what various ways did Ephrem, Francis, and Clare, Wesley, and Bonhoeffer communicate Christ's empowering presence to others?
4. In which ways do anchorites, cenobites, and mendicants follow the same values? In which ways do they diverge in their values?
5. Which of the saints or groups do you resonate with the most and why?

---

[14] Dietrich Bonhoeffer, *The Cost of Discipleship*, trans. R. H. Fuller, rev. ed. (New York: Macmillan, 1963), 47.

8

Contemporary Stories of Empowerment to Holiness, Service, and Witness

DeLonn L. Rance

EMPOWERED TO HOLINESS AND WITNESS[1]

In the fourth grade, Dan hated spelling tests. English spelling defied logic, requiring rote memorization, something that Dan loathed to do. Good grades in spelling eluded him. Then one Friday, he followed the lead of some of his classmates—even though he knew it was wrong—by concealing a cheat sheet for the spelling exam. Despite his deft deception, seemingly out of nowhere, the teacher walked up behind him, grabbed his exam and cheat sheet, and without saying a word, crumpled them up and deposited them in the trashcan by the desk at the front of the room. The consequences of Dan being caught cheating on a spelling exam brought shame and embarrassment to the son of the local pastor. At age

---

[1] The narratives of this chapter emerge from personal interviews. The author uses pseudonyms for the purpose of security.

five Dan had committed his life to Jesus, yet he seemed powerless to resist temptation.

A few months later, an evangelist came to Dan's rural church in North Dakota preaching on the baptism of the Holy Spirit. As Dan prayed at the altar, he fully surrendered his will to the Holy Spirit. Not long after that experience, when Dan's teacher stepped out of the room his classmates began sharing with one another answers for an exam. Even though Dan knew the correct answers, when the teacher collected the papers he explained, "Please mark this answer wrong because I heard someone say it when you stepped out of the room." The Spirit had quickened his conscience to live a holy life.

That same year the Holy Spirit called Dan to be a missionary. Though introverted and shy, the Spirit gave him boldness to witness. At age eleven, when Dan's missionary parents were studying at language school, he would walk to the Christian bookstore, and use all his "birthday" money—and any other income—to purchase gospel tracts to pass out to people on the streets of San Jose, Costa Rica. When the money ran out, Dan borrowed his father's typewriter and typed John 3:16 (very slowly) on small strips of paper that he then distributed in the neighborhood. The Holy Spirit's empowering presence in Dan's life motivated him toward holiness and witness so that others would come to know Jesus as their Savior and Lord.

EMPOWERED TO MISSIONARY SERVICE

In 1987, Katy accepted Christ as her Savior at twenty years of age in El Salvador. Yet she had not yet totally surrendered herself to the Lord. About three years later, the church she attended had a week of special services dedicated to seeking the baptism in the Holy Spirit. Though she did not fully understand, she watched as people went to the altar to receive the baptism with the evidence of speaking in tongues. She prayed, "Lord, I would like that experience." Katy relates that in her ignorance of spiritual and biblical truth during a meeting she prayed, "If you will baptize me with your Holy Spirit, I will serve you. Here is my life. If it is of use to you, take it. I will take it as a sign of your acceptance if you baptize me with your Holy Spirit." She then lifted her arms in praise and immediately began to speak in tongues.

Katy grew increasingly concerned for those who did not yet know Christ as she became active in her local youth group. The Lord Jesus constantly challenged her whereby she wanted to stand and proclaim, "Here I am." A missionary discipleship group formed, and though she knew little about missions, she joined the gathering desiring to learn how to better evangelize. In the group, Katy experienced intense discipleship in the word, in service, and in missions as they participated in Bible studies, street witnessing, evangelistic campaigns, church planting, and short-term missions trips.

Katy heard the Master's distinct call to missionary service on one of the short-term missions trips to the north coast of Honduras. The Lord said, "This is what I want you for. Look around you; this is what I want you for." Katy responded, "I can't. I have to finish my schooling. I have a family that depends on me. I can't. I can't." For a year, she told no one. She continued her education, yet took advantage of every opportunity to serve.

Subsequently, one January while Katy was at her bank withdrawing the money that she had sacrificially saved to pay for her final year of industrial engineering studies, she heard the Spirit say, "You are going to need that money. You should not give it up." Katy responded, "Lord, just this year, and after this year, I'll go into full-time service."

In April, Katy sat ready for her early morning class on project administration. The professor came in and said, "No class today. We are going to get to know each other. Everyone is going to come to the front, and tell a joke." Katy did not know what to do. One by one, the students told jokes, each one getting increasingly vulgar. Katy felt shame, and the conviction of the Holy Spirit. She began to cry. The Spirit spoke: "This is not the place where you belong. You are a person who is going to preach the word and teach others. This is not your place." She could not stop crying. Her classmates began to notice. In desperation, she fled to the restroom where she wept openly. The Holy Spirit took hold of her.

She heard these words: "This is the last time I will call you. If you don't do it now, then I'll never call you again. This is your opportunity. This is not where I want you." When the bell rang, she returned to the classroom, collected her books, and never returned. Thus began Katy's missionary service, an empowered journey that led her and her husband to Africa.

EMPOWERED TO CROSS-CULTURAL MINISTRY

At age fifteen, the Spirit began to work in Ana's life from the moment that she accepted Jesus as Lord. Yet when she experienced the baptism in the Spirit, she became fully engaged in ministry. A high school classmate invited her to a Sunday school class where she sought and received the baptism in the Holy Spirit. She clarifies:

> At that moment, the Lord began to speak to me, because I had never heard the voice of God. I had read the Bible and all that, but God had never spoken in that way.... But, the day I received the baptism in the Holy Spirit, God spoke to me. God spoke to my life, and from that moment, he began speaking into my life as a Christian, and I began to hear his voice.... My whole life changed—my actions, my conduct, my emotional and spiritual states.... I became more active. I began to participate in service to the Lord; to do something for him.

Ana began to participate in personal and street evangelism. She accompanied a ministry team from her local church to a mental ward, where they evangelized and prayed for the sick. Her burden for those separated from Christ grew. As she watched a televised Jimmy Swaggart campaign, her concern for the multitudes convinced her that God was calling her to ministry.

During the first missions convention at Ana's church in El Salvador—at sixteen years of age—she became aware of missions and her missionary calling. Yet she and her family had plans. She was going to go to college to become an architect. In confusion, Ana asked the Lord to confirm his call by providing a place in El

Salvador where she could train for missionary service. That same year the Christian University of the Assemblies of God opened a licentiate in theology with a specialization in missions. She states, "I knew it was of God. I had no doubt. It was the Lord preparing the place where I needed to go to prepare."

Ana's family counseled her to finish her degree in architecture and then enter the ministry. In fact, she studied both degrees concurrently and did well. Yet a decisive moment came as she registered for her second semester. Standing in line at the National University with her registration papers, and faculty advisors all around, the Lord spoke to her. "Ana, you can study architecture if you want. You can become the best architect in the country, but you will never practice that career because I am calling you to full-time ministry." Ana narrates, "Right there I surrendered. I gave up architecture, and committed myself solely to studying missions at the university [Christian University]. And that is how, in a word, I fully entered the world of missions."

At the university, Ana's call gained definition as she learned about the needs of the world and unreached groups of people. Even though the university professors often focused on reaching Muslims, Ana became more and more affected by tribal groups, especially those found in India. The local church shaped Ana in ministry, but at the university she acquired theological and missiological tools that enabled her to minister cross-culturally.

After graduation, she faced uncertainty. A missionary appointment seemed impossible, but she trusted the Lord, believing that he would provide the opportunity, and show her the next step. She participated in a missions trip to the Miskito Coast of Honduras to explore an unreached people group. On returning from the trip, the national missions president asked her if she would be willing to go to this remote region as a missionary. Ana says, "At that moment, I knew that this was my opportunity. It wasn't a city. It was exactly the kind of place I wanted to work. So I said, 'I am willing to go to the field, the mission field.' That is how I arrived on the Miskito Coast. I was waiting for the door to open, and the door opened, and I said, 'I'm ready.'"

To answer the call, Ana broke off her engagement to be married, raised her support in the churches of the Assemblies of God of El Salvador, said good-bye to family and friends, and moved to Puerto Lempira, Honduras. There she lived among the Miskito people learning their language, leading them to Christ, and planting a church. Her five years of service on the Miskito Coast resulted in the establishment of three church plants and a Bible school.

Later Ana served among the tribal peoples of India by incarnating Christ among the lost multitudes. She is convinced that life in the Spirit is critical. Without the experience, communion, and guidance of the Spirit, the missionary's life and ministry are at risk. She states with conviction,

> I believe that the Holy Spirit is the key in missions. When we allow the Holy Spirit to guide, we are walking in the right way, and this gives us surety to advance, to do, or not do something. Without the voice, without the guidance of the Holy Spirit, without hearing the voice of God, I believe it would be very difficult. . . . But, the fact that we have the Holy Spirit in our lives, means that we have that intimate communion with him; we can hear his voice—hear him. It allows us to overcome any obstacle. . . . We know how we should act and what we should be by the guidance of the Holy Spirit.

EMPOWERED TO START CHURCHES

Ray traveled the world as a ship's pilot but strayed from the ways of the Lord Jesus. He found himself docked for five months in the port city of Smyrna, Turkey. Each day he interacted with Muslims, serving tea and befriending them. Having never encountered a Muslim before, their religious rituals deeply impressed him. In the midst of a foreign religion, God called him to preach the gospel. On returning to his home country of El Salvador, he publicly recommitted his life to Christ but refused to give up the life of a sailor. Much to his chagrin, every attempt to sign on with another ship met with rejection. Desperate to leave El Salvador, he stowed away on a freighter bound for New York with the help of a friend. Before beginning the voyage, the captain conducted a search of the ship. When it appeared that Ray was going to escape detection, the captain heard a voice, and walked directly to where he was hiding.

Ray's expulsion from the ship led him to meet with his church pastor who was preparing to go to Bible school. Ray said, "Do you think that they would accept me in Bible School?" The pastor replied, "If I recommend you, they will." "Well, recommend me then. I want to study." Together, they went to a Bible school in San Salvador. His classmates nicknamed him the "sailor" on hearing of his travels. Though the itch to travel did not diminish, no doors opened. So he accepted the challenge to work in a difficult place known for the influence of its witches. There the Lord gave him the desire to practice his favorite spiritual disciplines of prayer, fasting, and Bible reading. He observes, "Prayer and fasting give one strength in such a way that the devil himself is unable to affect you." As a result, Ray founded a new church, the first of twenty-four churches that he would plant in the power of Christ.

Ray became the first missionary sent out by the national Assemblies of God in El Salvador when international leaders issued a call for church planters to participate in a concentrated evangelism effort in Paraguay. In Paraguay, and later in Ecuador and Colombia, Ray—along with his wife Dina—started churches by holding evangelistic tent campaigns characterized by the miraculous. Ray relates one occasion in Ecuador:

> The tent is a center that attracts many people by the miracles that God does. I remember that one day a mute person passed by in the street. I was preaching. When I invited the people who were sick and had problems forward for prayer, the mute was among them. God touched him, healed him, and made him speak. The mute jumped in the air three times and screamed saying, "I speak." People were frightened. Some said, "That man is drunk." But, as I looked in his face, he did not look like a drunk. I asked, "Who knows this man?" A young woman—who worked

in a bank—stood and said, "I know him. This man was mute. For thirty years he has not spoken." The Lord made him speak at that moment. The tent became famous for miracles.

As an evangelist, I have seen God manifest the gifts of faith, miracles, and divine healing. I have the privilege of saying that I have prayed for two people who were dead, and God raised them up. Of course, we do not attribute anything to man or ministry, because the ministries belong to God. But if God has desired to do this, the glory is his.... I have seen miracles of the resurrection of the dead, mutes who speak, the paralyzed who rise, the blind see, wondrous things.

The Spirit of Christ called a sailor to be a missionary. In Ray's words, "God has a plan. When one is guided by the Holy Spirit and when you do things under the guidance of the Spirit, he takes charge."

REFLECTION QUESTIONS

1. In the contemporary stories of Dan, Katy, Ana, and Ray, in what ways did they experience the empowerment of Christ in relation to salvation, holiness, service, and/or gospel witness?
2. How did Christ empower these people to discern God's direction for their lives?
3. According to the narratives, what is the relationship between the work of the Holy Spirit and missions?
4. In the stories of the chapter, what is the role of signs and wonders in cross-cultural ministry?
5. In what ways do these contemporary narratives draw you to seek more of the Holy Spirit in your life and ministry to communicate Christ to the nations?

PART III

CHRIST OUR HEALER

9

Healing as a Divine Testimony, Compassionate Act, and Coming Kingdom

Sarita Gallagher Edwards

When John [the Baptist], who was in prison, heard about the deeds of the Messiah, he sent his disciples to ask him, "Are you the one who is to come, or should we expect someone else?"

Jesus replied, "Go back and report to John what you hear and see: The blind receive sight, the lame walk, those who have leprosy are cleansed, the deaf hear, the dead are raised, and the good news is proclaimed to the poor."

—Mt 11:2–5

"We prayed for her, and then, right there in the dorm room, her leg grew." A few minutes before, I had asked the undergraduate students in my Life of Christ class if they had ever experienced a miracle of God. It was a spontaneous decision on my part. We had been discussing the miracles of Jesus as a class, and I wanted to provide an opportunity for students to share about their personal experiences with the miraculous healing power of Christ.

As a professor at a Christian liberal arts university in the United States, I had become accustomed to hearing an oft-repeated question from my students: "Why does God do miracles overseas, but not here in the United States?" This question was always asked with sincerity, and without fail I responded by sharing stories about how God does do miracles here in the United States as well. The frequency of this question, however, started to make me curious. God was clearly moving all around the world, including in the United States. Why then did my students think that this was not the case?

It was therefore with a mixture of inquisitiveness and faith that I stood before my students one fall morning at the beginning of my Bible class. Not knowing the outcome, I decided to ask my students to share specific times when Jesus had miraculously intervened in their lives in big or small ways. The first student to respond shared about a miracle that had taken place the night before in her college dorm room. She and a few friends had prayed for a young woman who was suffering from chronic hip pain. As the group prayed for their friend, one of her legs grew right in front of their eyes, relieving her from the chronic pain she had been experiencing. After the student had shared this narrative, the floodgates opened, and student after student shared personal stories about how Jesus had miraculously interceded in their lives or their family members' lives.

What started as a spontaneous exercise in one class session became a repeated activity in each of my Life of Christ courses. Every semester that I taught the course, I reserved an entire period of class for students to share their personal experiences of God's healing and transformative power in their lives. And, without fail, every semester, students filled the entire class time with powerful testimonies of the miraculous work of Christ in their lives. As I discovered in my academic classroom, it is in both testifying and listening to examples of Christ's power that our faith grows. The miraculous healing power of Christ is present in every corner of the world, including the United States. God calls us to testify about our personal encounters with the healing power of Christ and to share the Lord's transformative work in our lives with one another.

THEMES IN THE HEALING NARRATIVES

In the following chapters, we will engage with true stories of Christ's healing power in human history through biblical, historical, and contemporary narratives. As we consider the ongoing communal testimony of God's supernatural intervention, several significant and sometimes difficult questions start to emerge. Why, for example, does God heal some people and not others? Additionally, is faith a requirement for individuals to receive divine healing, or is healing available to all? And what is the purpose of these power encounters? Are they stand-alone occurrences, or do they have a broader eschatological importance?

While there is a certain mystery surrounding the supernatural activity of God, in analyzing the biblical accounts of divine healing and its ongoing expression in the life of the church, several consistent themes emerge in relation to the impetus, purpose, and outworking of divine healing. In this introductory chapter, I will briefly highlight the foremost of these biblical themes: (1) healing as a divine testimony, (2) healing as a compassionate act of God, and (3) healing as a foreshadowing of a coming kingdom. As we consider divine healing throughout human history and in our contemporary world, these motifs provide a theological framework and hermeneutical lens through which we can begin to comprehend the significance of God's acts of healing.

Healing as a Divine Testimony

In the Hebrew Scriptures, as in my classroom, God frequently reveals Godself to individuals through miraculous acts of healing. Whether it is the healing of Abimelech's household (Gen 20:1–18), the raising of the widow of Zarephath's son (1 Kings 17:17–24), or the healing of Naaman's leprosy (2 Kings 5:20–27), the restorative power of God provides a divine testimony about the authority of God over the spiritual and natural world. Naaman explains it well when, after being healed from his skin disease, he states, "Now I know that there is no God in all the world except in Israel" (2 Kings 5:15). It is through these divine acts of healing that God reveals God's universal sovereignty and omnipotence. When God heals people, they encounter the Lord. In the midst of their suffering, need, and pain, God brings restoration, provision, and healing.

In the biblical accounts, these sacred moments of divine healing are both intimate and communal. Each divine encounter changes the trajectory of the healed individual's life. However, it also affects the wider community, and, frequently, the surrounding nations as the news of God's power spreads throughout the region. In the New Testament, the gospel authors write of the extensive influence of Jesus's supernatural acts. They note how rapidly the news of Jesus's miracles spread throughout the regions of Galilee, Judea, and the surrounding areas.[1] As is true today, the news about Christ's miracles traveled fast in first-century Israel. While Jesus's miraculous acts profoundly affected those who witnessed them, even individuals who heard secondhand about the miracles responded with amazement, awe, and praise of God.[2] Therefore, when Jesus healed one person, more than their family, village, or town was impacted. Instead, the news about Jesus's miraculous acts reached a multicultural and multireligious audience as Hebrews, Gentiles, and Samaritans alike heard about the signs and wonders of Jesus, called the Christ.

In addition, Jesus's miracles confirmed to the Jewish community that he was the Messiah, the "Son of Man," of whom the prophets Daniel and Isaiah had spoken.[3] In the Gospel of Luke, the author explains that Jesus's miraculous acts were a fulfillment of Isaiah's prophecy about the coming Messiah. In a climactic narrative, Jesus returns to his hometown of Nazareth and standing in the crowded synagogue reads from the scroll of the prophet Isaiah:

---

[1] See Mk 1:23–28, 40–45; 7:31–37; Lk 7:11–18; Mt 9:18–31.

[2] See Mk 1:27, 7:37; Lk 7:16; 13:13; 17:15; Mt 9:8, 33.

[3] In the Hebrew Scriptures, the phrase "Son of Man" is used in prophetic literature to refer to the coming Messiah (see Dan 7:13–14; Is 51:12). In the New Testament, the phrase is used by Jesus to speak about himself (Mt 8:20; 9:6; 11:19; 12:8; 16:13, 27; 19:28; 26:64; Mk 2:28; 8:31; Lk 5:24; 24:7), and is also used by the gospel writers to refer to Jesus's divinity (Jn 1:49–51; 5:25–27; 8:28; 9:35–37; 12:34–36; Acts 7:54–57; Heb 2:6–9; Rev 1:12–13; 14:14).

> The Spirit of the Lord is on me,
> because he has anointed me
> to proclaim good news to the poor.
> He has sent me to proclaim freedom for the prisoners
> and recovery of sight for the blind,
> to set the oppressed free,
> to proclaim the year of the Lord's favor.[4]

As everyone's eyes turn to Jesus, he continues, "Today this Scripture is fulfilled in your hearing" (Lk 4:20–21). The Messiah, who was foretold by the prophets, had come. Isaiah's prophecy foretold both the spiritual and physical nature of Jesus Christ's ministry. While Jesus restored people's spiritual sight, he also healed those who were physically blind and enabled them to see.

Matthew repeats this prophetic description of the Christ in his gospel when John the Baptist sent his disciples to Jesus to find out whether or not he was the Messiah. Jesus responds to the men, "Go back and report to John what you hear and see: the blind receive sight, the lame walk, those who have leprosy are cleansed, the deaf hear, the dead are raised, and the good news is proclaimed to the poor" (Mt 11:4–5). Both biblical accounts identify the Messiah as the One who brings healing and restoration to individuals' bodies, hearts, and minds. For the Jewish community it was Jesus's physical acts of healing that confirmed for them that Jesus was the Messiah.

Healing as a Compassionate Act

Another consistent theme within the narratives of divine healing is God's compassion toward human beings. In both the Hebrew Scriptures and gospel accounts, when individuals cried out to God for help, they encountered the loving-kindness of God. The Lord's miraculous intervention in individuals' lives through divine healing is, at its core, intimate—a personal connection between God and humanity. In the New Testament, God's compassion is demonstrated in the narrative of the man healed of leprosy (Mk 1:40–45). Upon seeing Jesus, the afflicted man cried out, "If you are

---

[4] Lk 4:16–19. See Is 61:1–2; 58:6.

willing, you can make me clean" (Mk 1:40). Filled with compassion (Greek verb: *splagchnizomai*) Jesus immediately responded, "I am willing; be clean" (v. 41).

The Hebrew Scriptures embed compassion in the very character of God. As King David writes in Psalm 86, "But you, Lord, are a compassionate and gracious God, slow to anger, abounding in love and faithfulness" (v. 15). While an exhaustive analysis of God's acts of compassion is outside the scope of this introductory chapter, I will highlight several passages that exemplify the connection between healing and the compassion of God.

First, in the Hebrew Scriptures, the compassionate (Hebrew adjective: *rachum*) nature of God is repeatedly proclaimed by the prophets, and observed by the people of Israel. Despite the failings of the Hebrew people, God's compassion—as well as God's mercy, goodness, love, forgiveness, and justice—remains constant.[5] Even when Israel's sin and rebellion expose them to God's punishment, upon the nation's repentance, God once again responds to his people with forgiveness and compassion.[6] In the Bible, God's compassion is evident on a number of occasions. This includes when individuals cry out to Yahweh in repentance due to their sinfulness, such as King David (2 Sam 12) and the Ninevites (Jon 3–4). Also, God's compassion is witnessed in cases of impending death (Hagar and Ishmael [Gen 16, 21]) and illness (Hezekiah [2 Kings 20]). In each case, God meets the individual with compassion.

God's interaction with King Hezekiah of Judah is a poignant example of God's compassion toward an individual facing physical illness. In reading the biblical account, we encounter Hezekiah, son of Ahaz, who reigned as king from the age of twenty-five and "did what was right in the eyes of the Lord" (2 Kings 18:3). After only fourteen years, however, Hezekiah "became ill and was at the point of death" (2 Kings 20:1). Upon receiving a direct word from God through the prophet Isaiah that he was going to die from this illness (v. 1), Hezekiah pleaded with God for mercy, weeping bitterly (v. 2). God's reply to Hezekiah's petition came swiftly. Before

---

[5] See Ex 33:19; Ps 51:1; 86:15; 103:13; 116:5; 119:77; 145:8–9; Is 30:18; 49:10–13; 54:10; 63:7; Jon 4:2.

[6] See Deut 30:1–4; 1 Sam 7; 2 Sam 12; Neh 9:16–18; Dan 9.

the prophet Isaiah had left the palace grounds, God spoke to him with a new message: "Go back and tell Hezekiah . . . I have heard your prayer and seen your tears; I will heal you" (vv. 4–5). God's compassion toward Hezekiah resulted in the Lord's reversal of his divine decree regarding the king's death. God extended Hezekiah's life by fifteen years, and additionally granted the king's request for a miraculous sign to prove that the divine healing would come to pass (vv. 4–11). In this account, as in so many other biblical narratives, we witness a God who hears people's prayers, sees their pain, and acts swiftly with mercy and compassion.

In the gospel accounts, the connection between divine compassion and healing is evident throughout the ministry of Jesus Christ. Indeed, Jesus's compassion marks his ministry in Israel and the surrounding regions to both communities in need as well as individuals in distress. For example, as Jesus landed on the Galilean shore and saw the large crowd awaiting his arrival, "he had compassion on them and healed their sick" (Mt 14:13–14). On another occasion outside Jericho, "two blind men were sitting by the roadside, and when they heard that Jesus was going by, they shouted, 'Lord, Son of David, have mercy on us'" (Mt 20:30). Upon hearing the men's pleas, Jesus stopped, asked the men what they wanted, and learning that they desired their sight, "had compassion on them." Immediately Jesus healed them, restoring their sight (Mt 20:29–34).

Jesus not only feels the emotion of compassion, but he acts upon that sentiment. When Jesus shows compassion toward those in pain, he intervenes in their lives, and brings them healing and freedom from their ailments. In some instances, as in the case of the widow's dead son in Nain (Lk 7:12–15) and the Galilean crowd along the lakeshore (Mt 14:13–21), Jesus, full of compassion, intercedes on their behalf without the individuals having to request his intervention (Lk 7:13–15; Mt 14:14–21).

In these instances, the Greek term (*splagchnizomai*) used to describe Jesus's compassion refers to the Lord being moved in the depths of his being, or literally in Greek, his inward parts (*splagchnon*). The word reflects the first-century belief that one's emotions emerged figuratively from one's internal organs: the heart, intestines, lungs, and liver. In these acts of compassion, therefore, Jesus expresses empathy from the center of his being.

As was true of God the Father, Jesus's compassion is a core characteristic. As such, in Jesus's acts of divine healing, he reveals the heart of God, and the depth of the Lord's mercy and compassion toward humankind.

Healing as a Coming Kingdom

Lastly, Jesus's acts of healing in the Scriptures provide us with a glimpse of the full restoration of the creation to come. In the Lord's acts of mercy, he transformed individuals' lives on multiple levels—physically, socially, emotionally, mentally, and spiritually. These divine acts of healing brought life to withered hands, bent limbs, closed ears, and sightless eyes. Each of the individuals whom Jesus healed, however, ultimately grew old and died. Their bodies, while restored for a time, eventually succumbed to the inevitability of death. While these healings were singular events that spoke of the power and compassion of God, they also point to something much greater—the fullness of the resurrection of all believers through Jesus (see Jn 11:25–27, 43–44; 12:1–2, 9–11). The biblical acts of divine healing throughout human history are a taste of things to come. They are a foreshadowing of the fullness of Christ's resurrection. The resurrection of the physical body and eternal life after death can only come to the believer through the acceptance of the sacrificial death and resurrection of Christ.

With this eternal reality in mind, we can begin to answer the difficult question, why does God heal some people and not others? In the New Testament narratives, one needs to read between the lines. When Jesus healed the invalid man at the pool of Bethsaida, for instance, there were many people there that day who were blind, paralyzed, and lame whom the Lord did not heal (see Jn 5:1–15). Similarly, after the resurrection of Christ, when Peter and John walked toward the Gate Beautiful on the temple grounds to pray, they encountered a lame man who had been placed daily at the temple gate to beg for money (Acts 3:10). After the lame man was healed, the author observes, "When all the people [on the temple grounds] saw him [the healed man] walking and praising God, they recognized him as the same man who used to sit begging at the temple gate called Beautiful" (vv. 9–10a). In reflecting on this account, the reader is led to wonder if Jesus ever encountered this invalid man begging each day within the temple. If so, then why had not Jesus healed him? Likewise, after Jesus's healing ministry in Galilee and Judea, why were there sick and physically disabled people left in the region (cf. Mt 4:23–25)?

To answer these questions, we must turn again to the missional purpose of the ministry of Jesus Christ as well as to the unfolding nature of the kingdom of God. As exemplified in the account of the lame man in Acts 3, the natural outcome of Jesus's miracles through his disciples was missional. God was glorified (vv. 8–10) and revealed the divinity of Jesus Christ (vv. 6–8, 12–26) as well as providing an opportunity for people to repent and be saved (vv. 11–26; 4:4). Luke, the author, records that this one miraculous event resulted in 2,000 men believing in the truth about Jesus Christ (Acts 4:4).[7] An examination of the miraculous healings included in the gospel accounts and the writings of the early church repeat the motif that the healing miracles are most often evangelical in their purpose. As such, while these miracles bring holistic healing to the cured individual, their overarching purpose is to turn people toward repentance and the salvation available through Jesus Christ. Simply put, divine healings are signs directing people toward God.

Why then does God heal some people, and not others? Biblical teaching about the kingdom of God offers one answer to this question. While Jesus Christ ushered in the kingdom of God through his ministry, the complete fulfillment of that kingdom is yet to come.[8] This concept of the kingdom of God being "already here, but not yet" can be seen in both the gospel accounts and the writings of the early apostles. With the coming of the Messiah, the

---

[7] The number of individuals who believed in Jesus Christ after this event in Acts 3–4 may have been much higher since Hebrew custom only counted the males (see Acts 4:4).

[8] Theologians Geerhardus Vos and later George Eldon Ladd were the first to promote the contemporary discussion surrounding the kingdom of God being "already, but not yet," as they interpreted the theological teachings of Christ and the authors of the New Testament. See Geerhardus Vos, *The Teachings of Jesus Concerning the Kingdom of God and the Church* (New York: American Tract Society, 1903); and George Eldon Ladd, *A Theology of the New Testament* (Grand Rapids, MI: Eerdmans, 1974).

kingdom of God, which is not of this world (Jn 18:36), has come (Mt 4:17; 12:28; Mk 1:15; 10:15; Lk 10:9; 11:20), and yet is still coming (Mt 6:10; Lk 11:2; 17:20-21; Rev 11:15).

The early apostles expounded on this teaching, indicating that while everything is subject to God, "at present we do not see everything subject to him" (Heb 2:8). As believers in Christ, we also wait for the second coming to see the fulfillment of our place in the kingdom of God (1 Jn 3:2; Rom 8:30; Eph 2:6). In regard to miraculous signs and wonders, therefore, what we witness prior to Christ's second coming is a taste of what is to come. The time will come when "the sound of weeping and of crying will be heard . . . no more" (Is 65:19). However, that time has not yet arrived. For now, the miraculous intervention of Christ on earth reveals the beginning of the complete healing and wholeness that God will give all humanity after the second coming of the Messiah (Is 65:17-25).

The reality of this theological truth entered my life in 2001 when a routine medical examination revealed that my mother had stage-four colon cancer at the age of forty-nine. It was not until the malignant growth had almost fully blocked her colon that doctors diagnosed her illness. I was in graduate school at the time in Chicago, and from the occasion of her diagnosis to her death, seven months later, I was able to spend significant time with her as she underwent treatment for the disease. During this period, I prayed—along with many of my family members and friends—for my mum's full and comprehensive healing.

I knew from experience that if it was God's will, God had the power to heal my mum completely. As I prayed for her healing, I always received the same sense in my heart—that God had answered my prayers. The Lord would heal my mum, in either this life or the next. It was a consistent impression each time that I prayed for my mother's healing. Whether walking back home from work through the snow, or praying by her bedside at home, the sense I had in my spirit was always the same. Christ had answered my prayers. Indeed, God made my mum whole when she passed from this life to the next and was welcomed into the loving arms of Jesus.

Even though these experiences of earthly loss can be difficult, as followers of Christ we have the assurance that the fullness of God's kingdom will come. As such, we stand with longing and anticipation as we await the second coming of Christ when illness will be no more, death will not restrain us, and God's peace will reign over the whole earth (Is 65).

OVERVIEW OF CHRIST OUR HEALER

Perhaps the most compelling takeaway from my introductory chapter is the notion of the ongoing healing power of Christ to bring restoration to humanity through his Spirit and his church. In the midst of people's physical pain and suffering, Christ comes with power to heal and restore what was broken. I have shown that Christ our Healer is manifested through the scriptural themes of healing as a divine testimony, a compassionate act of God, and as a foreshadowing of the coming kingdom of Christ. Thus, as we reflect on Christ our Healer, which considers divine healing throughout human history and in our contemporary world, keep in mind these motifs. They allow us to have biblical guide rails by which we can begin to understand the character of God through God's healing acts of mercy and grace.

In the following narrative chapters, you will read several accounts of divine healing throughout the ages: from testimonies from agrarian villages in Galilee during the first century to urban centers in southern California in the twenty-first. While each context is distinct, these stories continue to reflect the biblical motifs of divine testimony, the compassion of the Triune God, and the coming kingdom of God. As you read these biblical, historical, and contemporary narratives, may the experiences of these women and men of God strengthen your faith in Christ. Similar to the students in my undergraduate classroom, may you have the privilege and joy of listening to these testimonies of Christ's healing power with new eyes and ears. The following is a summary of the contents of Part III, Christ our Healer.

Christ Our Healer in First-Century Palestine

Through Jesus's miraculous acts in first-century Palestine, we witness the depth of God's mercy and compassion toward humankind. In fulfilling the Messianic prophecies, Jesus reveals the heart of God. Jesus's acts of healing provide us with a glimpse of the full restoration of the creation to come. In the Lord's acts of mercy, he holistically renovates individuals' lives. In the two biblical narratives of chapter 10—the healing of the paralytic man in Capernaum and the demon-possessed man in the Gerasenes—the restorative power of Christ permanently transforms two individuals' lives as well as the communities around them.

Healing Works of Thaumaturgus, Cuthbert, the Blumhardts, and Kuhlman

Throughout church history, God has used many followers of Christ as instruments of divine healing. This is often within the context of the Lord separating a person unto himself, together with the empowerment of the Holy Spirit. How these healings take place and the theological understanding for each may somewhat differ. Chapter 11 displays a number of cameos of figures throughout church history such as Gregory Thaumaturgus, Cuthbert of Lindisfarne, Johann and Christoph Blumhardt, and Kathryn Kuhlman. These historical narratives pattern Christ our Healer. In turn, these people of God are models of ministry through the miraculous.

Contemporary Healings of Jennifer Matheny and Sarah Puckett

The testimonies of Jennifer Matheny and Sarah Puckett in chapter 12 of Christ's healing in their lives are similar, yet different. The narratives reveal different aspects of the character of God, yet the role of prayer is paramount in both scenarios. Their stories of Christ's miraculous healing provide valuable insights, which help to answer two questions. Why does God's healing occur quickly in some cases and slowly in others? In addition, why does the Lord heal some people and not others? As you read these contemporary stories of healing, may your faith rise within your heart to believe God for the miraculous in your personal life and ministry context.

10

Christ Heals the Paralytic and Demon Possessed

Sarita Gallagher Edwards

HEALING THE PARALYTIC MAN IN CAPERNAUM[1]

"There is a Jewish rabbi who heals people." The offhanded comment caught the group's attention immediately. "I saw it with my own eyes," the traveler continued. "In Capernaum, down by the Sea of Galilee, there is a man of God who heals the sick, the possessed, and even those with incurable diseases." "When I was in the city," the man explained, "I personally witnessed the rabbi cast out several evil spirits from people, and also restore the sight of a woman who was born blind." The traveler, noticeably still awed by the experience, added, "There was even a young boy who was completely paralyzed; absolutely no movement." The small group of listeners became even more attentive. The visitor continued, "The rabbi completely healed the invalid boy, and now he can walk." Hearing this last comment, the small group of friends

---

[1] I based my retelling of the biblical narrative on the accounts recorded in Matthew 9:1–8, Mark 2:1–12, and Luke 5:17–26.

caught each other's eyes. They decided immediately, without a word between them—they would leave for Capernaum tomorrow. Maybe this rabbi could heal their paralyzed friend.

* * *

As Jesus's disciples walked back into the quiet seaside town of Capernaum, they were not surprised to see the small throng of people waiting for them. Over the past few months, the news about Jesus's teaching and miracles had spread like wildfire throughout the regions of Galilee and Caesarea Philippi. Returning home to expectant crowds had now become a common occurrence. As Capernaum was situated on the Via Maris trade route, which extended from Egypt in the south to Syria in the northeast, the news about Jesus had traveled all the way to Judea, and even as far as Phoenicia, Samaria, Syria, and the Decapolis.

Looking around at the crowd, the disciples recognized some familiar faces—family and friends—who were excited about the group's return. Most of the people, however, appeared to be from out of town. Several of the visitors looked like they had traveled quite a long distance to reach the Galilean fishing village. Among the crowd were men and women who had brought their ailing relatives and friends to see Jesus. Others were clearly sick themselves. There was also a company of Pharisees and teachers of the law who were walking toward them from the direction of the synagogue.

Meanwhile, the group of friends arrived in Capernaum much later than they had anticipated. After hearing the traveler's stories about Jesus the rabbi who healed the sick and paralyzed, they immediately knew that they had to bring their friend to this man of God. Jesus would heal their crippled friend. They knew it. As sure as the sun rose in the east and set in the west, this rabbi would cure their friend. As the friends entered the town, they did not have to ask where the Jewish rabbi was staying. They could hear the distant murmur of the crowd as soon as they entered the village. Following the noise, they soon found an overflowing multitude of people gathered outside a modest fisherman's dwelling located in the center of town.

At first, Jesus's disciples did not notice the falling dirt. But after small bits of debris started dropping into the center of the packed room, it became difficult to ignore. There were obviously some people moving around on top of the roof. The disciples were used to bustling crowds, however, so they chose to ignore the additional disturbance. They turned again to Jesus, who was still preaching to the rapt audience.

A few minutes later, as the roof began to separate, a distinct beam of sunlight streamed into the darkened room. The disciples looked up again. It was evident now what was happening. Whoever was on the roof was breaking through the dense layer of branches and mud plaster. The hole got larger and larger. Finally, the disciples could see several faces peering into the house through the now alfresco ceiling. There was further commotion on the roof. Then the interlopers started lowering something into the middle of the gathered crowd. What were they lowering? It was a person—the men were lowering a man on a mat right in front of Jesus.

What in the world was happening? The teachers of the Law looked up at the commotion on the roof. This disturbance was not acceptable. They turned to the rabbi Jesus expectantly. The upcoming reprimand alone would make their trip to this rural outpost worthwhile.

As the sunlight spilled into the room, Jesus stopped teaching and looked up at the group of friends lowering their comrade before him. Jesus saw the men's faith, and turning to the paralyzed man who now lay hopeful before him, declared, "Son, your sins are forgiven."

When the teachers of the Law heard Jesus's words to the crippled man, "Your sins are forgiven," shock and anger gripped their hearts. They exclaimed, "Why does this fellow talk like that? He is blaspheming! Who can forgive sins, but God alone?"

Jesus immediately turned and faced the Jewish leaders. Did Jesus know their thoughts? Without hesitation, Jesus responded to their silent critiques: "Why are you thinking these things in your hearts? Which is easier to say, 'Your sins are forgiven,' or to say, 'Get up and walk?'"

Then, turning to the gathered crowd, Jesus continued, "I want you to know that the Son of Man has authority on earth to forgive sins." Looking at the paralyzed man Jesus said, "I tell you, get up, take your mat, and go home." Immediately the crippled man stood up. As everyone in the sunlit room stared in amazement, the man bent down, picked up his mat, and walked out of the house in full view of everyone. Those remaining in the room could hear the healed man continuously praising God as he navigated his way through the pressing crowds along the narrow alleyways of the village.

What had happened? The gathered crowd was astonished at what they had witnessed. Jesus had forgiven the paralyzed man and then healed him! Everyone was amazed and praised God. Filled with awe, the people said, "We have seen remarkable things today."

The healed man's friends felt the cool sea breeze on their backs as they walked away from the Galilean village. Still amazed at what had occurred, every now and then they would turn around, and check on their formerly paralyzed friend, now walking beside them. This Jewish rabbi, Jesus, was more than a prophet or a healer; he had the ability to forgive sins. And, as the teachers of the Law had proclaimed, only God could forgive sins.

HEALING THE DEMON-POSSESSED MAN IN GERASENES[2]

The herdsmen were the first to see the fishing boat moored to a piece of driftwood on the shoreline. They had been sitting on the hillside watching their drove graze lazily on the fresh grass, when they first saw the boat in the distance. Now, they observed, the fishermen were climbing out of the vessel. It was quite a large group. Clearly, they were not planning to catch any fish. Ten men appeared, maybe twelve. No, there were thirteen men in all. Who were they? Why were they here? Even from a distance, the herdsmen could tell that they were not from their region. The men

---

[2] I based my retelling of the biblical narrative on the accounts in Luke 8:26–39 and Mark 5:1–17.

must have come from the other side of the Lake of Gennesaret. Were they Romans? Clearly, they were foreigners. Perhaps they were Jews.

They had been staring at the men for a few minutes, when they first heard him. Their skin involuntarily bristled with fear. Where was he? He had been living in the hills near the lake as long as they could remember. As small children, they had heard the adults speak about him. "Stay away from him," they warned. "Do not go near that man. He is dangerous and unpredictable." His family locked him up near the tombs outside the village. His brothers, or maybe it was his uncles, took turns looking after him. Rumors floated around the village that his family had to restrain him with chains and shackles. Villagers sometimes noticed that the man's relatives had deep scratches on their faces. People whispered stories about the man's madness, his unhuman strength that could break chains, and the evil that spoke through him.

The herdsmen could still hear his screams. He was coming closer. Finally, they saw him. The demonized man tore wildly down the hillside toward the boat. They then saw the visitors look with shock as the man rushed toward them: naked, screaming, and running with increasing speed.

* * *

Following Jesus of Nazareth was definitely an adventure. It was unpredictable at the very least. After following Jesus for several months, though, the disciples had learned not to question Jesus's unusual instructions and directions. So, this morning, when Jesus had asked them to prepare for a trip across the Lake of Gennesaret to the region of Gerasenes, they did it. It was a largely Gentile area with only a few Jews living there.

As soon as they reached the shore, they realized that they were in Gentile territory. On the hillside, they saw a few herdsmen looking after a drove of pigs. Here were unclean Gentiles, looking after their unclean beasts. Had Jesus noticed the herdsmen? No, he had not. He was looking toward the left of them—at a man. Was the man yelling? He was swiftly running toward them, naked and bloody. Had people attacked him? As the man came toward them, his eyes became visible. He was not sick or injured. He was possessed. As Jesus stepped forward toward the sprinting man with purpose, the disciples witnessed the Lord exercise his divine authority.

Looking after the possessed man had become a job, which lay on the shoulders of the older men in the family. When the episodes first started, the men kept him downstairs with the animals. However, the small stable door could not restrain him, so they took him outside the village to dwell among the tombs. The men in the family looked after him in shifts, never going alone. Each shift involved two men, and sometimes three. It had been many years since the "evil" took over him. They did not use his proper name anymore. They called the demonized "him," or sometimes "the boy," even though he had long since become a man. The scars across their bodies were a constant reminder of the demonic strength—of his madness and the evil that had possessed him. They restrained him with ropes, chains, and shackles. Yet when they returned to visit him, the chains and shackles lay crushed on the floor. The family knew that the villagers talked about spirits cursing them or that they had sinned against one of the gods. Maybe that was true, maybe it was not. What the family did know, though, was that a ghost had taken over the boy's body. Perhaps it was the work of an evil spirit. Whatever was in him was definitely not from this physical world.

Jesus looked up and saw this screaming man running toward him. When the man was within a few feet of the Lord, he stopped abruptly and flung himself on the ground. He bowed before Jesus. Jesus immediately spoke with authority to the evil spirit within the man, "Come out of the man, you unclean spirit!" A deep voice from within the man started speaking: "What business do we have with each other, Jesus, Son of the Most High God?" Jesus repeated his command. The voice continued, "I beg you, do not torment me."

Jesus asked the evil spirit, "What is your name?" The spirit responded immediately: "My name is Legion, for we are many."

The disciples looked at each other. The possessed man had said, "Legion." There were usually 6,000 soldiers in a Roman

Legion. The fishermen looked at each other, and then at Jesus. The spirits were speaking again, begging Jesus not to command them to go into the abyss. They were asking Jesus for mercy—for him to cast them into the herd of pigs, still grazing on the nearby hillside. The disciples then heard Jesus give them permission to enter the swine. The poor tormented man suddenly jolted back, and then laid down at rest.

The herdsmen were too far away to hear the visitors' conversation by the shoreline. They thought about sending one of their party toward the group but thought against it when they saw "him" arrive. It appeared that one of the men, the leader, they thought, was having a conversation with the boy, naked as he was, crazy as he was. It was a confusing sight: the boy prostrating himself before this strange visitor. The Jew was clearly not afraid of him. They wondered what was happening.

Then, they heard the first piercing squeal. Then, the second, the third, the tenth, the twentieth, and the hundredth shrieking noise. Was it wolves? Perhaps it was bears. The herdsmen looked frantically around for the approaching predators. Suddenly, their herd of pigs started racing down the mountain—agitated, fearful, and possessed. Some of the herdsmen tried to stop them, but the fleeing drove struck them down. The herdsmen followed the pigs down the hill, racing behind the panicked animals. Then they watched helplessly as their livelihood rushed straight, with no hesitation, past the small group of foreigners, and into the water. They watched, now staring with shock, as their entire drove, 2,000 pigs, drowned in the lake.

When the herdsmen finally reached the edge of the lake, they saw the possessed man. He was sitting. Someone from among the Jewish group must have given him a robe to wear. He sat there, calmly, eating some bread, and talking with some of the men.

The man looked up at all the smiling and laughing men around him. He did not recognize any of them. He could tell from their accents that they were Jews from the Galilean region from across the sea. He felt so much peace—like a river rushing through his body. The strangers gave him some bread, and he ate. It seemed that he had not eaten in a long time. He was famished.

Apparently, evil spirits had possessed him for years as he lived in the tombs outside his village. He knew that this was true as he looked down at his scarred and bloodied body, and felt the filth on his long stringy hair and beard. The last few years appeared as a hazy dark dream. He remembered voices: so many voices in his head each speaking words that he did not understand. He remembered the cold wet tombs. He recalled villagers chaining him—holding him down with shackles. He thought of how he felt so afraid, because he was not able to overcome the voices in his head. Again, he looked at the man called Jesus. He had heard the words that had come out of his mouth moments before, "Jesus, Son of the Most High God."

It was midmorning when the villagers heard the commotion outside. Why were the herdsmen in town? Why had they left their animals alone and unprotected? At first, the story came as fragments. First, "The Jews came on a boat." Then, "Our pigs are all dead." Further, "The possessed man from the tombs is healed." The crowd of villagers grew larger, milling around the herdsmen. "We saw it all happen before our eyes," the men continued in a terrified tone. "The leader must be a powerful sorcerer," another added. "Yes, it's true; we witnessed it all," responded a third. "Come with us. They are still there by the shore." Encouraging the crowd to follow them, the herdsmen again entreated, "Come and see the possessed man for yourself. You will then know that it is all true."

When the village people finally reached the shore, there was already a small gathering around the Jewish men. The herdsmen must have told everyone within earshot of what they saw. It took a while to push through the crowd to see the boy. He was sitting still, as the herdsmen had said. He sat quiet, calm, and in his right mind. The boy's family was already making their way to his side. The shock in their faces was tangible.

Who was this man, who had the power to expel evil spirits from the boy? What human being had the power to cause the death of 2,000 pigs? As they stood there, the crowd grew—women, children, and men—all wanting to get a glimpse of the former possessed man and his healer. The air thickened with panic as the group started to realize what had taken place. "Legion," the tormented man had called himself. This Jewish rabbi, for that is who they now realized him to be, had cast out 6,000 evil spirits, and had caused the death of 2,000 pigs. Fear gripped the crowd as they looked at each other, whispering with increasing fervor, "Who was this man?" Finally, from the back of the crowd, a small group of village elders emerged. They walked up to the Jewish rabbi with purpose. Facing the healer, they told him, "You are not welcome here. You need to leave immediately."

A growing throng of people from the nearby village surrounded the boy. He stood up suddenly, and pushed through the gathered crowd. Why was Jesus leaving? The healed man increased his pace, walking toward the Jewish men who were pushing their boat back into the lake. "Wait! Wait for me," he yelled to them. "Take me with you," he implored his healer as he reached Jesus's boat. The rabbi turned to him. The peace of God flooded through the man's body once again. "You can't come with us," Jesus responded. "Go home to your people and report to them what great things the Lord has done for you. How he had mercy on you."

Jesus turned and helped his followers push the boat into the sea. The man walked determinedly through the crowd and prepared for his journey. He would tell of all the great things that the Lord had done for him. He would travel to each of the Roman cities of the east—Hippus, Raphana, Dion, Gadara, and beyond—and tell whoever would listen about how Jesus, the Son of God, had healed him. How Jesus, the Son of God, had released him with the power of God from a legion of evil spirits. How Jesus, the Son of God, had set him free from a tormented life of satanic captivity.

REFLECTION QUESTIONS

1. What impact do you think that Jesus's act of healing had on the healed individual, his immediate family, and his larger community in the narratives of the paralyzed man in Capernaum and the demon-possessed man in Gerasenes?
2. What do you notice about Jesus's reaction to and engagement with the sick individuals?

3. How has God brought holistic healing into your life—physically, socially, emotionally, and/or spiritually?
4. How have you witnessed Christ's healing power in your own family, church, and ministry? What short-term and/or long-term influence did Christ's healing have on your communities?
5. What role should Christ our Healer play in our lives and ministries today?

11

The Healing Stories of St. Thaumaturgus, St. Cuthbert, the Blumhardts, and Kuhlman

Paul W. Lewis

Throughout church history, God has used many followers of Christ as conduits of divine healing. Commonly, this is within the context of a person being holy or "set apart" by the Lord and being used by his Spirit. How these healings take place, however, and the theological understanding for each, may differ. Below are four vignettes of key figures throughout church history that are exemplars of following Christ our Healer. These stories are models of ministry through the miraculous.[1]

---

[1] The many resources that scholars use to describe the lives and healing ministries of the chapter's historical figures—such as biographies from within church history—can be works of hagiography, or "holy writing." These writings tend to highlight the positive aspects of the person without any careful critique. With this awareness, I have attempted to balance the narratives between the possibility of the miraculous and the apparent exaggerations of the original authors.

ST. GREGORY THAUMATURGUS (ca. 213–270)[2]

St. Gregory Thaumaturgus was an important theologian and bishop of the third century. He grew up in a wealthy yet pagan family in Neocaesarea, Pontus (present-day Turkey), and was a student of law and rhetoric. Around 233, he traveled with his brother Athenodorus to Caesarea in Palestine. There he met the theologian Origen, who was instrumental in his Christian conversion. He became a student of Origen while he was at Caesarea, where, along with the Christian faith, he studied logic, geometry, literature, philosophy, and ethics. Five to eight years later, the church appointed him the bishop of Neocaesarea (his native city), where he ministered until his death. In this capacity as bishop, he witnessed Roman Emperor Decius's persecution of the church (250–251), and the Gothic invasion of Pontus (253–254), as well as participating in the Synod of Antioch (264–265), in which church theologians rejected the heterodox teachings of Sabellianism, Tritheism, and those of Paul of Samosata.

Miraculous works were most prominent in the ministry of Gregory Thaumaturgus. His commonly used designation, Thaumaturgus, means miracle worker, or wonder worker. This was due to the miraculous activities that accompanied his ministry. Multiple sources in antiquity attest to descriptions of him and his

---

[2] All dates are Common Era (CE) unless otherwise specified. An important ancient source is St. Gregory of Nyssa, *The Life of Gregory the Wonderworker*. See this work and the writings of St. Gregory Thaumaturgus in Michael Slusser, trans., *St. Gregory Thaumaturgus: Life and Works*, The Fathers of the Church 98 (Washington, DC: Catholic University of America Press, 1998). Some helpful modern sources on Gregory Thaumaturgus are Stanley M. Burgess, ed., *Christian Peoples of the Spirit: A Documentary History of Pentecostal Spirituality from the Early Church to the Present* (New York: New York University Press, 2011), 38–39; Stephen Mitchell, "The Life and Lives of Gregory Thaumaturgus," in *Portraits of Spiritual Authority: Religious Power in Early Christianity, Byzantium and the Christian Orient*, ed. Jan Willem Drijvers and John W. Watt (Leiden, the Netherlands: Brill, 1999), 99–138; Frederick W. Norris, "Gregory Thaumaturgus," in *Encyclopedia of Early Christianity*, ed. Everett Ferguson (New York: Routledge, 1990), 403–404; W. Telfer, "The Cultus of St. Gregory Thaumaturgus," *Harvard Theological Review* 29 (1936): 225–344; and Raymond van Dam, "Hagiography and History: The Life of Gregory Thaumaturgus," *Classical Antiquity* 1, no. 2 (October 1982): 272–308.

miraculous works.³ While some modern scholars have questioned many of the stories about him, it seems to some other theologians that God genuinely used him in healing and the miraculous. The basis for their conclusion is the number of ancient stories about his ministry, his designation of Thaumaturgus, and his miraculous activity that caused many in his bishopric to become Christian believers.

One such historical witness was the healing of a demon-possessed boy. Early stories relay that Gregory was in an open-air gathering in a rural area, and while teaching the people, a boy started to scream. After the gathering had dispersed, a group brought the boy to the bishop. Gregory spoke to those around him that a demon possessed the child. Gregory then took a cloth from around his shoulders and flung it at the boy. Once this happened, the boy shook, cried out, fell to the ground, and the demon threw him about. When Gregory put his hand on him, the shaking stopped, the demon left him, and the boy became normal.⁴ This is one of many stories about the healings and miracles associated with Gregory of Thaumaturgus.

ST. CUTHBERT OF LINDISFARNE (ca. 636–687)⁵

St. Cuthbert grew up in Northumbria in northeast England. In 651, he became a monk in the monastery at Melrose, and adopted the Celtic Christian tradition.⁵ The Celtic practice calculated a

---

³ See Eusebius, *Historia Eccles.*, vi. 30, vii. 14; Basil, *De Spiritu Sancto*, xxix. 74, Epist., 28; Jerome, *De Viris Illustr.*, chap. 65; Rufinus, *Historia Eccles.*, vii. 25; Socrates, *Historia Eccles.*, iv. 27; and Sozomen, *Historia Eccles.*, vii. 27.

⁴ St. Gregory of Nyssa, *Life of Gregory the Wonderworker*, 77.

⁵ While St. Cuthbert of Lindisfarne is a lesser-known saint of European medieval times, we have a few ancient sources that describe his life and works. One distinguished source is The Venerable Bede, "Life of Cuthbert," in *The Age of Bede*, ed. D. H. Farmer and trans. J. F. Webb (New York: Penguin, 1983), 41–102. Also see The Venerable Bede, *The Ecclesiastical History of the English People*, intro. and ed. Judith McClure and Roger Collins (Oxford: Oxford University Press, 1994), 221–37. Another translation of Bede's *Life of Cuthbert* with another contemporaneous anonymous life of Cuthbert is in Bertram Colgrave, trans., *Two Lives of Saint Cuthbert* (New York: Cambridge University Press, 1985). Helpful works written about Cuthbert are "Cuthbert, St. (c. 636–87)," in *The Oxford Dictionary of the Christian Church*, ed. F. L. Cross, 3rd ed./rev. ed. (Oxford:

different date for Easter, and used a distinctive tonsure, which involved shaving the head from ear to ear. He helped start a new monastery at Ripon with his abbot Eata of Hexham. Partially due to Cuthbert's Celtic traditions, he and Eata returned to Melrose when Bishop Wilfrid, who was of the Roman tradition, became abbot. Cuthbert worked tirelessly to connect with the rural people in visitation and outreach. Yet he felt a call to a life of solitude. Eata, however, appointed him the Prior of Lindisfarne around 662.

During this time, there was major tension in many regions of England between the Roman Catholic and the Celtic Christian traditions. Church leaders called a synod at Whitby to settle the issue for Northumbria (664). Subsequently, the monastics and the church of Northumbria decided to follow the Roman tradition. Through patience and kindness, Cuthbert led the monastery at Lindisfarne—steeped in Celtic Christianity—to adopt the Roman Catholic traditions. Many commented about his character in slowly winning over the monks to the Latin forms. Later, the church allowed him to be a hermit on the island of Farne. His renown as a holy man, however, meant that many came to him for spiritual guidance and counsel. In 684, Cuthbert reluctantly accepted the role as the Bishop of Lindisfarne. The church hierarchy consecrated him on Easter 685. He served for approximately a year and a half, and then he withdrew to Farne, where he died on March 20, 687.

Cuthbert exemplifies a saint who devoutly followed the Lord Jesus. Stories about his life include many works of miracles and healings. People saw him as a man of prayer. In fact, the church directly tied his intercession and prayer to some of the miraculous events. To show this connection, let me relate the following two stories about Cuthbert.

Oxford University Press, 2005), 443–44; David Adam, *Fire of the North: The Life of St. Cuthbert*, 2nd ed. (London: SPCK, 2003); B. Colgrave, "Cuthbert of Lindisfarne, St.," in *New Catholic Encyclopedia*, vol. 4 (New York: McGraw-Hill, 1967), 553–54; and Margaret Donaldson, "Reflections on the Life of St. Cuthbert," *Journal of Theology for South Africa* 62 (1988): 62–67. One notable volume that has essays about Cuthbert himself, the later developed cult, and the tracking of his bones from Lindisfarne to Durham (where they currently reside) is Gerald Bonner, David Rollason, and Clare Stancliffe, eds., *St. Cuthbert, His Cult and His Community to AD 1200* (Woodbridge, Suffolk, UK: Boydell Press, 1989).

First, when Aethelwold was bishop of Melrose in England, Cuthbert was preaching in the villages, proclaiming the Good News of Jesus Christ. He came upon a village where nuns had taken refuge since barbarians had threatened their nunnery. One of the nuns, a relative of Aethelwold, started to get seriously ill with pains in her head and down her side, to the point that the doctors stopped treatment. Hearing the pleas of others on her behalf, Cuthbert had pity on her, and anointed her with oil. Immediately, she began to improve, and had a total recovery a few days later.[6]

Second, while Cuthbert was preaching in the hill country, which was a low socioeconomic region, there was no lodging available for Bishop Cuthbert's entourage. Therefore, the local people provided tents for them. Cuthbert preached to the crowds, and "brought down the grace of the Holy Ghost by imposition of hands on those newly regenerated in Christ."[7] In the midst of these services, people brought a youth on a stretcher who was wasting away with a nagging disease. The attending women positioned the youth near Cuthbert to ask permission to bring him forward for a blessing. Seeing the youth's plight, the bishop asked everyone to move further away. Cuthbert then proceeded, as what was his habit, in "prayer, gave a blessing and drove away the disease for which the doctors, despite their skill in concocting medicines, had been unable to devise a cure."[8] The Lord healed the youth, who gave thanks to God and returned home with the women who had brought him. The hallmarks of Cuthbert of Lindisfarne were healings and miracles, together with his virtuous character.

JOHANN CHRISTOPH BLUMHARDT (1805–1880) AND CHRISTOPH FRIEDRICH BLUMHARDT (1842–1919)[9]

Johann Christoph Blumhardt, and his son, Christoph Friedrich Blumhardt, had a significant religious impact in nineteenth-century Germany.[9] They pastored and ministered in a Christian commu-

---

[6] Bede, *Life of St. Cuthbert*, 30.
[7] Ibid., 32.
[8] Ibid.
[9] A helpful reader with a selection of the Blumhardts' works is Vernard

nity in Möttlingen. Johann Blumhardt grew up within a Pietist context in southern Germany and had a rigorous education, which included philosophy, theology, and biblical languages. Soon after he moved into pastoral ministry, he arrived at Möttlingen, where he ministered for many years. Furthermore, believers knew Christoph, his son, as an evangelist and faith healer. After reducing the number of his evangelistic crusades, he put more energy into the political dynamics of helping people, with an emphasis on democratic socialism. Yet he devoutly followed the Lord, seeing his political activity as a part of his life's work.

Theologically, the Blumhardts trusted that Christ's victory resulted in healing: "Jesus is Victor." Christ's victory subjugated Satan's work among the demonic forces and the realm of sickness. The Blumhardts believed, contrary to the contemporary Christian thinking of the time, that the Lordship of Christ meant that people did not have to accept evil in the world. Rather, it was necessary for Christians to oppose evil. This notion was true because God poured out the Holy Spirit on all humanity; God's Spirit provides the hope and victory.[10]

The testimony of Gottliebin Dittus is a noted story related to the Blumhardts' healing ministry. Dittus's aunt raised her in the occult and dedicated her to Satan. She was suffering from demonic torment as well as psychological and physical issues. In 1842, she came to Pastor Johann for help. During a prayer session, she manifested demonic voices and hysterical fits. Johann

---

Eller, ed., *Thy Kingdom Come: A Blumhardt Reader* (Grand Rapids, MI: Eerdmans, 1980). Several works on the thought and ministry of the Blumhardts have been written, including several dissertations such as William G. Bodamer, Jr., *The Life and Work of Johann Christoph Blumhardt* (PhD diss., Princeton Theological Seminary, 1966); and Frank D. Macchia, *Spirituality and Social Liberation: The Message of the Blumhardts in the Light of Württemberg Pietism with Implications for Pentecostal Theology* (PhD diss., University of Basel, 1989). Also see Ronald Kydd, *Healing through the Centuries: Models for Understanding* (Peabody, MA: Hendrickson, 1998), 34–45; Ronald Kydd, "J. C. Blumhardt: Another Kind of Healer," *Historical Papers 1994: Canadian Society of Church History* (1994): 25–42; and Roger Newell, "Blumhardt, J. C. (1805–80) and C. F. (1842–1919)," in *The Dictionary of Historical Theology*, ed. Trevor A. Hart (Grand Rapids, MI: Eerdmans, 2000), 76–77.

[10] Newell, "Blumhardt, J. C. (1805–80) and C. F. (1842–1919)," 76–77.

urged her to ask Jesus to come to her aid. However, ministerial colleagues recommended that Blumhardt commit her to a mental institution. Nevertheless, he desired to help her, and considered her need to be that of demonic deliverance. During a late-night prayer meeting, Johann Blumhardt witnessed her being delivered of demons. The Lord Jesus dramatically changed her. Shouting, she declared, "Jesus is Victor, Jesus is Victor!" This led to a revival in the town of Möttlingen, with a focus on repentance and spiritual renewal. Later, Gottliebin Dittus married, and lived a productive life, including involving herself in Christian ministry.

This story of the Blumhardts' healing and deliverance ministry affected European theology for the next century and a half.[11] The impact was such that Rudolf Bultmann commented that it was "*mir ein Greuel*" ("an abomination to me").[12] Yet Karl Barth defended the story in his "Freedom for Life" section in *Church Dogmatics*, highlighting that "Jesus is Victor."[13] The Blumhardts provided both the theological framework and practical expression for healing in the modern age.

---

[11] While relatively unknown in North America, the theological impact of the Blumhardts, including specifically the above story, is evident in the writings of Karl Barth, Dietrich Bonhoeffer, Emil Brunner, Oscar Cullman, Jacque Ellul, Gerhard Sauter, Paul Tillich, and Eduard Thurneysen. See Donald Dayton, "The Radical Message of Evangelical Christianity," in *Churches in Struggle: Liberation Theologies and Social Change in North America*, ed. William K. Tabb (New York: Monthly Review Press, 1986), 215–16; Eller, *Thy Kingdom Come*, xii–xvi; Kydd, "J. C. Blumhardt," 31; and Newell, "Blumhardt, J. C. (1805–80) and C. F. (1842–1919)," 76–77.

[12] Theologians also translate the phrase "to my mind preposterous." See Rudolf Bultmann, *Kerygma and Myth: A Theological Debate*, ed. Hans Werner Bartsch (New York: Harper Torchbooks, 1961), 120.

[13] Karl Barth, *Church Dogmatics: The Doctrine of Creation*, III:4 § 55, ed. G. W. Bromiley and T. F. Torrance (Peabody, MA: Hendrickson, 2004), 370–71. Karl Barth also dedicates a chapter to J. C. Blumhardt in his seminal work, *Protestant Theology in the Nineteenth Century: Its Background and History* (Valley Forge, PA: Judson Press, 1973), 643–53.

KATHRYN KUHLMAN (1907–1976)[14]

At fourteen, Kathryn Kuhlman had a spiritual experience with God that led her toward itinerate preaching in Colorado, Idaho, and Utah. Later she expanded her evangelistic travels to other parts of the United States and around the world. She became a well-known radio and television presence. Without any formal theological training she became known as the "world's most widely-known female evangelist."[15] Moreover, she was not only a preacher but also a celebrated healing evangelist. Kuhlman conducted "miracle services," whereby in the midst of a service, God would heal people. She gave credit to the Holy Spirit for the miraculous healings in her meetings and ministry, and became a significant voice and representative of the Charismatic-Pentecostal movement of 1960s and 1970s. The following story demonstrates Kuhlman's healing ministry.

Raised in a traditional Christian home, Marjorie Close suffered from stomach cancer. In 1967, the doctors gave her six weeks to live. Her weight was decreasing so rapidly that she was too sick to cook. A friend, Phyllis Diller (the famous comedian), recommended a number of books for Marjorie to read, including Kathryn Kuhlman's *I Believe in Miracles*. Larry Ahlborn, a local gospel pianist who accepted Christ in a Kuhlman meeting, then encouraged Close to attend a Kuhlman healing service in Pittsburgh, near her hometown of Greensburg. Marjorie turned down Ahlborn's invitation four times before accepting. Even then, while

---

[14] Kathryn Kuhlman wrote several books on miracles and healing, including *God Can Do It Again* (New York: Pyramid Family Library, 1974); *I Believe in Miracles* (Englewood Cliffs, NJ: Prentice-Hall, 1962); and *Nothing Is Impossible with God* (North Brunswick, NJ: Bridge-Logos, 1992). In addition, several works were written about Kuhlman including Wayne E. Warner, *Kathryn Kuhlman: The Woman Behind the Miracles* (Ann Arbor, MI: Servant Publications, 1993); D. J. Wilson, "Kuhlman, Kathryn," in *New International Dictionary of Pentecostal and Charismatic Movements*, rev. ed., ed. Stanley M. Burgess (Grand Rapids, MI: Zondervan, 2002); Amy Collier Artman, *The Miracle Lady: Kathryn Kuhlman and the Transformation of Charismatic Christianity*, Library of Religious Biography Series (Grand Rapids, MI: Eerdmans, 2019); and Grant Wacker, "The Forgotten Female Preacher," *Christianity Today* 63, no. 8 (2019): 46–50.

[15] Wilson, "Kuhlman, Kathryn," 826.

on the bus to the meeting, she tried to back out of the opportunity. It was her daughter, Janie, who encouraged her mother to continue.

While in the Kuhlman service, she experienced a "warm sensation coming over her head, and then to her stomach . . . [and] a lemon-sized lump disappeared from her stomach."[16] One of the ushers saw what was happening, and escorted Marjorie onto the stage to meet Kathryn Kuhlman, and give a testimony. Kuhlman asked Marjorie if she knew what it was like to "pass from death unto life." The Greensburg native replied that she did not. Kuhlman then led her in the sinner's prayer, and prayed for her and her daughter. Both fell to the floor. Marjorie later testified that it was the most wonderful feeling. Her heart and body had changed. When she went back to the doctor who had diagnosed her cancer, he testified to the miracle. He wrote a report comparing her medical condition before and after the Kuhlman service, which officially verified the physical healing. After her miracle, Marjorie participated in prayer meetings and lived to serve her Lord another twenty-five years beyond her life expectancy. Kathryn Kuhlman continued to minister evangelistically through healing services until her death.

REFLECTION QUESTIONS

1. In what ways are the stories of Christ our Healer in the lives of St. Thaumaturgus, St. Cuthbert, the Blumhardts, and Kuhlman similar to each other?
2. In what ways are the Christ our Healer stories different from each other?
3. How are the stories instructive in their different missions contexts?
4. What do these stories tell us about engaging the members of the church?
5. How can these stories of Christ our Healer help us encounter non-Christians in various settings?

---

[16] Warner, *Kathryn Kuhlman*, 164.

12

Contemporary Stories of Christ Our Healer

Sarita Gallagher Edwards

CHRIST HEALS JENNIFER MATHENY[1]

A sharp stab of excruciating pain shot through Jenny Matheny's body as she woke with a start. Shaking from the agony, Jenny crawled out of bed and slowly made the harrowing journey to the bedroom door to find help. A few days before, she had driven two hours from her central California home to Fresno, California, where she was enrolled in a Masters of Marriage and Family Therapy program at a local seminary. Earlier that year, Jenny and her husband, Art, had moved to the town of Atascadero. Art had accepted a new pastoral position at Atascadero Christian Church. After enrolling in graduate school that fall, Jenny had begun the weekly commute to Fresno to attend her classes. While in town, she was staying with Danielle—her best friend—as had become her custom.

---

[1] The author conducted the interview on August 29, 2019. The events took place between October 30 and November 1, 1999, in Fresno, California. The interviewees gave permission to use their real names.

At 4:30 in the morning, Art received the urgent call from Danielle. As he listened, he immediately sensed the seriousness of the situation. Ambulance personnel had rushed Jenny to the emergency room where she continued to be in intense, crippling pain. Danielle's words resounded on the phone: "They think it's a tubal pregnancy. They are going to have to abort the baby to save Jenny's life." She continued quickly, "I have to return to the hospital room. I will call you back when I have more information." Sitting alone in the dark room, Art immediately fell to his knees and cried out to God. Thoughts tumbled out haphazardly as he struggled to find the words to pray. Not only was Jenny's life in danger, but their unborn child was at risk. They had found out two days before that Jenny was six weeks pregnant. Art was overwhelmed at the thought of losing both his wife and baby.

What Is Causing Jenny's Pain?

When Art arrived at the hospital in Fresno, he found Jenny lying on the hospital bed perspiring and writhing in pain. Since the time he had first spoken to Danielle, the medical staff had been able to rule out an ectopic pregnancy. The doctors were still unable, however, to identify the cause of Jenny's suffering. Sitting by her bed, Art watched helplessly as a nurse tried to find a vein to take blood from his wife's dehydrated body. Finally removing a vial of blood from Jenny's foot, the nurse quickly retreated to continue the medical tests. When the on-call doctor returned to the hospital room, Jenny was unable to speak due to the extreme pain and her physical exhaustion.

The doctor shared that the medical tests had finally identified the problem. Jenny had acute appendicitis. To save her life, the doctor continued, an immediate operation was necessary to remove her appendix. This was a high-risk surgery because Jenny was pregnant. Any use of anesthesia, which was required for the surgery, would put the baby at risk. If they did not proceed with removing Jenny's appendix, conversely, the resulting rupture could kill her. If they did proceed with the surgery, the unborn baby would most likely die.

As the nurse prepared Jenny for surgery, Art called various church communities around the United States to pray for his wife and child. He entreated his close friend in Missouri: "Would you pray? Christ needs to heal Jenny. There is no good alternative. If Jenny lives, then the baby dies." The urgent prayer request spread rapidly among the groups. Friends and family began interceding on behalf of Jenny and their unborn child—their home church in Iowa, former pastorate in Missouri, and current church in Atascadero. As the doctor returned to Jenny's bedside, Art informed him, "We are praying about this situation." The flash of skepticism in the doctor's eyes was immediately apparent. As the physician touched Jenny's side, a new shockwave of pain radiated throughout her body. "This is an acute appendicitis," the doctor responded. "And we have to immediately go in for surgery."

A Turn of Events

A flurry of organized activity surrounded Jenny as the nurses prepared to move her from the room to the surgery. Still in excruciating pain, the nurses carefully shaved her stomach, and wheeled her into the operating theater. Turning to the surgeon, Jenny started joking, as she always did when she found herself in an awkward situation. After some back-and-forth banter, it dawned on her that something was different. Puzzled, Jenny wondered, "How in the world am I joking right now?" Looking at the doctor, she remarked, "I think I don't have any more pain." The medical staff had not yet given Jenny any medication. Thus, the doctor pressed her side. Yet there was no discomfort. At that moment, Jenny realized that she had experienced an instant healing. The surgeon paused before replying, "As this is a high-risk surgery due to your pregnancy, if your pain is gone, I would rather observe you through the night and wait to see what is going on."

After Jenny returned to her hospital room, she fell asleep. Art made his way downstairs to the cafeteria. It was late in the evening, and the cafeteria was empty, except for one other person—the nurse who had drawn blood from Jenny's foot earlier that day. As Art sat down at a table next to the nurse, she turned to him and inquired about Jenny's surgery. "She didn't go into surgery," Art replied. "What?" The nurse responded in confusion. "Yeah," Art answered. "I think Christ healed her. She's no longer in any pain." As they began to talk together, the nurse confided in Art that she used to attend church as a child and had faith in God. Sitting in the empty cafeteria, they talked about faith, life, and God. Eventually, Art felt the physical exhaustion of the day creeping upon him and, taking his leave, returned to Jenny's hospital room to rest before the morning.

Two days later, after a series of tests and monitoring Jenny's progress, the doctor delivered his final prognosis. Jenny no longer had acute appendicitis. She was completely healthy. Her vital signs had continued to stabilize, and the hospital could release her that day. As the doctor shared the good news with Jenny and her husband, Art pressed the doctor for clarification. Art enquired, "Okay, so is this something that is going to come back? Does appendicitis do this: come and go?" "No," the doctor replied, "you either have appendicitis, or you don't. And Jenny does not have appendicitis." Holding Jenny's medical chart in his hand, the doctor looked back and forth between the chart and Jenny as he spoke. "Everything is fine. She can go," he concluded. As the doctor started to leave the hospital room, he turned to Jenny, still puzzled by the outcome. He inquired with a mixture of curiosity and incredulity, "What God do you pray to?" As the doctor walked out of the room, Art jumped out of his seat and ran to the door to answer the doctor's question. "It's Jesus! Jesus is the one," Art declared with enthusiasm. "That's who we were praying to!"

CHRIST HEALS SARAH PUCKETT[2]

After a full day of exploring Disneyland, ten-year-old Sarah was standing next to her father waiting for their final amusement ride. As they weaved through the long line, the pain that had been building up in Sarah's feet reached an excruciating level—she found herself starting to lose her balance. She quickly caught herself,

---

[2] The author conducted the interview on September 7, 2019. The interviewee gave permission to use her real name.

almost falling to the ground. Unsure of what was happening, Sarah turned to her Dad in concern. "Dad, I can't walk anymore." Tears were starting to form in Sarah's eyes as the father picked up his crying daughter to take her home. "Maybe it's because we were walking around all day," he said, trying to console his distraught daughter. "I don't know," Sarah exclaimed through the now-searing pain. "It feels like something is really wrong. It is so painful."

The next day the pain had not gone away. Whenever Sarah was on her feet for more than an hour, she would feel shooting pains radiate up both legs, from her heels all the way to her shoulders. In the weeks and months after the Disneyland visit, Sarah would wake up each morning in agony. By the end of the day, she would lie down in pain. As her parents looked for answers, they took her to their local medical doctor, then specialists, physical therapists, dermatologists, and even a homeopathic doctor. Each medical practitioner conducted a thorough examination. However, the doctors could only speculate as to why Sarah was in so much pain. They explored many possible causes: plantar fasciitis, curved Achilles tendons, allergies, and shingles. None of the treatments for the suggested diagnoses, though, eradicated the discomfort. Months turned into years.

Daily Pain Remained

One evening Sarah woke up in the middle of the night to find the tops of her feet covered with boils. Now thirteen, Sarah had become accustomed to the chronic pain, yet never before had her feet erupted in hot, painful boils. Covering Sarah's burning feet with ice, her parents quickly took her to the emergency room of the local hospital. The doctors could not identify the cause of the boils, however. They suggested that it might be an allergic reaction, and sent Sarah home with instructions to keep a cold compress on the affected areas. The boils went down a day later, but the daily pain remained.

During this time, Sarah's family and church community had been praying for her healing. Both of Sarah's parents were in ministry at their local church, where her dad was the youth pastor.

Through prayer, it became apparent to Sarah's parents that the cause of her suffering was more than a physical ailment. It was an attack from Satan. Over the years, hundreds of believers had prayed for Sarah's complete healing. Nothing had changed. The chronic pain remained. Oftentimes it would even get worse during prayer.

One day at church, Sarah was once again in physical distress. In response, her parents gathered a group of people from their congregation to pray for her. The pain was particularly severe that day—a mixture of sharp, stabbing sensations on the bottom of her feet together with hot fire radiating through her entire foot. As the congregants prayed, Sarah cried out in agony, "Stop! It's only getting worse." Turning to her parents, she exclaimed, "Stop, please stop. It's only making it worse. It's only hurting more when you are praying."

Following God's Mission Call

Despite the often-debilitating agony, Sarah was determined to continue to follow God's call upon her life to be a missionary. This was a call that she had first heard when she was ten years old. Throughout her ordeal, a biblical passage that had encouraged Sarah was Isaiah 52:7: "How beautiful on the mountains are the feet of those who bring good news, who proclaim peace, who bring good tidings, who proclaim salvation, who say to Zion, 'Your God reigns!'" When she first heard these words, Sarah declared, "I don't care. This is never going to hold me back. I believe that Christ has called me to be a missionary. My foot pain is never going to change that call. I may be in excruciating pain, but it doesn't matter."

Growing up in a church community where she had seen Christ heal people, Sarah wondered, "Why can't I be healed?" She had even prayed for people who had received healing. While pursuing Christian ministry, the question was ever present in her mind: "Why is God healing other people but not me?" Over the years, believers had provided a variety of spiritual hypotheses concerning Sarah's ailment. For example, one person proposed, "You obviously have some big sin in your life. And God is punishing you for it." These unsolicited comments were often hurtful to Sarah. They also did not reflect the truth of what God had spoken to her over the course of her life.

As the years passed, the prayers of Sarah's family and church continued. Still, the painful ailment persisted. One morning when Sarah was sixteen, red, square marks appeared on the tops of her feet, and did not fade for several months. During Sarah's senior year of high school, the boils returned with a vengeance, forcing her to seek hospital treatment. Again, there was no concrete diagnosis for the painful pustules. She moved to Oregon for college, but the pain persisted and continued to plague Sarah's daily life. By this stage, Sarah was twenty years old, and she had suffered from chronic pain for half of her life. Throughout college, rather than getting better, her pain got progressively worse. The medical practitioners continued to puzzle over her condition.

Prayer for Inner Healing

In December 2014, Sarah graduated from college, and moved back to southern California, where her mother had joined an inner-healing prayer ministry at the Pasadena International House of Prayer (PIHOP). At her mom's invitation, Sarah started attending PIHOP to provide prayer support during the healing sessions. In these sessions, Sarah repeatedly witnessed people encountering Jesus in real and tangible ways. Upon hearing that Sarah had been suffering from chronic pain for eleven years, the PIHOP director invited Sarah to seek healing prayer the following week. While Sarah immediately accepted the invitation, she was not optimistic about the outcome. "Sure," Sarah thought to herself. "If you want to try and help me, go ahead. Tons of people have already prayed for me with no results." At twenty-one years of age, Sarah knew that Christ could heal, yet she had started to wonder whether healing was a part of God's plan for her life. Sarah's mom, on the other hand, was already rejoicing. "This is it," she exclaimed to Sarah. "You are going to be healed. It's going to be amazing!"

The next week, Sarah found herself in the small prayer room at PIHOP at the beginning of her inner-healing prayer session.

Sarah started by talking about the pain in her feet. "Since I was ten years old . . ." she began, as she shared her story. As the prayer time progressed, the facilitator asked Sarah, "Do you have any significant memory of the first time you had pain?" "Yes," Sarah recalled. "I was at Disneyland with my Dad." As Sarah started talking about this experience, she saw herself walking around the theme park with her father, with whom she had always been close. Then she observed Satan trying to harm her relationship with her dad. In that instant, Sarah realized that the enemy had come and caused the physical pain, which had never left her body. Sarah shared what she had seen with the prayer-team leader. He then affirmed that he also had the same impression. This spiritual attack when she was ten years old had caused Sarah's pain.

Jesus Washed Sarah's Feet

The pain in Sarah's feet intensified as she continued to witness the scene. The prayer leader encouraged her to picture herself in a peaceful place. In Sarah's mind, she now perceived a cool stream as she walked toward the water's edge. Then she saw Christ sitting by the water. "Jesus wants to wash your feet," the team leader interjected. As Sarah saw Jesus, she thought in amazement, "What in the world is going on? This is crazy!" In her vision, however, Jesus started washing her feet. Then she heard Jesus speak to her. "You know, Sarah, this has been really hard. But it's okay. I am going to bring healing, and this pain is not going to be anymore. It is going to be over." As Jesus washed her feet, the pain disappeared. The prayer team was praying throughout this time. The leader said, "Sarah, Jesus wants to know if you want your scars to go away." After years of pain and struggle, she thought about the many scars that marred the tops of her feet. Sarah quickly replied, "No! Because I don't ever want to forget this experience. Ever."

As the prayer time ended, the prayer facilitator looked up in amazement. "Wow!" he exclaimed. Although he had been leading people in inner-healing prayer for years, he had mostly prayed for people facing emotional and spiritual issues—not those with physical ailments. "How do you feel?" he asked Sarah. "I don't feel anything," she replied. "I don't feel any pain at all." As Sarah reflected on what had happened, it was hard to believe that the pain was gone. She had experienced ten pain-free minutes against a backdrop of eleven years of constant suffering. "Even if I'm not permanently healed," Sarah thought, "that was the most amazing thing that has ever happened in my life." Before leaving the prayer room, one of the team members turned to Sarah and declared, "You know, when we have inner healing and Christ has healed us, sometimes the enemy will try to come back. You have to know that you have power over the enemy. And you have to say, 'No!'"

The next morning Sarah woke up and, for the first time in eleven years, she had no discomfort. Thinking about what had occurred, Sarah realized that only God could have done something so unbelievable. No doctor had ever been able to identify her ailment. No specialist had ever been able to determine its cause. Then, all of a sudden, Christ had healed her. Over the next five months, Sarah experienced no pain, and soon she found herself in ministry. While on a missions trip to Kenya with her family, the PIHOP team member's words about an attack of the enemy came to her mind.

Enemy Attack

One evening after a conflict had arisen among the missions team, Sarah went to bed, only to wake up the next morning in excruciating pain. Looking down at her feet, she saw that they were bright red, and burning hot to the touch. Disappointment gripped her heart. "Oh well," she thought. "I guess this is it. The healing lasted for a few months; and it was a great few months." Sarah asked her fiancé and parents to come to her room. Sarah's mother immediately called the small group into action. They needed to pray for Sarah straightaway. As her fiancé started praying, Sarah could feel that familiar feeling of hopelessness rise in her heart. "Why are we here again?" she wondered. She thought determinedly, "I'll say what I always say. This pain is never going to hold me back. It's never going to change how I live."

Pushing through the pain, Sarah spent the entire day ministering in the local Kenyan community with the missions' team.

Returning home that evening, her family started praying again for her feet. Lying in bed that night, Sarah remembered the words of the PIHOP team member. She declared throughout the night, "No. Not again. I do not have to willingly submit to this." The next morning Sarah woke up, and the pain was gone.

* * *

At the time of this interview, September 2019, Christ had brought healing to Sarah for four years. Now a teacher at a local Christian school, Sarah and her husband Kaleb, are both prayerfully moving toward international ministry. Reflecting on this time, the gracious power of Jesus in Sarah's life still amazes her. While many questions remain, Sarah is committed to sharing with others the true freedom that she has found in Christ.

REFLECTION QUESTIONS

1. How are the testimonies of Christ's healing similar and different in the lives of Jennifer Matheny and Sarah Puckett?
2. What do these narratives reveal about the character of God?
3. What is the role of prayer in these two stories of divine healing?
4. Why do you think that God's healing occurs quickly in some cases and slowly in others? Furthermore, why does God heal some people and not others?
5. How has Christ our Healer been evident in your personal life and ministry context?

PART IV

CHRIST OUR HOPE

13

Living with Christ in Purpose, Hope, and Expectancy

DeLonn L. Rance

But in keeping with his promise we are looking forward to a new heaven and a new earth, where righteousness dwells. So then, dear friends, since you are looking forward to this, make every effort to be found spotless, blameless and at peace with him.

—2 Pet 3:13–14[1]

The doctrine of the second coming has failed, so far as we are concerned, if it does not make us realize that at every moment of every year in our lives Donne's question, "What if this present were the world's last night?" is equally relevant.

—C. S. Lewis,
"The World's Last Night and Other Essays."

---

[1] Further supporting scriptures are Ephesians 1:18–21 and Matthew 24:14.

This chapter introduces the section on Christ our Hope (our soon-coming King) by highlighting the themes of living with purpose by serving Christ, the King; living with hope through the promises of Christ; and living with expectancy because of the soon-coming King. Furthermore, at the end of the chapter, I will provide an overview of Part IV that deals with these themes of Christ our Hope as they emerge in biblical, historical, and contemporary narratives.

In Pentecostal circles, proclaiming Jesus Christ as the soon-coming King has several implications for the believer, including living with purpose, hope, and expectancy. For a person to accept Jesus Christ as Savior requires repentance from sin and self-rule, and a surrender and submission to the Lordship of Christ. Meaning and purpose emerge from this change. No longer can a worshipper of Christ serve his/her own will, but he/she must live and pray, "Your kingdom come, your will be done, on earth as it is in heaven" (Mt 6:10). The individual's story finds meaning and significance living in service to the King within his grand narrative. Believers exist to worship the Lord in surrender to his will that he might be known and glorified. J. Hudson Taylor contends, "If the Lord is coming soon, is this not a very practical motive for greater missionary effort? I know of no other motive that has been so stimulating to myself."[2]

A focus on the second coming of Christ constantly reminds his followers that the God of the universe knows every thought, attitude, and action, and that when he comes, every individual will give an account of his/her life. Believers will stand before the judgment seat of Christ (Rom 14:10; 2 Cor 5:10).[3] The criterion for judgment is obedience to the will of God, including obedience to (1) the Great Commandment, "'Love the Lord your God with all your heart and with all your soul and with all your mind.' This is the first and greatest commandment. And the second is like it: 'Love your neighbor as yourself'" (Mt 22:37–39); and (2)

---

[2] J. Hudson Taylor quoted in Ron Rhodes, *The Key Ideas Bible Handbook* (Eugene, OR: Harvest House Publishers, 2016), 375. [Ed. note: primary source unavailable.]

[3] "See also Rev 19:11–16.

the Great Commission, "Therefore go and make disciples of all nations, baptizing them in the name of the Father and of the Son and of the Holy Spirit, and teaching them to obey everything I have commanded you. And surely I am with you always, to the very end of the age" (Mt 28:19–20). This reality should shape and guide the believer's life for the glory of God. One finds the meaning and purpose of human existence in serving and worshipping the soon-coming King, Jesus Christ.

Christ's imminent return fills the Christ worshipper with hope. This world of sin, division, decay, and death is not the final word because this world is not the believer's home. Those under the rule of Christ live with hope as strangers and foreigners in this world (1 Pet 1:17, 2:11; Heb 11:10, 13–16), living as children of promise (Gal 4:28). In anticipation of his coming, the believer lives in the "already but not yet" of the kingdom of God. The church, the missionary people of God, live in community demonstrating that they are Christ's disciples by their love of one for another, and by signs and wonders that give witness to the kingdom that has come (Mt 12:28; Mk 16:17, 20; Acts 14:3; Heb 2:4).

The hope of Christ's return produces great expectancy and a sense of anticipation in the hearts of his followers. For many Pentecostals the immediacy of Christ's return spurs missionary efforts. The church should be on the move because at his coming, those without Christ, those who have never heard, are condemned to an eternity in hell. The King's just wrath will be unleashed on the unrepentant unbeliever. This eschatological longing for the return of Christ is linked directly to the completion of the missionary task (see Mt 24:14).[4]

---

[4] In October 2010, Christian leaders gathered in Cape Town, South Africa, for the Third Lausanne Congress to discuss critical issues of the time as they related to the church and evangelization. Written chiefly by Christopher J. H. Wright and serving as a roadmap for the Lausanne Movement, *The Cape Town Commitment* presents a statement of shared biblical convictions, and calls Christians all over the world to action. *The Commitment* states, "We love the mission of God. We are committed to world Mission because it is central to our understanding of God, the Bible, the Church, human history, and the ultimate future. The whole Bible reveals the mission of God to bring all things in heaven and earth into unity under Christ, reconciling them through the blood of his

The experience of the baptism in the Holy Spirit initiates an empowering love of Jesus and his return, and an empowering love of those spiritually lost, thus motivating missionary efforts to reach all nations for Christ. At Pentecost, the outpouring of the Holy Spirit and the experience of tongues-speech were directly related to giving witness to the nations of the world in anticipation of Christ's return. Daily intimacy with Jesus through the spiritual disciplines of prayer, reading the Word, and fellowship with the community of believers produced the fruit of the Spirit and unleashed the gifts of the Spirit to empower the apostolic people of God to reach the world before his return.

LIVING WITH PURPOSE: SERVING CHRIST, THE KING

Between the first and second comings of Christ, God tasks the church with continuing Jesus's ministry of revelation and reconciliation in the power of the Spirit (2 Cor 5:11–21). The church, the bride of Christ, lives out the Lordship of Jesus giving witness to the world in word, deed, and sign as demonstrated in the Book of Acts. Gordon D. Fee asserts, "Luke singles out the Spirit as the power for Jesus's life and mission; and it is by that same Spirit that he ties together his Gospel and Acts in terms of the ongoing proclamation of good news to the poor—and thus to the ends of the earth."[5]

---

cross. In fulfilling his mission, God will transform the creation broken by sin and evil into the new creation in which there is no more sin or curse. God will fulfil his promise to Abraham to bless all nations on the earth, through the gospel of Jesus, the Messiah, the seed of Abraham. God will transform the fractured world of nations that are scattered under the judgment of God into the new humanity that will be redeemed by the blood of Christ from every tribe, nation, people, and language, and will be gathered to worship our God and Savior. God will destroy the reign of death, corruption, and violence when Christ returns to establish his eternal reign of life, justice, and peace. Then God, Immanuel, will dwell with us, and the kingdom of the world will become the kingdom of our Lord and of his Christ, and he shall reign forever and ever." *The Cape Town Commitment*, www.lausanne.org, 1–10.

[5] Gordon D. Fee, "The Kingdom of God and the Church's Global Mission," in *Called and Empowered: Global Mission in Pentecostal Perspective,* ed. Murray

The missionary agenda of Jesus becomes the missionary agenda of the church and its members. When a person accepts Jesus as Savior, God immediately sets him/her free from sin, death, and eternal punishment. Yet this acceptance also requires surrendering to and obeying Jesus as King, as the Lord of his/her life. The purpose of life transforms to serving the King. Every thought, every attitude, every decision, and every action must submit to the will of the One who sits on the throne. In encountering the King, our response should be like Isaiah, "'Woe to me!' I cried. 'I am ruined! For I am a man of unclean lips, and I live among a people of unclean lips, and my eyes have seen the King, the Lord Almighty'" (Is 6:5). In this personal encounter with Jesus, God's live coal (Is 6:6–7) of the Lord's purifying life, death, and resurrection frees the sinner and calls him/her to holiness and service: "Here am I, send me" (Is 6:8).

In explaining the second coming of Christ, Scripture admonishes, "Since everything will be destroyed in this way, what kind of people ought you to be? You ought to live holy and godly lives as you look forward to the day of God and speed its coming" (2 Pet 3:11–12). The accountability required by the immediacy of Christ's return moves his followers to lives separated from fallen human nature, and dedicated to walking in obedience and service to the ways of the Lord. This holiness and service give witness to the world of the good news and the coming kingdom of Christ. R. E. Neighbour tells this story of A. J. Gordon, which illustrates this statement:

> Dr. A. J. Gordon of Boston used to tell how, once, when he was about to make a preaching tour his two little girls asked him the day of his return, desiring to meet him at the train. He told them that he would return the next week, on a certain train, on either Tuesday or Wednesday or Thursday or Friday. When the stated Tuesday arrived the children dressed in their best Sunday white and went

---

W. Dempster, Byron D. Klaus, and Douglas Petersen (Peabody, MA: Hendrickson Publishers, 1991), 16.

down to meet their father. But Dr. Gordon did not arrive. Wednesday and Thursday was just as disappointing to the children. Friday came, and, as the girls, clothed with the same white dresses, knew that papa must come, their hearts were filled with joy. After the happy greeting was over, Dr. Gordon said his wife remarked, "The next time you leave the city, tell the children that you will come home Tuesday or Wednesday or Thursday or Friday—it was never so easy to keep the children's dresses white." And what manner of persons ought we to be, seeing that we are looking for Christ's return? Certainly, we should give ourselves over to holy behavior and to godliness.[6]

Empowered by the Spirit (Acts 1:8), this holy witness to the world (from a human perspective), "speeds" his second coming.[7] While only God knows the time of the Lord's return and when he will reach all the peoples of the earth, Jesus directly links his return with the fulfillment of the missionary task when he says, "And this gospel of the kingdom will be preached in the whole world as a testimony to all nations, and then the end will come" (Mt 24:14).[8]

Consider the Dominion Mandate ("God blessed them and said to them, 'Be fruitful and increase in number; fill the earth and subdue it. Rule over the fish in the sea and the birds in the sky and over every living creature that moves on the ground'" [Gen 1:28)]) and the Great Commission ("Then Jesus came to them and said, 'All authority in heaven and on earth has been given to me. Therefore, go and make disciples of all nations, baptizing them in the name of the Father and of the Son and of the Holy Spirit, and teaching them to obey everything I have commanded you. And surely I am with you always, to the very end of the age'" [Mt 28:18–20]). In these we observe that the Trinity invites human participation in God's story and mission through movement ("fill-

---

[6] R. E. Neighbour, *Biblia*, www.biblia.work/sermons/0610-the-purifying-hope/.

[7] See Acts 1:6–8.

[8] See George Eldon Ladd, *The Gospel of the Kingdom: Scriptural Studies in the Kingdom of God* (Grand Rapids, MI: Eerdmans [1959] 2000).

ing" and "going"), through reproduction ("be fruitful" and "make disciples"), and through representation of the King ("subdue . . . rule" and "baptizing in the name . . . teaching them to obey"). To live with purpose and meaning requires participation in God's missionary story through service to the soon-coming King.[9]

LIVING WITH HOPE: THE PROMISES OF CHRIST

In a world tormented by global pandemics, natural disasters, violence, war, injustice, brokenness, alienation, pain, and death, Christ—the believers' hope—promises that his return will usher in the fullness of the kingdom of God characterized by health, life, reconciliation, unity, justice, and intimacy with the Godhead, one another, and a renewed creation. His victory at Calvary grounds this future promise in history, and in the power of the resurrection (Eph 1). One cannot earn an entry into the kingdom, but Christ offers it as a gift of revelation and reconciliation: a promise. Ephesians 2:8–9 states, "For it is by grace you have been saved, through faith—and this is not from yourselves, it is the gift of God—not

---

[9] In 1974, *The Lausanne Covenant* emerged from the First Lausanne Congress at Lausanne, Switzerland, with John R. W. Stott as its lead composer, serving as a call to the evangelical church around the world. It defined what it means to be evangelical, and challenged Christians to work together to make Jesus Christ known throughout the world. On the return of Christ, *The Lausanne Covenant* states, "We believe that Jesus Christ will return personally and visibly, in power and glory, to consummate his salvation and his judgment. This promise of his coming is a further spur to our evangelism, for we remember his words that the gospel must first be preached to all nations. We believe that the interim period between Christ's ascension and return is to be filled with the mission of the people of God, who have no liberty to stop before the end. We also remember his warning that false Christs and false prophets will arise as precursors of the final Antichrist. We therefore reject as a proud, self-confident dream the notion that people can ever build a utopia on earth. Our Christian confidence is that God will perfect his kingdom, and we look forward with eager anticipation to that day, and to the new heaven and earth in which righteousness will dwell and God will reign forever. Meanwhile, we re-dedicate ourselves to the service of Christ and of people in joyful submission to his authority over the whole of our lives" (Mk 14:62; Heb 9:28; Mk 13:10; Acts 1:8–11; Mt 28:20; Mk 13:21–23; 1 Jn 2:18; 4:1–3; Lk 12:32; Rev 21:1–5; 2 Pet 3:13; Mt 28:18). *The Lausanne Covenant*, www.lausanne.org.

by works, so that no one can boast." The task of the church is not to bring about the kingdom of God, a work only Christ can accomplish. Rather, the church is to proclaim the Good News of the kingdom by giving witness to Christ.

God's missionary people live in hope as children of promise, as foreigners and aliens in this world, taking courage and comfort in his promises. Paul declares in Ephesians, "Remember that at that time you were separate from Christ, excluded from citizenship in Israel, and foreigners to the covenants of the promise, without hope and without God in the world. . . . Consequently, you are no longer foreigners and strangers, but fellow citizens with God's people and also members of his household" (2:12, 19).

Reminiscent of the Psalmist, hope wells up when God's people put their trust in God's word (Ps 119:43, 49, 74, 81, 114, 147). God delivered God's children so that "the blessing given to Abraham might come to the Gentiles through Christ Jesus, so that by faith we might receive the promise of the Spirit" (Gal 3:14). He did this so that, like Isaac, believers would be children of promise (Gal 4:28). Therefore, Christ includes every person when he/she hears the message of truth, the gospel of his/her salvation. When people believe, they are marked in him with a seal, the promised Holy Spirit (Eph 1:13).[10]

In this age between the first and second comings of Christ, the church, the body of Christ, must give witness by being a clear manifestation of living under the rule of Christ: walking according to his promises. In the already-but-not-yet of the kingdom, John declares, "Dear friends, *now* we are children of God, and what we will be has *not yet* been made known. But we know that when Christ appears, we shall be like him, for we shall see him as he is" (1 Jn 3:2; italics added).

Every local community of faith should overflow with his love, declaring in word, deed, and sign that Christ rules here. "By this everyone will know that you are my disciples, if you love one another" (Jn 13:35). Paul further explains in Ephesians 2:10,

---

[10] Further supporting scriptures are Heb 11:9; Eph 3:6; 2 Pet 3:9; Jn 2:25; 2 Pet 3:13.

"For we are God's handiwork, created in Christ Jesus to do good works, which God prepared in advance for us to do." And again, in Romans 14:17–18, "For the kingdom of God is not a matter of eating and drinking, but of righteousness, peace, and joy in the Holy Spirit, because anyone who serves Christ in this way is pleasing to God and receives human approval."

Local churches are not to be optional in their missions, but should serve in contextually appropriate ways as tangible witnesses to the revelation, reconciliation, and unity found in Christ. As countercultural communities engaged in society, local churches should demonstrate the righteousness and justice of the King. Planting an indigenous local church among unreached peoples releases powerful expressions of social justice. We should surrender to the Spirit to govern, propagate, and support these indigenous communities of faith.[11]

Christ's apostolic people live as salt and light in the world (Mt 5:13–16), yet are not of the world (Jn 17:14–16). The miracles that occur in and through the lives of God's missionary people represent the first fruits of the coming kingdom (Rom 8:23; 2 Thess 2:1). Miraculous signs—for example, healings, exorcisms, liberation from oppression, supernatural provision, gifts of the Spirit, and salvation itself—demonstrate Christ's authority and authenticate the communication of the gospel (Mk 16:17, 20). John S. Piper confirms:

> The center of Christianity is the coming of the Son of God into the world as a real man to destroy the works of the devil, and create a new people for His own glory. The very heart of our faith is that he did this by obeying the law of God, dying for the sins of His people, rising victorious

---

[11] For additional reading on the principles of the indigenous church, see DeLonn L. Rance, "Historical Perspectives on Pentecostal Mission Theology," in *Contemporary Mission Theology: Engaging the Nations*, ed. Robert L. Gallagher and Paul Hertig (Maryknoll, NY: Orbis Books, 2017), 180–90; Melvin L. Hodges, *The Indigenous Church and the Indigenous Church and the Missionary* (Springfield, MO: Gospel Publishing House, 2009); and Roland Allen, *Missionary Methods: St. Paul's or Ours?* (Grand Rapids, MI: Eerdmans, 1962).

over death, ascending to God's right hand with all His enemies under his feet. The second coming of Christ is the completion of his saving work. If you take it away, the whole fabric of his saving work unravels.[12]

LIVING WITH EXPECTANCY: THE SOON-COMING KING

At the turn of the last century, the participants in the Pentecostal revivals understood their experience as a part of a sovereign move of God to evangelize the world in the "end times" in anticipation of the second coming of Christ. Their experience of the baptism of the Holy Spirit and the manifestation of signs and wonders signaled the restoration of the church to the New Testament pattern so that it might reach the lost. The urgency to "work while it is day" (Jn 9:4) continued the ministry of Jesus in the world through the power of the Holy Spirit. In view of the coming wrath of the King, the apostolic people of God also live with this sense of urgency to complete the task of global mission.[13]

---

[12] John S. Piper, www.desiringgod.org.

[13] In 1989, *The Manila Manifesto* arose from the Second Lausanne Congress at Manila, Philippines, with John R. W. Stott leading the production task force. "Proclaim Christ until he comes," the conclusion of *The Manila Manifesto* states, "That has been the theme of Lausanne II. Of course, we believe that Christ has come; he came when Augustus was Emperor of Rome. But one day, as we know from his promises, he will come again in unimaginable splendor to perfect his kingdom. We are commanded to watch and be ready. Meanwhile, the gap between his two comings is to be filled with the Christian missionary enterprise. We have been told to go to the ends of the earth with the gospel, and we have been promised that the end of the age will come only when we have done so. The two ends (of earth space and time) will coincide. Until then he has pledged to be with us.

"So the Christian mission is an urgent task. We do not know how long we have. We certainly have no time to waste. And in order to get on urgently with our responsibility, other qualities will be necessary, especially unity (we must evangelize together) and sacrifice (we must count and accept the cost). Our covenant at Lausanne was 'to pray, to plan, and to work together for the evangelization of the whole world.' Our manifesto at Manila is that the whole church is called to take the whole gospel to the whole world, proclaiming Christ until he comes, with all necessary urgency, unity, and sacrifice" (Lk 2:1–7; Mk 13:26, 27, 32–37; Acts 1:8; Mt 24:14; 28:20). Lausanne, *The Manila Manifesto*, www.lausanne.org.

God the Father sought Adam in the garden (Gen 3:9), and the Son came "to seek and to save the lost" (Lk 19:10). Further, "The Spirit and the bride say, 'Come!' And let the one who hears say, 'Come!' Let the one who is thirsty come; and let the one who wishes take the free gift of the water of life" (Rev 22:17). This same end-time urgency finds expression in Albert B. Simpson's hymn, "The Missionary Cry."

> The Master's coming draweth near.
> The Son of Man will soon appear,
> His Kingdom is at hand.
> But ere that glorious day can be,
> The Gospel of the Kingdom, we
> Must preach in every land.
> Must preach in every land.
>
> Oh, let us then his coming haste,
> Oh, let us end this awful waste
> Of souls that never die.
> A thousand millions still are lost;
> A Savior's blood has paid the cost,
> Oh, hear their dying cry,
> Oh, hear their dying cry.[14]

L. Grant McClung describes this passion for lost souls as an emerging Pentecostal missiology. William J. Seymour admonished his flock at the Azusa Street Revival: "Now, do not go from this meeting and talk about tongues, but try to get people saved."[15] McClung observes:

> At the heart of early Pentecostals' missiology was their personal experience with the Holy Spirit found around an

---

[14] Albert B. Simpson, "A Missionary Cry," vv. 3–4, www.hymnary.org.
[15] L. Grant McClung, "'Try to Get People Saved:' Revisiting the Paradigm of an Urgent Pentecostal Missiology," in *The Globalization of Pentecostalism: A Religion Made to Travel*, ed. Murray W. Dempster, Byron D. Klaus, and Douglas Petersen (Irvine, CA: Regnum Books International, 1999), 30–51, 35.

altar of prayer with fellow seekers. This profound experience was integrated with an eschatological urgency and a passion for souls. Apparently, their earliest understanding of the experience that came to be known as the "Baptism in the Holy Spirit" was that it produced a missiological fervor and ministry, and it provided the empowerment for the same.[16]

As on the day of Pentecost, speaking in tongues demonstrates the need to communicate the gospel to people from every nation, tribe, people, and language. This divine communication only occurs as motivated by God's love and empowered by God's Spirit. Dependency on the Spirit in missions requires intimacy with Christ as a lifestyle nurtured by the spiritual practices of prayer, saturation in the Word, and life in the community of faith.

In turn, intimacy with Christ produces an increasing desire to see him face to face. God's people long for the arrival of the King to share with him in paradise restored—a new heaven and a new earth, with no more tears, no more separation, no more disease, suffering or pain, reunited with loved ones and basking in the glorious presence of the King. Like John, the revelator, the missionary people of God say, "Come, Lord Jesus" (Rev 22:20). Russell D. Moore describes this desire as "joy," following the reflection of C. S. Lewis:

> C. S. Lewis, looking back over his life, summed all of it up as being "surprised by joy." If we see "joy" only in the way the word is used most often around us, we might surmise that what Lewis meant by "joy" was what most people call "happiness" or "contentment." For him, though, joy was a sense of longing, something bittersweet, having a sense of home, but not really finding it. The awakening of joy is what led him, the long way around, to the God and Father of the Lord Jesus Christ. In this, Lewis perceived pointers to the world beyond the one

---

[16] Ibid., 36.

he could see. "When we are lost in the woods the sight of a signpost is a great matter," he wrote. "He who first sees it cries, 'Look!' The whole party gathers round and stares. But when we have found the road and are passing signposts every few miles, we shall not stop and stare."[17]

God's apostolic people live with a paradox: they desire Christ to delay his coming so that they may take advantage of every moment in communicating the gospel to the lost, but they also have an expectation and intense anticipation of experiencing his immediate return in order to stand in the fullness of his presence. These two paradoxical desires converge in missional action to "bring back the King."

OVERVIEW OF CHRIST OUR HOPE

After this introduction, Part IV explores living with Christ in purpose, hope, and expectancy in the biblical narratives of Genesis, 1 Samuel, and the Gospel of Luke (chapter 14); the historical narratives of Irenaeus, Joachim of Fiore, André Crouch, and Jürgen Moltmann (chapter 15); and the contemporary narratives of believers in Central and South America, as well as on the west coast of central Africa (chapter 16).

Living with Purpose, Hope, and Expectancy in Biblical Narratives

In the narratives of Abraham, Sarah, and Hagar (Gen 16, 21), Hannah and Samuel (1 Sam 1–2), and Anna and Simeon (Lk 2), God gave these biblical figures purpose and meaning by calling, affirming, and empowering their lives of holiness and service for the glory of God. Abraham entered into a covenant with God as a servant, blessed by the Lord to be a blessing (Gen 12:2–3). His descendants,

---

[17] Russell D. Moore, *The Storm-Tossed Family: How the Cross Reshapes the Home* (Nashville, TN: B&H Publishing Group, 2018), Kindle loc. 4534. See also C. S. Lewis, *Surprised by Joy: The Shape of My Early Life* (London: Geoffrey Bles, 1955).

the missionary people of God, were to live with purpose, as a holy nation and a kingdom of priests. "Now if you obey me fully and keep my covenant, then out of all nations you will be my treasured possession. Although the whole earth is mine, you will be for me a kingdom of priests and a holy nation" (Ex 19:5–6).

In what seemed like impossible circumstances, the promises and words of God moved Abraham, Sarah, Hagar, and Hannah from despair to hope, from the impossible to hope in God's intervention, and from barrenness to fruitfulness. In Anna and Simeon's case, the promise resulted in a king whom they held in their arms, with the kingdom of God breaking into the present.

Hannah's anticipation grew with each passing day of her pregnancy with Samuel. Anna and Simeon lived in intimacy with God in prayer, in the Word, and in the temple, resulting in an expectancy that "today could be the day."

Living with Purpose, Hope, and Expectancy in Historical Narratives

The early church father Irenaeus directly linked his responsibilities and purpose as a bishop, pastor, theologian, and missionary to the eschatological and prophetic perspective that he found in Scripture. Joachim of Fiore's commitment to holiness and a contemplative life emerged from his understanding of the Revelation to John and the end times. In the context of Christ's return, the music and lyrics of André Crouch set the purpose of his age in the communication of the gospel. Moltmann highlights the connection between eschatological hope and historical praxis by giving meaning and purpose to suffering.

In persecution, Irenaeus prophetically and pastorally articulated hope from the biblical text. "Living in the last days," expresses Joachim of Fiore's lived hope. Crouch's music challenges us to live in hope. Moltmann's personal history and theological writing affirms the impossibility of living without hope, because hope sustains life.

Irenaeus lived with the expectation that the return of Christ would be the end of persecution and suffering. Joachim of Fiore longed for the understanding of the age of the Spirit. André Crouch's songs "Soon and Very Soon" and "It Won't Be Long," reverberate with the anticipation of Christ's coming. Moltmann wrote his theology "in the dawn of the expected new day."[18]

Living with Purpose, Hope, and Expectancy in Contemporary Narratives

In the story of Miguel of El Salvador surrendering to Christ, his life's purpose changed, affecting his attitudes, decision-making, and actions. Discerning how God broke into history, doing the impossible, allowed Ruth and Carlos of Nicaragua and Peru to give testimony to the authority of the King. The story of Katy, Roberto, and Christina in Equatorial Guinea affirms God's divine purpose for every individual. God "does it more."

The promise of the Spirit revealed to Carlos and Ruth demonstrates the authority of Christ over the already-and-not-yet of his kingdom, making the impossible possible. Similar to Hannah, Carlos and Ruth's expectancy grew each day as the births of their two miracles approached. In the story of Katy, Roberto, and Christina, the local church became a source of hope and promise to the entire community as God performed a miracle that brought life and gave witness to the resurrected Christ.

As you read the narrative chapters of this section, celebrate Christ our Hope, who breaks into history providing meaning, significance, and purpose to our days on earth. Celebrate his promises in anticipation of his coming to establish the fullness of his kingdom, when every nation, every people group, and every knee shall bow, and every tongue confess that Jesus Christ is Lord, the soon-coming King.

---

[18] Jürgen Moltmann, *Theology of Hope*, trans. James Leitch (London: SCM Press, 1964; HarperCollins, 1991), 16.

14

Blessing Our World with Messianic Hope

Sarita Gallagher Edwards

God foretold the birth of the coming Messiah long before the first century CE. The Lord first proclaimed the revelation to an immigrant traveling through Mesopotamia in the second millennium BCE. It must have come as a surprise to Abram (son of Terah) when God spoke to him. Genesis 12:2–3 records Yahweh's declaration to Abram:

> I will make you into a great nation,
> and I will bless you;
> I will make your name great,
> and you will be a blessing.
> I will bless those who bless you,
> and whoever curses you I will curse;
> and all peoples on earth
> will be blessed through you.

It was the final divine promise in verse 3, "And all peoples on earth will be blessed through you," which caught the eye of the apostle

Paul. In Paul's letter to the Galatian church he affirms, "Scripture foresaw that God would justify the Gentiles by faith, and announced the gospel in advance to Abraham: 'All nations will be blessed through you'" (Gal 3:8).

Echoes of this promise, the hope of the Christ (or the Messiah), are present throughout the Hebrew Scriptures. In these texts, the miraculous birth of a child is often a motif that foreshadows the coming birth of Jesus Christ, the hope of the world. The following narratives are stories of hope and promise. In all three, the power and compassion of God is evident. Just as God spoke creation into existence, so in each narrative God brings life after barrenness, hope after despair, and joy after waiting. Each story—the narratives of Abraham, Sarah, and Hagar; Hannah and Samuel; and Anna and Simeon—follows the journey toward the fulfillment of God's greatest hope for the world, Jesus Christ.

ABRAHAM, SARAH, AND HAGAR
(GEN 16, 21)

Was this a good place to die? Hagar looked around the wild and unforgiving landscape of the desert of Beersheba with a despondent gaze. Her son, Ishmael, was weak and lethargic in her arms. His breathing was shallow. She couldn't stand the thought of hearing his final breath. Hagar didn't want to see her only son die. The waterskin they had been relying on had run dry a few days before. This was it. Hagar wearily led her son to a small bush and then walked away. She couldn't bear to let Ishmael die alone. So, she stopped about one hundred yards away, sat down, and waited for both of them to die.

* * *

Sarai was sure that it was a good plan. Many women had done it before, and now she would join them. After explaining the idea to her husband Abram, he agreed to what she had proposed. According to their Mesopotamian customs, Abram would take a new wife, Hagar, the servant of Sarai. Sarai and Abram had spent their entire marriage trying to have a child. Yet even after Yahweh promised them a son in Haran, nothing happened. So maybe Yahweh had intended for them to play a different role than what they had anticipated. The couple made the decision. Abram would take Hagar to be his second wife. Actually, Hagar would be more like a concubine than a wife. Any offspring that Hagar bore would be Sarai and Abram's child. Perhaps this was God's plan all along—that another woman would finally produce a child for Abram and Sarai.

As soon as Hagar knew that she was pregnant, Sarai could sense a change of attitude in her maidservant. Hagar started to despise her mistress. Sarai could feel it each morning as Hagar helped her to dress. She sensed it each afternoon as Hagar went to fetch water. Sarai immediately spoke to Abram about Hagar's disrespect. Sarai's anger still vibrated through her body as she thought about it. "You are responsible for the wrong I am suffering," Sarai had snapped at her husband. "I put my slave into your arms, and now that she knows she is pregnant, she loathes me. May the Lord judge between you and me," Sarai concluded. Yes, that was right. It was God's role to determine who had caused this catastrophe. After listening to Sarai's critique, Abram placed Hagar's fate in his wife's hands. A few days later Hagar ran away. Then, in two weeks she was back; still heavily pregnant with Abram's child.

* * *

As Sarai watched young Ishmael run around the camp, she reflected again on her deep desire to have a child. That intense longing that she first felt as a young bride had not dissipated over the years. Yet it seemed to Sarai, now in her twilight years, that she would never bear a child for Abram. Yet one day her hope rekindled. God Almighty appeared to her husband Abram, promising him a son through Sarai, not another woman. God spoke many promises over Abram, and gave him the new name of "Abraham," which means, "father of a multitude of nations." Moreover, God gave Sarai a new name, "Sarah," and declared that "she will be the mother of nations" and that "kings of peoples will come from her." Then, one day, it came to pass. At the age of ninety, Sarah discovered that she was pregnant; she couldn't believe that she would finally give Abraham a son in his old age. God heard her desperate cry. Their son was born during Abraham's hundredth year and Abraham named him Isaac, which means "he laughs." For indeed they both laughed with joy and shock when they found that Sarah was pregnant at ninety. Holding her small infant, and surrounded by the women of the household, Sarah exclaimed again, "God has brought me laughter, and everyone who hears about this will laugh with me." In amazement she added, "Who would have said to Abraham that Sarah would nurse children? Yet I have borne him a son in his old age."

When Sarah's son Isaac was born, Hagar and her son Ishmael continued to live in Abraham's household. Ishmael faded into the background as Isaac emerged as the true firstborn. It was on a special feast day to celebrate the birth of Abraham's promised son that Sarah observed Ishmael mocking Isaac, his half-brother. The next morning Abraham came to Ishmael's tent carrying some food and a waterskin. Sarah had witnessed the exchange between the boys, and had issued an order of banishment. Now Hagar and her son—Abraham's son—were being sent away.

* * *

As Hagar sat in the heat of the day, she thought about the last few years. She had almost perished once before in a desert. At the time, she was a few months pregnant with Abraham's son, Ishmael. She had thought she was going to die then, too. Hagar remembered that she was near a spring of water in the wilderness of Shur when the angel appeared to her. It still amazed her that the angel knew her name. "Hagar, slave of Sarai," the angel had proclaimed. "Where have you come from, and where are you going?"

Hagar could still recall the rush of fear and surprise that had passed through her body when she saw the angel and heard those words. As a young child living in Egypt, she remembered the legends about the vast pantheon of Egyptian gods and goddesses—stories about Isis, Horus, Osiris, Ra, and many other divinities. Even Egypt's powerful deities, however, were not able to extend their reach beyond the national borders. What deity had the power to speak to her in this barren wasteland? What god had sent a messenger to her? What divine being knew her name?

In the desert of Shur, Hagar had named the God who spoke to her, *El Roi*. She had declared aloud, "You are the God who sees me." There in the wasteland, alone and pregnant, *El Roi* had seen her, and had spoken hope into her daunting plight. The angel of God had told her that the Lord had heard her misery, and that she should call her unborn son Ishmael. He had also told her to return to her mistress, Sarai, and she obeyed that direction. When her son was born, Abram named the child Ishmael, which means, "God hears."

Now, Hagar looked into the distance at her son Ishmael still lying under the bush. Hagar began to cry as she watched her son. It was then that she heard the voice. It was strong and clear; the air appeared to resonate with the sounds of each word. "What's the matter, Hagar?" There it was. Her name written on the wind. "Do not be afraid," the voice continued. "God has heard the boy crying as he lies there. Lift the boy up and take him by the hand, for I will make him into a great nation." It felt like the breath of God opened her eyes. A short distance away was a well of water. She ran to it, filled her water skin, and rushed back to her son to relieve his thirst. Once again, God had saved them. *El Roi*, the God who sees, had preserved their lives once again, and had given them hope.

HANNAH AND SAMUEL (1 SAM 1–2)

Eli heard the wailing before he saw her. Why was someone drunk on the tabernacle grounds? The woman was young and dressed in the style of the local Ephraimites. He looked at her again. Now she was throwing herself around frantically and mumbling wildly. She was definitely drunk.

Hannah didn't notice the priest standing there until he came close to her. His stern rebuke followed. "Woman, how long are you going to stay drunk? Put away your wine." It was then that she looked up and saw him—the head priest of the tabernacle at Shiloh—staring at her with obvious disgust.

The tears rushed down Hannah's face as she looked at Eli. It was hard to speak. Finally, the words tumbled out, "I'm not drunk," she uttered in a barely audible voice. "I'm not drunk," she repeated to the priest with more strength now. As she confessed to the priest, the weight of her grief hit her deeply, "I'm a woman who is deeply troubled. I haven't been drinking wine or strong drink. I was pouring out my soul to the LORD. Do not take your servant for a wicked woman. I have been praying out of my great anguish and grief."

The young woman was praying. She was not drunk. Eli straightened up. The frustration that he had felt moments before began to fade away. Compassion and empathy took its place. He felt a bit foolish. He had seen his sons—Hophni and Phinehas—disrespect the sacred space of the Lord's tabernacle so many times that he had just automatically made that assumption. This woman's tears, however, were real. Her sorrow and pain were almost tangible.

* * *

Elkanah remembers his wedding day with great joy. His father Jeroham arranged his marriage to Hannah according to Hebrew wedding customs. As soon as Elkanah saw Hannah for the first time, he knew that he would love her. He could not predict, however, the challenging years to come: the tears, miscarriages, and sheer disappointment of each lost opportunity for a child. As the months passed without children, Elkanah's parents pressured him. "You need to remarry," they urged. "We have already spoken with a well-respected family, and they are willing to give their daughter, Penninah, in marriage for the right bride price. Just say the word and it is done."

At first Hannah resigned herself to the fact that Elkanah had married a second wife. In both their extended families, it was normal for a man to marry again when his first wife was barren. Hannah even looked after the young girl, taking her under her wing as

Penninah adjusted to the household duties. When Penninah's pregnancy began to show, however, the new bride's demeanor changed. The insults started to flow as soon as she knew she was pregnant. Penninah, not Hannah, was going to give Elkanah his first child. Hannah loved Elkanah. She was his first wife. Yet she was not able to give him a child.

The provocations of Penninah increased with each new pregnancy. How could she be pregnant again so quickly? She seemed to gloat in her ability to give Elkanah children—son after son, daughter after daughter. The worst of the affronts took place when Hannah traveled to worship the Lord along the fifteen miles from Ramah to Shiloh. When she first married Elkanah, she loved traveling to the tabernacle. She was proud of her new husband. The entire community knew his faithfulness and dedication to the Lord God. And he loved her. That fact was especially obvious on their trips to Shiloh.

It was clear that Elkanah still deeply loved Hannah even after Penninah delivered his first child. Every year at Shiloh, Elkanah would give Hannah a double portion of the meat offered in the temple, even though he was only required to give her one helping. Elkanah gave this to Hannah because he loved her. Yet she knew it was also because she could not have a child. Elkanah's generosity continued, year after year. Hannah's deep ache to have a child persisted. Each year Penninah's insults continued, as did her ability to bear a seemingly endless number of children. The years went by and nothing changed. Hannah was still barren, and Penninah was still producing offspring.

* * *

Filled with compassion, the head priest Eli looked at the weeping woman with new eyes. He finally responded to her: "Go in peace and may the God of Israel grant you what you have asked of him." Standing in the tabernacle that morning, Hannah had hope for the first time. Her prayer to God had been desperate and raw; emerging in an effortless manner out of years of bitterness and disappointment. Her words to God reverberated in her heart.

"Lord of Hosts, Jehovah Sabaoth, if you will only look on your servant's misery and remember me, and not forget your servant, but give her a son, then I will give him to the LORD for all the days of his life, and no person will ever use a razor on his head." Could it be that God heard her prayer and vow?

Eli's response was so absolute. She repeated the priest's words again in her head: "Go in peace and may the God of Israel grant you what you have asked of him." Hannah picked herself up. Hope seemed to flood back into her body. She had not eaten for days. All of a sudden, she was hungry. Her sadness had fled. Her heart was no longer heavy. Her spirit was uplifted. She had hope.

* * *

It was hard for Hannah to believe that several years had passed so quickly. Her first-born Samuel, her little boy, was a constant reminder of God's faithfulness. She had promised God in this very tabernacle in Shiloh only a few years before, that if God granted her petition, she would dedicate her child to God; and here she was. She had named her son Samuel, "God hears," as a constant testament to God's answer to her prayer.

With all the worshippers milling around the tabernacle, it took Hannah a while before she found Eli the high priest. Then, there he was right in front of her. Approaching the elder priest with Samuel circling her legs, she addressed him, "Excuse me, my lord. As surely as you live, I am the woman who stood here beside you praying to Yahweh." She could see the recognition start to emerge in Eli's eyes. Yes, he did remember her. Pointing at Samuel, she continued, "I prayed for this child, and the LORD has granted me what I asked of him. So now, I give him to God. For his entire life he will be given over to the LORD."

Hannah smiled at the priest's surprise. The joy of God's gracious answer to her prayer filled her heart once again. The only adequate response to what had happened was to sing praises to the Lord. God had heard her. The God of hosts, the God of Israel, had responded to her desperate cry for help.

A song of praise arose in her heart. Hannah sang:
My heart rejoices in the LORD;
in the LORD my horn is lifted high.
My mouth boasts over my enemies,
for I delight in your deliverance.
There is no one holy like the LORD;
there is no one besides you;
there is no Rock like our God. . . .

She who was barren has borne seven children,
but she who has had many sons pines away...

It is not by strength that one prevails;
those who oppose the LORD will be broken.
The Most High will thunder from heaven;
the LORD will judge the ends of the earth.

He will give strength to his king
and exalt the horn of his anointed.[1]

ANNA AND SIMEON (LK 2:21–38)

Simeon felt a prompting from the Holy Spirit that morning. Going to the temple in Jerusalem that day was not on his schedule. Yet he could not dismiss the quiet, yet persistent feeling that he should go to the temple courts. Simeon learned to attune himself to these small nudges of God. Sometimes they would lead him to comfort an old widow. At other times, the prompting would result in a smile to a child. Simeon brushed off the last feelings of sleep and prepared himself for the short walk to the temple.

* * *

The temple was bustling that day, with Jews coming from near and far to pray and burn offerings. Joseph led his small family

---

[1] 1 Sam 2:1–2, 5b, 9c–10.

through the gathered crowd and then through the gate into the outer court of the temple. Looking down at little Yeshua in his wife's arms, he was reminded of the angel that had first appeared to him in Nazareth before his son's birth. Etched in his memory were the angel's words: "Joseph son of David, do not be afraid to take Mary home as your wife, because what is conceived in her is from the Holy Spirit. She will give birth to a son, and you are to give him the name Yeshua, because he will save his people from their sins."

According to the Law of Moses, Joseph and Mary had come to Jerusalem to present Yeshua, their infant son, to God. Mary had also completed the additional thirty-three days of recuperation required after her son's birth and circumcision. She was now ready to go through the Jewish ritual of purification for new mothers. Joseph held the two pigeons tightly. He could not afford to buy a year-old lamb for Mary's ceremony, but he knew that the birds would be acceptable before God—one as a burnt offering, and the other as a sin offering.

* * *

Simeon entered the Court of the Women in the Jerusalem temple and looked around at the penitents. He immediately saw the man and woman—a young couple holding a child. The Spirit of God prompted him forward. A warm feeling overcame Simeon as he walked purposefully toward the pair. Many years before, the Holy Spirit had revealed to him—declared to him—that he would see the promised Messiah before he died. Today, it was happening.

* * *

Mary was clutching Yeshua tightly in her arms as she walked through the Court of the Women. She saw the older man approaching her from the corner of her eye. Then he was right there, standing in front of her and her husband. The man reached out, and took her son out of her arms. She did not panic. The action felt natural and right.

Holding Yeshua in his arms, Simeon started proclaiming loudly, "Sovereign Lord, as you have promised, you may now dismiss your servant in peace. For my eyes have seen your salvation, which you have prepared in the sight of all nations: a light for revelation to the Gentiles, and the glory of your people Israel."

* * *

Joseph stared at the man holding his son. The older man was clearly overjoyed. In fact, he was rejoicing. Singing praises aloud to God, the devout man's eyes sparkled with hope. What had he declared over their child? That Yeshua would be "God's salvation . . . a light for revelation to the Gentiles . . . the glory of God's people Israel."

* * *

Simeon felt overwhelmed by joy as he held the promised Messiah of Israel in his arms. Blessing the young child, Simeon turned to the mother and prophesied: "This child is destined to cause the falling and rising of many in Israel, and to be a sign that will be spoken against, so that the thoughts of many hearts will be revealed." He paused. Looking into the young woman's eyes, he added, "And a sword will pierce your own soul too."

* * *

Mary marveled at the elder's words. Turning to Joseph, she could tell he was also trying to process the prophetic words spoken over their newborn son. An aged woman approached them right at that moment. She also started praising God upon seeing the child, speaking about the "redemption of Jerusalem."

* * *

Anna loved being in the presence of God at the temple. Since her husband died eighty-four years ago, leaving her a young widow, she had come daily to the temple to fast and pray. Now she spent all her time in the temple courts—praying to God and fasting for the redemption of Jerusalem. Anna rejoiced as she looked upon the sleeping infant in Simeon's arms. The joy of the Lord filled her heart. The parents told her that the baby's name was Yeshua, or Jesus in Greek. The Hebrew name, Yeshua, means "God saves." Yes, it was a very appropriate name. Anna's hope of God's salvation had indeed come.

REFLECTION QUESTIONS

1. In the three biblical narratives of Abraham, Sarah, and Hagar, Hannah and Samuel, and Anna and Simeon, why do you think the Scripture uses the motif of barrenness and childbirth to foreshadow the coming Messiah?
2. What do these narratives reveal about God's character and engagement with humanity?
3. How does God reveal God's faithfulness in these narratives?
4. In each of these narratives, the Lord fulfills hope after a long period of waiting. How have you navigated times of waiting in your spiritual journey? What has God taught you during these times of waiting on the Lord?
5. The Bible embeds the coming of the Messiah in human story. How does this enrich and affect our understanding of Jesus Christ being the hope of the world?

15

Historical Glimpses into Christ Our Hope

Paul W. Lewis

A prominent theme throughout church history is the second coming of Christ. This is the "blessed hope." This hope is not just wishful thinking, but rather the complete certainty of his return. It is currently unrealized, however. The importance of this hope and the surety of the Lord's return are related concerns. Christians hope for the Lord's return, but the hope runs deeper. It is a hope of the coming Lord and all that that entails, but it is also about hope in this life. It is a hope that helps Christians endure hardship, to live in deplorable situations, and not to live in despair. Ultimately, it is tied to the Lord's return (the Ultimate), but we are living in the time before (the Penultimate), a time in need of hope.[1] The lives of

---

[1] Several scholars have written on this tension, such as Dietrich Bonhoeffer, *Ethics*, ed. Eberhard Bethge (New York: Macmillan, 1955), 122–87, and in the multiple works of George Eldon Ladd and Gordon Fee. For example, George Eldon Ladd, *The Gospel of the Kingdom* (1959 repr.; Grand Rapids, MI: Eerdmans, 1990), and Gordon Fee, "Kingdom of God," in *Called and Empowered: Pentecostal Perspectives on Global Mission*, ed. Murray A. Dempster, Byron D. Klaus, and Douglas Petersen (Peabody, MA: Hendrickson, 1992), 7–21.

Irenaeus, Joachim of Fiore, André Crouch, and Jürgen Moltmann demonstrate this hope in Christ, our soon-coming King.

ST. IRENAEUS (ca. 130–202)[2]

St. Irenaeus was from Smyrna in Asia Minor, which was Polycarp's hometown. Irenaeus would have seen and heard Polycarp (d. 155), whom the apostles—most notably John—converted to Christianity. Unlike other bishops of his time, Irenaeus grew up in a Christian family. Later, he moved to Lyon in Gaul (present-day France), and was sent from Lyon with a letter to Pope Eleutherius in Rome in 177. While he was in Rome, a persecution broke out in Lyon. Upon his return from Rome, church authorities selected him as the second Bishop of Lyon. At this time Christianity, being a minority religion, was under great persecution.

We must see Irenaeus through the three lenses of his ministry: pastor/bishop, theologian, and missionary. However, for him they are an integrated whole. The city of Lyon appreciated his contribution in his role as pastor and bishop to assist the church and its environs in the aftermath of the persecution (which included the martyrdom of the previous bishop, and other Christians), and in the role of guarding against heresy.

This leads to his second role, as a theologian. Irenaeus took seriously the issues of false teaching that seemed to abound in his region, and throughout the Roman Empire. Of his many

---

[2] St. Irenaeus is an influential early church father. You can find his works in Alexander Roberts and James Donaldson, eds., *Ante Nicene Fathers: The Writings of the Fathers Down to A.D. 325, Vol. 1, The Apostolic Fathers including Justin Martyr and Irenaeus*, American Reprint of Edinburgh Edition, revised by A. Cleveland Coxe (New York: Charles Scribner's Sons, 1903). Works about him include Mary T. Clark, "Irenaeus," in *Encyclopedia of Early Christianity*, ed. Everett Ferguson (New York: Routledge, 1990), 471–73; Mary Ann Donovan, *One Right Reading? A Guide to Irenaeus* (Collegeville, MN: Michael Glazier, 1997); Douglas B. Farrow, "Irenaeus of Lyons (c. 130–c. 200)," in *The Dictionary of Historical Theology*, ed. Trevor A. Hart (Grand Rapids, MI: Eerdmans, 2000), 273–75; and Denis Minns, *Irenaeus* (London: Georgetown University Press, 1994). A helpful work of various scholars is Paul Foster and Sara Parvis, eds., *Irenaeus: Life, Scripture, and Legacy* (Minneapolis, MN: Fortress Press, 2012).

theological works (some are extant, while others are lost), the noted five-volume *Against Heresies* is still one of the best resources for understanding various second-century heresies, including Valentinian Gnosticism. Irenaeus also articulated how to adjudicate between heresy and orthodox Christianity. In his writings, he demonstrated and delineated how to recognize genuine orthodoxy with the use of Scripture (he used most of what is now the New Testament, especially the Pauline corpus), emphasis on the apostolic "rule of faith" (which were traditions passed down from the Lord's disciples), and apostolic authority and succession.

Finally, in his role as missionary, Irenaeus was a strong articulator of prophetic perspective. He used Daniel and Revelation extensively in his eschatological vision and discourse. Irenaeus was significantly missionary in his approach to his bishopric responsibilities. He saw his role as ministering to those "in the fold," together with those outside who needed to be in. In this way, his missionary work is inseparable from his eschatological (theological) perspective, and his pastoral role.

JOACHIM OF FIORE (ca. 1135–1202)[3]

Joachim of Fiore grew up in a notary's house, and planned to be a clerk himself. It was around 1159 that he took a pilgrimage to Jerusalem and had a conversion experience. Thereafter, he assumed a religious lifestyle. First, he was a hermit, then a lay brother in a Cistercian abbey. Later, he became an ordained priest in 1168, and then an abbot around 1177. When he was later relieved of his role as an abbot, he focused on the spiritual life through prayer and through writing books on interpretations of the Book of Revelation. People valued his holiness, and a branch of the Franciscans considered his work to be a prophetic ministry. Personages sought

---

[3] Helpful introductions to Joachim of Fiore are Stanley M. Burgess, ed., *Christian Peoples of the Spirit: A Documentary History of Pentecostal Spirituality from the Early Church to the Present* (New York: New York University Press, 2011), 104–11; and Marjorie Reeves, "Joachim of Fiore (c. 1135–1202)," in *The Dictionary of Historical Theology*, ed. Trevor A. Hart (Grand Rapids, MI: Eerdmans, 2000), 284–86. Also see Delno C. West, *Joachim of Fiore in Christian Thought*, 2 vols. (New York: Burt Franklin, 1975).

audience with him, such as Empress Constance, Queen of Sicily, and King Richard I of England (Richard the Lionheart).

In Joachim's theology, he divided history into three ages: the age of the Father (Old Testament times); the age of the Son (from the birth of Christ to 1260, based on his interpretation of the Apocalypse); and the forthcoming (for him) age of the Holy Spirit, which is when the impending Spirit's dispensation of universal love would transpire. The Roman Catholic Church later condemned his teachings, which included a refutation by Thomas Aquinas, the Italian Dominican theologian. Yet he was highly esteemed by Dante Alighieri, the Italian poet and philosopher.

For Joachim, the focus on progressive spirituality was in harmony with church theology. His passion and emphasis were on living life based on the Book of Revelation. Today, theologians would call his approach "living in the last days." He also highlighted that the personal contemplative life was a journey leading through tribulation (such as the exodus) to greater heights and noted the need to connect with the concrete aspect of scriptural depths. Through the contemplation of the mind, clarity and understanding (of the Book of Revelation) are possible. In essence, one's journey would include digging into the depths of Scripture, and understanding the Triune Godhead through study, contemplation, prayer, being open to God, and progressively, one's personal pilgrimage. Following Joachim's teaching would mean to live with a passion and conviction of Scripture and God, and notably, a belief that we are living in the last days.

ANDRÉ CROUCH (1942–2015)[4]

Church historians can state many things about the modern Pentecostal movement. Yet one definite focus since its origin is the emphasis on the soon-coming King. The imminent return of Christ

---

[4] See Bob Gersztyn, "Crouch, Andrea," in *Encyclopedia of American Gospel Music*, ed. W. K. McNeil (New York: Routledge, 2005), 91–92, and "Crouch, André Edward (1942–2015)," in *Dictionary of Pan-American Pentecostalism*, vol. 1, North America, ed. Estralda Y. Alexander (Eugene, OR: Cascade, 2018), 124–25.

was front and center. It is one of the pillars of Pentecostalism.[5] It is both the why and the when of missions and evangelism—to reach the lost as soon as possible since he is coming soon.[6]

Singer and songwriter André Crouch is one representative voice of Pentecostalism who impacted the world. Crouch was born, with his twin sister, Sandra, in 1942, in California. Their father was a business owner, who was a Church of God in Christ street preacher, and later a bishop. Early in his life, André sang and played the piano in church services. He wrote his first notable song, "The Blood Will Never Lose Its Power," when he was fourteen. While in college, he felt the call to ministry, and formed a music group called The Disciples. The group had both black and white members, a composition very unusual in America in the 1960s and '70s. Throughout Crouch's life, he continued to write songs, and was involved in several collaborative efforts with both gospel and secular music artists. Some of the musicians he worked with included Elvis Presley, Michael Jackson, Quincy Jones, and Stevie Wonder, to name a few. After his father's death in 1994, André and Sandra took over the pastoral responsibilities of their father's church—Christ Memorial Church of God in Christ in Pacoima, California.

Crouch's theological influence was through his music. Christians still sing many of his songs around the world today. Several themes are prominent within these songs. For example, his testimony of the grace and salvation of God, and from where Christ brought him, is evident in the lyrics of "My Tribute (to

---

[5] See Donald W. Dayton, *Theological Roots of Pentecostalism* (Peabody, MA: Hendrickson, 1987), 143–71; D. William Faupel, *The Everlasting Gospel: The Significance of Eschatology in the Development of Pentecostal Thought*, Journal of Pentecostal Theology Supplemental Series 10 (Sheffield, UK: Sheffield Academic Press, 1996); and Keith Warrington, *Pentecostal Theology: A Theology of Encounter* (London: T&T Clark, 2008), 309–23.

[6] The prominent motif was that the soon-coming King is both the motivation and a key theme of missions and evangelism. See L. Grant McClung, "'Try to Get People Saved': Revisiting the Paradigm of an Urgent Pentecostal Missiology," in *The Globalization of Pentecostalism: A Religion Made to Travel*, ed. Murray A. Dempster, Byron D. Klaus, and Douglas Petersen (Carlisle, UK: Regnum, 1999), 30–51.

God Be the Glory)," "Take Me Back," and "Through It All." In addition, he wrote several songs praising God, such as "Bless His Holy Name," and about his salvation, "I Don't Know Why Jesus Loved Me."

The need for missions/evangelism and the second coming of the Lord are also two key themes found in his music. Crouch's songs about evangelism and missions include "We Are Not Ashamed," "Jesus Is the Answer," and "Tell Them." In "Tell Them," Crouch emphasized the need for proclamation whether or not the audience believed the message or even received the message. In whatever state they are in, God's people need to proclaim the message of his love. We are to "Tell Them."

Likewise, Crouch repeatedly highlights the emphasis on the second coming of Christ in songs such as "Soon and Very Soon," "It Won't Be Long," and "Just Like He Said He Would." In these songs, he highlights that the return of Christ is very soon; it is imminent. As noted in "It Won't Be Long," the return will be "Any Day Now," and God will transform us into the image of Christ. In many of his songs, what Christ promised—his return—will take place in a moment. Crouch steeps his lyrics in New Testament imagery. Christ's return will be "in the twinkling of an eye" (1 Cor 15:52), and "when the trumpet sounds" (1 Thess 4:16). In addition, Christ has prepared a place for the believers to be with him (Jn 14:1–4). Crouch saw the hope in Christ as both real and imminent. His return is soon, at any moment, but it also impacts how we are to live. We should be grateful for salvation, proclaim the love of God, and live in divine hope.

André Crouch knew that his ministry was through song. Hope provided by Christ and his return should be and would be reaffirmed through song and our singing. Outreach and the hope in Christ for salvation and his return were and are all intertwined. The concerns of this life should not preclude concern for those who do not know Christ, and the awareness of the soon return of Christ.

JÜRGEN MOLTMANN (1926–)

Jürgen Moltmann[7] was born and raised in an enlightened, yet unbelieving German family. In 1944, the Nazi army drafted him, where he fought until captured in 1945. It was during his life as a prisoner of war (POW) that he underwent a conversion experience and settled upon a religious vocation. In an English POW camp, he informally studied Hebrew and other rudimentary religious subjects from religious professors who were also captives. After his release in 1948, he started his formal theological training. Later, he pastored in Wasserhorst near Bremen. In 1958, he started his academic career, eventually becoming—from 1967 until his retirement in 1994—a professor of systematic theology at the University of Tübingen, Germany.

Moltmann was one of the most prominent voices in Protestant theology in the latter half of the twentieth century. While other theologians in 1960's America were propounding the "death of God" following Friedrich Nietzsche's declaration, Moltmann proclaimed a theology of hope. Moltmann highlighted the connection between eschatological hope and historical praxis. In *Theology of Hope* he states, "The eschatological is not one element of Christianity, but it is the medium of Christian faith as such, the key in which everything in it is set, the glow that suffuses everything here in the dawn of the expected new day.... A proper theology would therefore have to be constructed in the light of its future goal. Eschatology should not be its end, but its beginning."[8]

---

[7] There are many major works on Jürgen Moltmann. His autobiography can be found in Jürgen Moltmann, *A Broad Place: An Autobiography*, trans. Margaret Kohl (Minneapolis: Fortress, 2008), and a brief interview can be found in Michael Bauman, *Roundtable: Conversations with European Theologians* (Grand Rapids, MI: Baker, 1990), 31–41. An introduction about Moltmann is in Richard Bauckham, "Moltmann, Jürgen (b. 1926)," in *The Dictionary of Historical Theology*, ed. Trevor A. Hart (Grand Rapids, MI: Eerdmans, 2000), 376–78. For a helpful volume on Moltmann's eschatology (and hope), see Richard Bauckham, ed., *God Will Be All in All: The Eschatology of Jürgen Moltmann* (Minneapolis, MN: Fortress, 2001).

[8] Jürgen Moltmann, *Theology of Hope*, trans. James Leitch (London: SCM Press, 1964; HarperCollins, 1991), 16. Also see Moltmann, "My Theological Career," in *The History of the Triune God*, trans. John Bowden (New York: Crossroad, 1992), 168–71.

Another concern of Moltmann was about God and suffering, which he answered in his second major work, *The Crucified God*. Then followed his reflection on how the church is empowered in his next volume, *The Church in the Power of the Spirit*.[9] In his writings, Moltmann went from the resurrection (Christ our hope), to the cross (the crucified Christ), and then to Pentecost (the empowerment of the Spirit of Christ). Therefore, for Moltmann, the resurrection offers the hope that Christ provides in the cross, which God enlivens within us personally and ecclesiastically through the Spirit.

In his personal story, Moltmann emphasizes the depth of hope. In 1945, he was captured by the Allies, who sent him to a POW camp in Belgium. At the prison, Allied soldiers came and showed photographs of the concentration camps. Initially, many of the German POWs thought it was British propaganda. Eventually most came to the realization, however, that this was happening throughout the Third Reich of Nazi Germany. Moltmann notes the shock of many of his POW colleagues as they concluded that these horrors were not the reason why they fought. He starkly remembers that many of his coprisoners lay down, and gave up their will to live. Subsequently, they died in the POW camp. They had lost hope.

However, a chaplain distributed to the POWs small New Testaments, which included the Psalms. Upon reading the Scriptures, Moltmann moved toward his conversion experience. He saw firsthand how hope is central to life. Christ provides that hope. After this occurrence, he studied and developed his theology of hope.[10]

---

[9] Jürgen Moltmann, *The Crucified God*, trans. R. A. Wilson and John Bowden (London: SCM Press, 1974; HarperCollins, 1991), and Jürgen Moltmann, *The Church in the Power of the Spirit*, trans. Margaret Kohl (London: SCM Press, 1977; HarperCollins, 1991).

[10] Jürgen Moltmann, *Experiences of God*, trans. Margaret Kohl (Philadelphia: Fortress Press, 1980), 6–11; Jürgen Moltmann, "My Spiritual and Theological Pilgrimage," in *Following Jesus Christ in the World Today* (Elkhart, IN: Institute of Mennonite Studies, 1983), 9–18; Jürgen Moltmann, "My Theological Career," in *The History of the Triune God*, trans. John Bowden (New York: Crossroad, 1992), 165–67. This is also found in a different translation in A. J. Conyers, *God, Hope and History*, trans. Charles White (Macon, GA: Mercer

Moltmann understood that people could die without hope. Christ brought hope through his crucifixion. God took upon himself the suffering of humanity so that we could, can, and will have hope in the power of his Spirit through his church. This hope brings life: the life of Christ.

REFLECTION QUESTIONS

1. Hope is powerful in life. How did St. Irenaeus, Joachim of Fiore, André Crouch, and Jürgen Moltmann view and express the hope of Christ that they found in their lives?
2. How are hope in Christ and his return tied together?
3. Is hope possible apart from Christ?
4. What are the different ways Irenaeus, Joachim of Fiore, André Crouch, and Jürgen Moltmann showed or communicated hope to others?
5. How can hope help you not only in theology but also in your daily living as you move forward in life's journey?

University Press, 1988), 203–23; A. J. Conyers, "Politics and the Practice of Hope," *Christian Century* 87 (1970): 88–91; and Miroslav Volf, "An Interview with Jürgen Moltmann," in *Communities of Faith and Radical Discipleship*, ed. G. MacLeod Bryan (Macon, GA: Mercer University Press, 1986), 5–11. Note that Moltmann stresses the importance of the POW experience for his personal life and theological thought. For example, Jürgen Moltmann, "Foreword," in M. Douglas Meeks, *Origins of the Theology of Hope* (Philadelphia: Fortress Press, 1974), xi–xiii; and Jürgen Moltmann, *Passion for Life*, trans. M. Douglas Meeks (Philadelphia: Fortress Press, 1978), 96–97.

16

Christ the King: Our Purpose and Hope

DeLonn L. Rance

SERVING CHRIST WITH PURPOSE: MIGUEL OF EL SALVADOR

El Salvador's civil war forced Miguel's nominally Christian family to immigrate to the United States for a period of five years. When they returned to El Salvador, facing severe economic problems, Miguel's parents began to seek the things of God. Miguel attended the Josue Church in San Salvador occasionally just to keep the peace at home but did not commit to Christ. A series of problems and events led to a moment of crisis. Work, university studies, family, friends, and weekend drinking binges did not fill the void in Miguel's heart. He narrowly escaped a bullet during a traumatic robbery, which only exacerbated his financial problems. One day at work, as he raised a steel rod to place a commercial sign, a voice spoke to him, "Look up." When he did, he realized that he had come within inches of high voltage power lines and electrocution.[1]

---

[1] The narratives cited in this chapter emerge from personal interviews and correspondence. The author uses pseudonyms for the purpose of security.

That night, loneliness and sadness crushed Miguel. He held a gun and contemplated suicide. Messages heard at church came into his mind. He said to himself, "If it is true that Jesus Christ exists, and that you gave your life for us, and that you can change me and do something in me, here is my life; I surrender it to you." The following day he left for work. He remembers that as he drove, he put a piece of gum in his mouth and threw the wrapper out the window. Something made him stop his car, go back, and pick it up. He thought, "What am I doing? I can throw whatever I want out the window." The Holy Spirit spoke to Miguel: "Do not destroy my creation." He remembered the commitment from the previous night and the start of his new life under the rule of Christ.

Miguel's hunger and thirst for the things of the Lord grew. In a prayer retreat, the Lord spoke to him: "Do you want to serve me, or do you want to work for the world? I will bless what you do, but make a decision." Miguel committed to serve him. When an opportunity arose to travel to Nicaragua on a short-term missions assignment with King's Castle—an Assemblies of God ministry of evangelism, discipleship, and missions focused on children and youth in El Salvador—he accepted. When he returned, his commitment deepened. Miguel left his job, and entered an internship with Master's Commission, a leadership discipleship program of King's Castle. For a year, he lived by faith, serving in full-time ministry while being a disciple in life and ministry. The one-year commitment extended to three. During his third-year missions internship, he intended to spend nine months ministering in Belgium, but due to problems with his visa documents, he ended up in Africa.

While in Africa, the Lord made it very clear to Miguel that his missionary call was to serve in that land. He states, "When I got to Africa, God moved my heart in such a way that I cannot even find words to express it. Now that I'm back [in El Salvador] I feel like I've left my home; like I'm not where I'm supposed to be."

CHRIST THE SOURCE OF AN IMPOSSIBLE HOPE: CARLOS AND RUTH OF NICARAGUA AND PERU

August 1998 marks an important moment in Ruth's life.[2] A day prior to Ruth's eighth surgery in three years due to an atypical endometriosis, the head of the gynecology department at the Social Security Hospital of Lima, Peru, requested authorization to remove her second ovary due to a malignant tumor. Doctors had removed the first ovary two years earlier. All hope of having a baby died with the likelihood of this eighth surgery.

Ruth asked the Lord Jesus for one thing after signing the authorization and before the surgery. "Give me the strength to leave this hospital, and return to the streets of my country to continue sharing your love with the children. And when I hug them, may they feel the love of a mother who can never hug her own children."

In October 1999, Ruth and I (Carlos) began a beautiful friendship during a missions trip to Peru, where Ruth served as the National Director of King's Castle, a children's ministry. We worked for three weeks with Master's Commission at King's Castle in Nicaragua, the country where I served as a missionary for eight years.

In December 2000, taking a step of faith, we formally began our relationship as a couple. We both had consecrated our lives to serve Christ to champion the children of the world. We placed our present and future in his hands, having given the Lord the best years of our youth.

A few months before the wedding I contacted Ruth and said, "God has spoken to me, and has given me the name of our first child!" Immediately she replied, "It will be the name we give to the first child we adopt." I said to my fiancé with conviction and sweetness, "This is the name we will give to the first child who God gives us, a son of our own blood."

I think Ruth wanted to prepare my heart so that I would not suffer so much after we got married. Thirty-five gynecologists over a period of six years had conducted ten surgeries on Ruth, eventually

---

[2] Carlos is the narrator of the story in this section of the chapter.

informing her that she could not bear children. Because of this she said, "If you want to have your own children, there are still a few months left before the wedding. You are free to look for a healthy woman with ovaries who can give you biological children, but I am not that person."

I knew who had spoken to me, despite this difficult conversation. I did not marry Ruth just to have children. I intended to marry her because I loved her and knew we were in God's perfect will. I knew for sure in whom I had placed my trust. I insisted, "His name will be Isaac Adonai—the laughter of my God."

Ruth and I joined our lives before the Lord and our families on October 20, 2001, in Peru. A month later, we arrived in Nicaragua. Ruth's health collapsed at the end of January 2002, during a World Summit of King's Castle in Managua, the capital and largest city in the nation. This seemed to have occurred because of all the intense preparations for the Summit, which included receiving delegates from many regions in Nicaragua. A number of our friends took Ruth to the emergency room of the local hospital since I was to minister at one of the plenary meetings.

Your "Culture Shock" Is Six Weeks Old

At the hospital, the doctors did rigorous tests on my wife. In front of one of the doctors, Ruth said, "Doctor, I know I have problems. Something is not right because I vomit every morning. The food in this country is very fatty. Because of the work responsibilities, my husband and I haven't been eating at home. Also, I've had liver problems since I was single. I feel dizzy because I've had three surgeries on my right ear. I want to cry all the time. It's been three months since I left my country. What I have is culture shock."

Then the doctor told her that her "culture shock" was about six weeks old. "No, doctor. You do not understand. I've only been living here for three months." A little desperate, the Cuban doctor raised his voice and said, "Madam, I don't know what 'culture shock' is, but you are six weeks pregnant!"

Ruth reacted with anger, disbelief, and outrage. She took the written results, and left the doctor's office telling our friends, "You brought me to the wrong place. This hospital is old. The doctor is crazy. They have made a mistake with these results. That man says I am six weeks pregnant. Please do not say a word of this to Carlos." Of course, they ignored her.

Isaac Adonai

Outside the hospital, our friends glorified the Lord, and later they gave me the news. Against all human prognosis, we rejoiced as we watched each month the "culture shock" grow in Ruth's womb. Our first child was born by caesarean section on September 6, 2002, at the Santa Ana Social Security Hospital in El Salvador. Ruth took Isaac Adonai to Peru when he was four months old.

Ruth and my son received a medical checkup with the chief of gynecology at the same hospital where my wife had had nine out of her ten surgeries. As Ruth entered the office, they greeted each other affectionately, as Ruth's friend pushed the baby's stroller. "You have a beautiful nephew, Ruth!" She replied, "No, doctor. This baby is not my nephew. He's my son." The doctor answered, "Ah, good! Well young lady, I'm going to ask you the million-dollar question. How did you adopt a baby with a face just like yours?" Everyone laughed.

While Ruth climbed onto the bed for her medical examination, she gave the specialist the documentation from the hospital in Santa Ana where Isaac was born. It stated, "This baby was born by a caesarean section." The doctor then checked the ten-centimeter scar where the incision should be. The doctor took off his glasses. He rubbed his eyes. There were tears. "I do not get it." A few seconds of silence. "I do not get it. If I were not the one who took out your second ovary five years ago; if I had not operated on you four times; I would say that you are lying to me."

There in front of the doctor's desk Ruth told the doctor, "In this same hospital, you and your colleagues did everything that medical science could do. They told me the logical outcome that I could never bear children. But the God who formed me in my mother's womb, the one who knows the deepest desires of the heart, told me that if the doctors closed all hope for me, he would open a door for me, so that his Name may be glorified." What is impossible for humankind is possible for God.

Entrusted with Two Children

Ruth and I suffered the loss of two babies in November 2004 and March 2006. My wife was four-and-a-half and three-months pregnant, respectively. In March 2008 in our third month in India, however, we confirmed a fourth pregnancy. It was a difficult time. We were walking a lot, traveling on trains and in rickshaws (three-wheeled bicycles, driven by one person, with two or three passengers), and exposed to very high temperatures. Yet God took care of Kevin Ariel, our second son, who was born on December 3, 2008.

God did not entrust us with these two children because we are better than other couples who have faced similar health problems. By the Lord's mercy, God has given us two sons to form and prepare them for God's glory. When God pleases, God works miracles and wonders to exalt God's name, and to strengthen our faith and trust in God.

CHRIST THE RESURRECTION AND THE LIFE: KATY, ROBERTO, AND CHRISTINA OF EQUATORIAL GUINEA

> God is going to do it more, God is going to do it more,
> God is going to do it more, God is going to do it more,
> Hallelujah.
> He heals the sick, raises the dead,
> He lives forever and will change us,
> He is the God of miracles, of miracles.
> God is going to do it more.[3]

In the churches in Equatorial Guinea (located on the west coast of Central Africa), people sing the above traditional song in Fang, Spanish, and French with great joy and exuberance.

---

[3] Katy is the narrator of the story in the last part of the chapter.

Now the Assemblies of God Church in Andohasi sings this chorus with the absolute certainty that this God of miracles will do more.

We finished the week's seminar on inner cleansing on a Sunday, with thirty-four people accepting Christ as Savior and Lord. On Thursday, we started a new seminar focusing on the subject, "What do we believe?" The first lesson talked about God, and about God's relationship with us. Roberto preached about the topics of God's Son, Word, and the Holy Spirit—all provided by God to establish the Lord's relationship with us. He declared, "The same power that raised Christ from the dead is in us, and with us today." The congregation responded, "Amen!"

At that exact moment, outside the church, a crying woman came down the road, fell to the ground in front of the building, and began to scream in her Fang dialect. She carried a little girl in her arms and released her on the ground. Women from the neighborhood and the church gathered around her. I got up from my seat and asked what was happening. They explained that Christina, a sister (member) of the church, had brought her dead daughter to the service. Her husband was in the congregation. When he realized what was happening, he went outside, and took his daughter in his arms. He brought her to the church altar where I then picked her up in my arms. The girl was dead! There was no time to do anything. Roberto instructed the church to start praying. We did not say a long prayer. We simply said, "Spirit of death, we bind you in the name of Jesus." And to the little girl, "Receive life in the name of Jesus." After the prayers, I opened my eyes, took the girl to her crying mother, and said, "Get up! Have faith, your daughter is alive!" Right then the girl cried, and sat up in my arms.

Upon seeing this miracle, some of the bystanders cried, others trembled, while others shouted *akibá*, which means thank you. We continued the service by worshipping God. That night, twenty visitors accepted the Lord Jesus as their Savior. Then we praised God with the song, "God is going to do it more; he is the God of miracles."

REFLECTION QUESTIONS

1. What does Miguel's story tell us about the relationship between Christ the King and the purpose for each of our lives?
2. What does the story of Carlos and Ruth denote about Christ our Hope and our faith and trust in the Lord?
3. What does the miracle that Katy, Roberto, and Christina witnessed signify about our present and future hope in Christ?
4. What do these three narratives indicate about our strategic priorities in missions?
5. Are signs and wonders optional in giving witness to Christ the King among the nations? Discuss why you agree, or do not agree, with this statement.

Conclusion

Communicating the Transforming Global Mission of Christ through Story

Robert L. Gallagher

I settled in my seat with a heightened expectation, attracted by the topic of a prominent missiologist—the importance and implications of narrative in mission theology—at the plenary session of the Evangelical Missiological Society in southern California. Nevertheless, I became increasingly restless as the presentation progressed. At the end of the lecture, the first few sentences in the question-and-answer time shed light on the reason for my edginess. The late Ralph D. Winter[1] asked the keynote speaker, "You well elucidate the influence of narrative in biblical theology of mission. Why is it, though, that you have not given one story in your presentation?"

Throughout *Christ among the Nations*, each of the authors are faithfully consistent in using narrative to convey the splendor and majesty of Christ our Savior, Empowerer, Healer, and Hope. In the conclusion, I do not want to drop the ball, relying solely

---

[1] Ralph D. Winter was the founder of the U.S. Center for World Mission, William Carey International University, and the International Society for Frontier Missiology in Pasadena, California.

on propositional truth without using any stories to illustrate my claims. In other words, I do not want the last chapter of our volume to read like Leviticus—a list of rules and regulations—lacking the vibrancy of Luke-Acts (my favorite book), which is the account of the mission of Jesus and the early church.[2]

In this chapter, I will follow the structure of the volume by dealing with the themes of biblical, historical, and contemporary narratives as they emphasize issues and trends of particular interest and uneasiness. With regard to biblical narratives, my concern is right reading and interpretation of the Bible. As such, I enlarge this portion because it is imbued with such personal apprehension. For historical narratives, my focus is on Bartholomäus Ziegenbalg of chapter 3, and his enthusiastic ability to communicate the story of missions in southern India to Europe and America—a promotional and marketing model to emulate. Lastly, in the piece on present-day narratives, I will share the effect of epic in my own life as a metaphor for the need to enhance narrative within the global mission community.

LEARNING TO GROW IN THE SCRIPTURES

The first section develops an approach to interpreting scriptural narratives that focuses on the gospel of Christ. My strong attention to biblical exegesis stems from my deep concern for the alarming decline in biblical literacy among Western Christians.[3] In the past few decades, I have often heard theology professors from Christian tertiary institutions lamenting the lack of biblical understanding

---

[2] For an understanding of the narratives in Acts, see Robert L. Gallagher and Paul Hertig, "Background to Acts," in *Mission in Acts: Ancient Narratives in Contemporary Context*, ed. Robert L. Gallagher and Paul Hertig, American Society of Missiology Series, no. 34 (Maryknoll, NY: Orbis Books, 2004), 1–17. Also, for a commentary that incorporates both Luke and Acts, see Robert C. Tannehill, "Introduction," in *The Narrative Unity of Luke-Acts: A Literary Interpretation*, vol. 1 (Philadelphia, PA: Fortress Press, 1986), 1–12. The genre of narrative comprises 43 percent of the Scripture.

[3] For further understanding of modern biblical illiteracy, see Glenn R. Paauw, *Saving the Bible from Ourselves: Learning to Read & Live the Bible Well* (Downers Grove, IL: IVP Books, 2016), 12–17.

among their students. These college students—often from Christian homes, schools, and churches—know a few Scriptures in the New Testament, but they do not know how the Bible joins them together. Within the Hebrew Scriptures, they have little understanding of any of the ancient stories. This is a distressing situation since these undergraduates are the Christian leaders of tomorrow in both the secular and ecclesial domains. Without a proper understanding and application of God's inspired Word, the church remains stunted in its maturity and effectiveness in spreading the gospel of Christ in our world. In learning to grow in the Scriptures, I first need to explain my suggested exegetical technique.[4]

Responsibility, Community, and Mission

In our growth in reading and interpreting the Bible—prayerfully and rightly—there are different translations, strategies, and theologies for understanding the Word of God. Still, in encountering Scripture, reading and studying should involve the contexts of responsibility, community, and mission. God asks us to embrace the responsibility of feeding on his Word, and in doing so we will mature in our understanding.[5] Without a growing relationship with Jesus and his Word, there is the risk of drifting toward

---

[4] See examples of this methodology in Robert L. Gallagher, "The Spirit's Revolution: Breaking through the Boundaries of Superiority (Peter in Acts 10–11)," in *Breaking through the Boundaries: God's Mission from the Outside In*, Sarita Gallagher Edwards, Robert L. Gallagher, Paul Hertig, and Young Lee Hertig, American Society of Missiology Series, no. 59 (Maryknoll, NY: Orbis Books, 2019), 145–70; Robert L. Gallagher, "Transformational Teaching: Engaging in a Pneumatic Teaching Praxis," in *Thinking Theologically about Language Teaching: Christian Perspectives on an Educational Calling*, ed. Cheri L. Pierson and Will Bankston (London: Langham Global Library, 2017), 135–62; Robert L. Gallagher, "Engaging in Pneumatic Mission Praxis," in *Transforming Teaching for Mission: Educational Theory and Practice*, ed. Robert A. Danielson and Benjamin L. Hartley, Association of Professors of Mission Series (Wilmore, KY: First Fruits Press, 2014), 117–49; and Robert L. Gallagher, "Missionary Methods: St. Paul's, St. Roland's, or Ours?," in *Missionary Methods: Research, Reflections, and Realities*, ed. Craig Ott and J. D. Payne (Pasadena, CA: William Carey Library, 2013), 3–22.

[5] See Deut 17:18–19; Josh 1:7–8; Ps 119:97.

modern-day relativism. Eugene H. Peterson writes that the spiritually mature person needs to continue in rigorous exegesis and that "this is not a task from which we graduate."[6]

N. T. Wright proposes that if the mission of God is "to make the deep, life-changing, kingdom-advancing sense it is supposed to, it is vital that ordinary Christians read, encounter, and study Scripture for themselves, individually and in groups."[7] Followers of Christ need to seek both individual and communal interpretation of Scripture. Henri J. M. Nouwen also encourages individuals to cultivate a personal spirituality through reading the Bible. He contends that unless we protect our own "inner mystery" we will not be able to form community.[8] Moreover, unless we nurture a genuine individual spirituality,

> Our relationships with others easily become needy and greedy, sticky and clinging, dependent and sentimental, exploitive and parasitic, because we cannot experience the others as different from ourselves, but only as people whom we can use for the fulfillment of our own, often hidden needs.[9]

In simpler terms, we are personally responsible for biblical study and obedience within a Christian community through the help of the Holy Spirit.

As a final point in this segment, we need to comprehend the Bible in the context of God's mission to redeem and restore all creation. The Bible is the Spirit's instrument for transforming followers of Christ for the mission of God. N. T. Wright in *Scripture and the Authority of God* recommends reading the Bible within the larger context of the authority of God set by the biblical authors.[10]

---

[6] Eugene H. Peterson, *Eat This Book: A Conversation in the Art of Spiritual Reading* (Grand Rapids, MI: Eerdmans, 2006), 53.

[7] N. T. Wright, *Scripture and the Authority of God: How to Read the Bible Today*, rev. ed. (New York: HarperOne, 2011), 133.

[8] Henri J. M. Nouwen, *Reaching Out: The Three Movements of the Spiritual Life* (New York: Image Books-Doubleday, 1975), 31.

[9] Ibid., 44.

[10] N. T. Wright, *Scripture and the Authority of God*, 26.

God's authority stems from God's sovereign power accomplishing the divine mission of redeeming and renewing the entire cosmos. For Wright, the authority of the Bible over the church is shorthand for the authority of God exercised through Scripture, which, as an extension of God's authority over all creation, is made manifest in God's mission.[11]

God's cosmic mission is the central narrative of the Hebrew Scriptures with its origin in the story of the people of God. The climax of Israel's chronicle comes with the death and resurrection of Jesus, which serves as the inauguration of the kingdom of God, and will come to full consummation in the future redemption and renewal of the cosmos.[12] Empowered by the transformative agency of the Holy Spirit, the church is God's vehicle for advancing God's kingdom in the world. The early church believed that God accomplished God's purposes "through the 'word'; the story of Israel now transmuted into God's call of God's renewed people."[13] The Bible invites and nurtures the church for this mission. The Word transforms Christ's disciples, led by the Holy Spirit as they gather in Christian community to advance the mission of God in the world.[14]

Principlizing Hermeneutics

Believers read the Bible and learn the universal truths and commands found therein, which are then applied in current situations bringing God's reality into the world. The Bible is God's spoken revelation disclosing all the necessary truths of life, especially regarding the death and resurrection of Christ. The certainty found within the Scriptures carries the authority of God into the world. The "Word" is the Son of God, Jesus Messiah, made flesh, and it is through his death and resurrection that the world's sins were paid and forgiven.

An overemphasis on principlizing, nonetheless, can separate the reader from the wider context of the church and the kingdom of

---

[11] Ibid., 21, 24.
[12] Ibid., 41.
[13] Ibid., 50.
[14] Ibid., 115–16.

God. Accompanying this assumption is the notion that the Bible's authority comes from its essence as a perfect book, carrying perfect truths, and given by a perfect God—however, in the process of proper interpretation, it is challenging for the Christian to determine a contemporary application from these truths. Believers find the Bible's authority in God's mission to the world, which the Lord invites the church to join. The reader should not only extract principles from the text but also seek understanding of how the biblical text portrays wisdom in action. Biblical understanding is more than an intellectual exercise since it requires participation in the report of God. The Bible is not primarily a set of commands and doctrines, but rather a call to participate in the theodrama.[15] Peterson asserts,

> The Bible does not present us with a moral code and tell us, "Live up to this"; nor does it set out a system of doctrine and say, "Think like this and you will live well." The biblical way is to tell a story and in the telling invite: "Live *into* this—this is what it looks like to be human in this God-made and God-ruled world; this is what is involved in becoming and maturing as a human being."[16]

Followers of Jesus do not simply study the Bible, but the Word changes their lives (in their thinking and behavior) as they demonstrate concrete acts of love and mission in God's world.[17]

Missional Hermeneutics

Christopher J. H. Wright suggests that interpreting the Bible should find a healthy rhythm between a principlizing and missional hermeneutic, since the two views are complementary. He maintains that we need to address how obedience to the Scrip-

---

[15] See Kevin J. Vanhoozer, "A Drama-of-Redemption Model," in *Four Views on Moving Beyond the Bible to Theology*, ed. Stanley N. Gundry and Gary T. Meadors (Grand Rapids, MI: Zondervan, 2009), 151–99.

[16] Peterson, *Eat This Book*, 43–44.

[17] Ibid., 18.

tures in our present world actually takes place. Some method of principlizing is necessary. Equally, the principlizing hermeneutical approach needs the contribution of knowing the fullness of the biblical metanarrative.[18]

Similar to N. T. Wright, Christopher Wright maintains that it is important for readers to understand that the mission of God provides the authoritative context of the Bible and to allow that realization to permeate their reading methodology. The church participates in God's determinations, "and the only access that we have to that mission of God is given to us in the Bible. This is the grand narrative that is unlocked when we turn the hermeneutical key of reading all the Scriptures in the light of the mission of God."[19] At the same time, students of the Bible should desire to follow specific commands and truths in their daily lives.

A missional hermeneutic, therefore, views the Scriptures with a missiological eye since mission is the central thrust of both the First and Second Testaments.[20] Richard J. Bauckham describes this inclination as "a way of reading the Bible for which mission is the hermeneutical key. . . . A missionary hermeneutic of this kind would not be simply a study of the theme of mission in the biblical writings, but a way of reading the whole of Scripture with mission as its central interest and goal."[21]

Viewing the Panorama

What follows is a brief exploration of the above hermeneutical approach, using the Gospel of Luke and Book of Acts as a case study for learning to grow in the Scriptures. Four historical–critical

---

[18] Christopher J. H Wright, "Reflections on Moving Beyond the Bible to Theology," in Gundry and Meadors, *Four Views on Moving Beyond the Bible to Theology*, 321–22.

[19] Christopher J. H. Wright, *The Mission of God: Unlocking the Bible's Grand Narrative* (Downers Grove, IL: IVP Academic, 2006), 534.

[20] David J. Bosch, "Reflections on Biblical Models of Mission," in *Toward the 21st Century in Christian Mission*, ed. James M. Phillips and Robert T. Coote (Grand Rapids, MI: Eerdmans, 1993), 175–78.

[21] Richard J. Bauckham, "Mission as Hermeneutic for Scriptural Interpretation," unpublished lecture given at Cambridge, England, in November 1999, 1.

questions are helpful throughout this procedure: What was the first author saying to the first audience? What does the audience understand about the meaning of the original author? What response does the author want from the audience? Moreover, after wrestling with the answers to the three previous questions: What should be our response?[22]

Pursuing the hermeneutical claims of the two Wrights, an essential ingredient in recovering the missiological message of Christ is to view the narratives of the Bible as an entire panorama. Because of the unrealistic expectations of modern religious culture, those responsible for feeding God's people with God's complete message seldom embrace the necessary tempo and liberty needed to do so. The pastoral route chosen in sermon and teaching preparation is often the shortest distance between baptisms, weddings, hospital visitations, funerals, conflict management, financial burdens, and endless board meetings. There is an alternative way, however.

In Wellington, the capital of New Zealand, I had the opportunity to facilitate a Pentecostal-leadership conference based on the Book of Acts, with a special directive to emphasize the work of the Holy Spirit. In response to the appeal, I released a list of seventy-three documented scriptures in Luke-Acts that speak of the Spirit, rather than give the participants a pneumatological treatise, which may have challenged their expertise on the topic. Dividing the leaders into small groups, I asked the question, "What is the first author's understanding of the role of the Holy Spirit in Luke-Acts?" In case the group reacted negatively to my personal interpretation and ostracized me as a result, I hesitated to tell them what I thought, but instead allowed the Spirit time and freedom to reveal himself.

Forty minutes later, the pastors began to communicate their findings group by group, with bullet points written with thick-dark markers on large sheets of butcher paper. It took over seventy

---

[22] See Edgar Krentz, *The Historical-Critical Method* (Philadelphia, PA: Fortress Press, 1975), and I. Howard Marshall, "Historical Criticism," in *New Testament Interpretation: Essays on Principles and Methods*, ed. I. Howard Marshall (Grand Rapids, MI: Eerdmans, 1977), 126–38.

minutes to complete the exercise—twice the normal time allowed. In spite of that, what was astonishing to me was that not one of the groups mentioned the expression, "speaking in other tongues." This was remarkable, considering that this is a foundational belief for the movement's dogma: the Spirit fills a believer and the immediate, initial evidence is the ability to speak in other languages (see Acts 2:4; 10:46; 19:6).[23]

How did this unusual occurrence happen? I believe that instead of defaulting to the five to seven biblical verses of Luke-Acts that support the leaders' doctrinal stance, the panoramic view of the mission of God positioned the Pentecostal influencers to consider the author's unabridged message, which took into account the repeated theological pattern.[24] In community, they prayerfully decided to consider over seventy verses on the work of the Spirit and not to feed themselves only with their denominational limitations. To clarify, I am grateful for the gift of a prayer language to edify my spirit (1 Cor 14:2).

Still, I am encouraging a broader approach to biblical exegesis, which includes examining whole books of the Bible instead of studying truncated portions squeezed into the mold of our theological traditions. Furthermore, as the small groups delivered their findings, there was much light-hearted joviality despite a painful

---

[23] Luke refers to "the baptism with the Holy Spirit" (Acts 1:5)—which the early church experienced at Pentecost (Acts 2:1–4)—by different expressions such as "the promise of my Father upon you" (Lk 24:49), "clothed with power from on high" (Lk 24:49), "the promise of the Father" (Acts 1:4 cf. Lk 24:49), "the Holy Spirit comes upon you" (Acts 1:8), "filled with the Holy Spirit" (Acts 2:4), "poured forth this" (Acts 2:33), "Holy Spirit fell upon" (Acts 10:44), "the gift poured out upon" (Acts 10:45), "received the Holy Spirit" (Acts 10:47), "Holy Spirit fell upon" (Acts 11:15), and "baptized with the Holy Spirit" (Acts 11:16). Furthermore, the Holy Spirit came through the laying on of hands of Peter and John to the Samaritans (Acts 8:17–19), Ananias of Damascus to Saul (Acts 9:12, 17), and Paul to the followers of John the Baptist at Ephesus (Acts 19:6). Compare Acts 6:6; 13:3.

[24] For further theological patterns concerning the Spirit, consider the following: The apostle Peter received the Holy Spirit (Jn 20:22), yet was subsequently filled with the Spirit in Acts 2:4, 14, 38 and Acts 4:8, 31. Likewise, Stephen was full of the Spirit and wisdom (Acts 6:3), full of faith and the Holy Spirit (Acts 6:5), full of wisdom and the Spirit (Acts 6:10), and even at his stoning, was again full of the Holy Spirit (Acts 7:55).

history of factions and dissent among the national movement. That afternoon in Wellington, God brought a measure of love, acceptance, and forgiveness to the national leaders as they prayerfully worked together to consider the panoramic view of a Lukan tapestry on the role of the Spirit of Jesus in the first-century church.

Recovering the Scriptures as a Whole

The modern Western church has not appropriately trained its church leadership to study and present the complete message of the Bible within its historic and sociocultural contexts. Hence, those responsible often do not retell the foundational biblical anecdotes in a way that communicates meaningfully to the current culture, which has resulted in the waning of vibrant Christianity in the minority world. Embodying the gospel to a people that have turned their back on Jesus and who "are choked by life's worries, riches, and pleasures" (Lk 8:14) will empower Western Christianity to retell the Bible's metanarrative, and to faithfully fulfill its missional calling. Lesslie Newbigin claims, "I do not believe that we can speak effectively of the gospel as a word addressed to our culture unless we recover a sense of the Scriptures as a canonical whole, as the story which provides the true context for our understanding of the meaning of our lives—both personal and public."[25] Michael W. Goheen agrees:

> A missionary encounter requires that the church live fully in the biblical story and contextualize the gospel in its culture in a way that is faithful to that story. This will involve a critical participation that embraces the creational good while opposing the destructive idolatry that can exist in any culture. Thus, central to the church's mission is an offer of the gospel as a counter story as the true way of life, a call for radical conversion, an invitation to understand and live in the world in the light of the gospel.[26]

---

[25] Lesslie Newbigin, "Response to the Word of God?," *The Gospel and Our Culture Newsletter* 10, no. 2 (1991): 2.

[26] Michael W. Goheen, "The Biblical Story of Narrative Theology," in *Con-*

There is a fundamental problem, all the same, with the Western church recovering "the Scriptures as a canonical whole." Our lifestyle of muchness and manyness does not allow us the time to "live fully in the biblical story" and thus to contextualize the gospel to our culture.[27] The ethos of our Western society has infiltrated and contaminated the church with pride.[28] David Brooks—an op-ed columnist for the *New York Times*—writes, in *The Road to Character*, of fourth-century Augustine of Hippo: "The problem, Augustine came to believe, is that if you think you can organize your own salvation you are magnifying the very sin that keeps you from it. To believe that you can be captain of your own life is to suffer the sin of pride."[29] Brooks continues,

> Pride can come in bloated form. This is the puffed-up Donald Trump style of pride. This person wants people to see visible proof of his superiority. He wants to be on the VIP list. In conversation, he boasts, he brags. He needs to see his superiority reflected in other people's eyes. He believes that this feeling of superiority will eventually bring him peace.[30]

Far too many church leaders have their triumphal chariots waiting outside the church building to parade themselves before adoring

---

temporary Mission Theology: Engaging the Nations, ed. Robert L. Gallagher and Paul Hertig, American Society of Missiology Series, no. 53 (Maryknoll, NY: Orbis Books, 2017), 33.

[27] Richard J. Foster, *Celebration of Discipline: The Path to Spiritual Growth*, rev. ed. (San Francisco: Harper & Row, 1988), 15.

[28] For an understanding of humility in the leadership of Jesus Christ, see Robert L. Gallagher, "Rome: God's Mission That the Wolf and the Lamb Live and Eat Together," in *God's Mission in the Cities of the Bible*, ed. Jude Tiersma-Watson, Christina T. Accornero, and Charles E. Van Engen (Skyforest, CA: Urban Loft Publishers, 2021), 202–09.

[29] David Brooks, *The Road to Character* (New York: Random House, 2015), 199.

[30] Ibid., 199–200. Also see Michael Austin. "Humility, Pride, and the Presidency of Donald Trump," in *The Spiritual Danger of Donald Trump: 30 Evangelical Christians on Justice, Truth, and Moral Integrity*, ed. Ronald J. Sider (Eugene, OR: Cascade Books, 2020), 42–46.

fans as they organize their brand of salvation and captain the treadmill of VIP success, while devoting little attention to prayer and the ministry of God's Word.[31] I have observed elsewhere:

> So often, the church has accepted Western society's definition of success without critical evaluation. Multiple seminars and conferences promote steps to success for a healthy church body based on the social axiom that bigger is better. Yet this is the secular business model, found nowhere in the Scriptures. Godly success is finding the will of God and doing it, whether this means a life of prosperity or hardship.[32]

Tossing Morsels under the Table

Time is a precious commodity, and pop-cultural sound bites sideline patient biblical meditation. Because of the chaotic traffic of overcommitment, we chop the Bible into little bits and pieces of theology, morality, and ethics, tossing morsels under the table to our starving congregations. Augustine of Hippo writes that such a person "heeds himself, and he who pleases himself seems great to himself. But he who pleases himself pleases a fool, for he him-

---

[31] Dietrich Bonhoeffer declares, "The figure of the Crucified invalidates all thought that takes success for its standard," in *Ethics* (New York: Simon & Schuster, [1949], 1995), 78. Cf. the attitude of the Apostles in Acts 6:3–4. "Brothers and sisters, choose seven men from among you who are known to be full of the Spirit and wisdom. We will turn this responsibility over to them, and will give our attention to prayer and the ministry of the Word." For a description of a Holy Spirit revival in the 1970s and 1980s in Papua New Guinea, see Sarita D. Gallagher, "Seeing with Church-Growth Eyes: The Rise of Indigenous Church Movements in Mission Praxis," in *The State of Missiology Today: Global Innovations in Christian Witness*, ed. Charles E. Van Engen, Missiological Engagements Series (Downers Grove, IL: IVP Academic, 2016), 62–63, 76–83; and Sarita D. Gallagher, *Abrahamic Blessing: A Missiological Narrative of Revival in Papua New Guinea*, American Society of Missiology Monograph Series, vol. 21 (Eugene, OR: Pickwick Publications, 2014), 154–84.

[32] Robert L. Gallagher, "From 'Doingness' to 'Beingness': A Missiological Interpretation of Acts 4:23–31," in Gallagher and Hertig, eds., *Mission in Acts*, 55. Also see in the above volume the topic of biblical success on pages 45, 54–56.

self is a fool when he is pleasing himself."³³ Is it any wonder that university students in Christian institutions of higher learning in the United States know a few Bible verses from the New Testament, yet do not know how they fit together, and when they are asked about the Old Testament, lack any basic understanding of the ancient narratives? As I stated earlier, current biblical literacy among Christian college students continues its downward spiral of the last thirty years.³⁴

Let me illustrate a possible solution to this dilemma from a Melanesian experience. Every year for nearly fifteen years, I taught for three to six weeks at an indigenous Bible School in Port Moresby, the capital of Papua New Guinea. My only means of communicating with my family in Australia (before Internet) was via postal mail. Imagine if upon receiving my six-page letter my children first turned to the third page and only read the second paragraph before putting it down. Then a few days later, they picked up my letter again, and read the fourth paragraph on the fifth page, and only then a few words before returning it to the kitchen table. Then a week or so later, my daughters resume my heartfelt communication, reading another small portion of the six-page letter. The rhetorical question arises: Would my family receive the full message of my letter by using this hermeneutical approach? Goheen answers my question by discussing how some of us read the Bible:

> If we fragment the story of the Bible into bits, we can easily domesticate the reigning cultural story. When we only have bits—moral bits, systematic-theological bits, devotional bits, historical-critical bits, narrative bits, and

---

³³ Augustine of Hippo, "Psalm 122: God Is True Wealth," in Mary Clark, *Augustine of Hippo: Selected Writings* (Mahwah, NJ: Paulist Press, 1984), 250.

³⁴ See George Barna, "Most Twentysomethings put Christianity on the Shelf Following Spiritually Active Teen Years," September 11, 2006, www.barna.org; Gary A. Tobin and Aryeh K. Weinberg, *Profiles of the American University*, vol. 2, *Religious Beliefs and Behaviors of College Faculty* (San Francisco, CA: Institute for Jewish and Community Research, 2007); and Howard Kurtz, "College Faculties a Most Liberal Lot, Study Finds," *Washington Post* (March 29, 2005), C01.

homiletical bits—there is no comprehensive grand narrative. The all-embracing cultural story accommodates the Bible bits, and it becomes *that* story that shapes our lives.[35]

Before I read, observe, interpret, and apply the narratives of the Word of God, I need to pray and refrain from dissecting the Bible into bits and pieces by viewing the panorama and thus recover the Scriptures as a whole. In other words, the big-sky perspective of the Scripture moves us into a position that allows a suitable understanding of the first author's intent to the original audience, concerning a particular biblical tapestry of God's mission under community investigation.[36] My concern for right reading and interpretation of biblical narrative thus dispensed, I now move to a historical model of promoting mission through story.

ZIEGENBALG MODELS PROMOTION OF MISSION IN ASIA AND EUROPE

In addition to the five Pietistic missional principles of Bartholomäus Ziegenbalg and Heinrich Plütschau (the first Protestant missionaries in Asia)—articulated in chapter 3 of this volume—their missionary effort also marks the significance of promoting missions through narrative. On their commissioning, Frederick IV, King of Denmark and Norway (r. 1699–1730), instructed the missionaries to send letters concerning the work, development, and plans of the Royal Danish Mission in Tranquebar, southern India, whenever a ship returned to Denmark.[37]

---

[35] Michael W. Goheen, "The Urgency of Reading the Bible as One Story in the 21st Century," public lecture given at Regent College, Vancouver, BC, Canada (November 2, 2006), 4.

[36] For a further understanding of the panoramic view of the Bible, see Gordon D. Fee and Douglas K. Stuart, *How to Read the Bible Book by Book* (Grand Rapids, MI: Zondervan, 2002); and Gordon D. Fee and Douglas K. Stuart, *How to Read the Bible for All Its Worth* (Grand Rapids, MI: Zondervan, 1981).

[37] J. F. Fenger, *History of the Tranquebar Mission—Worked out from the Original Papers. Published in Danish and Translated into English from the German of Emil Francke—Compared with the Danish Original*, trans. Emil Francke (Madras, India: M. E. Press, 1863), 238.

At Merseburg in Saxony, Ziegenbalg made a vow that predicted his vocational call in southeast India. He vowed that he would seek nothing in this world but the glorification of the name of God, the extension of his kingdom, the spread of the divine truth, and the salvation of humanity in whatever part of the world he found himself, and no matter what amount of affliction should befall him on account of his commitment to Christ.

Subsequently, Ziegenbalg wrote and sent descriptions of their cross-cultural ministry in Danish Tranquebar. Pietists circulated these letters in the *Halle Reports* (the first German Lutheran missionary magazine), and later published them in Berlin in a book entitled *Notable News* (1708). A year later, Anton Wilhelm Böhme (the German Pietist chaplain at St. James's Palace, London) translated these descriptions into English for the Society for Promoting Christian Knowledge (SPCK).

Christian publishers renamed the letters *Propagation of the Gospel in the East*, for distribution to Pietist communities in Germany, Denmark, and England.[38] This compilation of letters reached the royal courts of Denmark and England as well as farther afield. For example, they were read by John Wake (the Archbishop of Canterbury), Cotton Mather (an influential Puritan in the New England colonies), and Susanna Wesley (the mother of John and Charles), to name a few; and they served as a catalyst to encourage financial giving and sending to the mission field. By 1712, six years after the commencement of the Tranquebar Mission, the organization supported twenty-two workers.

Prince George of Denmark and Norway (r. 1702–1708), the Danish husband of Queen Anne of Great Britain (r. 1702–1714), along with Böhme, his Lutheran chaplain, had a strong interest in the Danish Tranquebar Mission. Böhme suggested to the SPCK that they should send a printing press to India for the service of the mission and that they might translate the Scriptures into the languages of southern India. The main languages included Gujarathi, Marathi, Portuguese, Sanskrit, Tamil, and Telugu. This

---

[38] H. M. Zorn, *Bartholomäus Ziegenbalg*, Men and Missions Series, ed. L. Fuerbringer (St. Louis, MO: Concordia Publishing House, 1933), 101, 103.

resulted in an ecumenical partnership whereby a German Lutheran (in the service of a Danish sovereign) translated the Tamil New Testament, which was then printed by Indian workers on an English press funded by an Anglican mission society.[39]

Owing to pressures from Johan Sigismund Hassius Lillienpalm, the governor of Danish East India, Ziegenbalg returned to Europe for a promotional tour (1714–1716), whereupon he married Maria Dorothea Salzmann.[40] During his home leave, he visited Plütschau in Holstein,[41] King Frederick IV of Denmark, and Prince George of England, and founded two institutions: a missionary society at Halle University, Saxony, for the propagation of the gospel (the Order of the Grain of Mustard Seed); and the Royal College of Missions for training missionaries in Copenhagen (1714). Ziegenbalg thus directly contributed to European opportunities for promoting and marketing missions in southern India.

Three years after returning from Europe, Ziegenbalg died in Tranquebar at the age of thirty-six. Following his 13 years of ministry in India, he left a legacy of 250 members in the New Jerusalem Church, studies of the Hindu religion and culture that aided later missionaries, two church buildings and a seminary for the training of national leaders, and the New Testament and Genesis to Ruth translated into the Tamil language.[42] Brijrai Singh argues, "His [Ziegenbalg] impressive knowledge of Hinduism, high regard for Hindus as human beings, desire to preserve the integrity of the Tamil language and culture as he presented Chris-

---

[39] For Pietist primary sources of Ziegenbalg, see Ernst Benz, "Pietist and Puritan Sources of Early Protestant World Missions (Cotton Mather and A. H. Francke)," *Church History* 20, no. 2 (1951): 28–55, esp. 34–38.

[40] For the missionary life of Maria Dorothea Salzmann (c. 1693–1722), see Helen H. Holcomb, *Men of Might in Indian Missions: The Leaders and Their Epochs—1706–1899* (London: Oliphant, Anderson, and Ferrier, 1901), 32; and Daniel Jeyaraj, "Maria Dorothea Ziegenbalg, the First German Lutheran Female Missionary to the Tamil People in South India," *International Journal of Asian Christianity* 2, no. 1 (2019): 101–21.

[41] In 1713, Heinrich Plütschau returned to Germany due to ill health, and became a Lutheran country pastor at Beyenflieth in Holstein in northern Germany.

[42] The New Testament Tamil translation of 1715, and the church building constructed in 1718, are still in use by the Tamil Evangelical Lutheran Church.

tianity, and the lack of racist attitudes coupled with his repudiation of the racism of other Europeans towards Indians," gained him commendable respect from many Hindus.[43] On Ziegenbalg's death, Johann Ernest Gründler[44] wrote a grieving letter to August Hermann Francke (a professor of theology at Halle University, Saxony), who, upon reading the letter to his students, moved many to become missionaries to India.[45]

In considering the missionary Bartholomäus Ziegenbalg, I would propose that in pioneering the Western study of south Indian culture, society, and religion, he modeled a ministry philosophy to generations of Pietist missionaries who followed his path.[46] Not only did he demonstrate how to bring an uncompromised gospel to the Indian people with Christian care and concern, but through his letters depicting stories of the mission field, he also brought an awareness of the importance of global missions to Protestant Europe and Asia.

Furthermore, through Pietism's continued correspondence, the Tranquebar Mission's influence extended to emerging mission movements such as Count Nicolaus Ludwig von Zinzendorf's

---

[43] Brijrai Singh, *The First Protestant Missionary in India: Bartholomäus Ziegenbalg* (New Delhi, India: Oxford University Press, 1999), 22–23.

[44] Bartholomäus Ziegenbalg, with the help of Johann Ernest Gründler (a former schoolteacher at the Francke Foundations in Halle, Saxony), translated the entire New Testament into Tamil in less than five years after his arrival at Tranquebar, southern India, in 1706.

[45] During the existence of the Royal Danish Mission (1706–1845), European missionaries (forty-nine Germans, six Danes, and one Swede) worked in India mostly following Ziegenbalg's missionary methods. In 1727, the forerunner's successor, Benjamin Schultze, completed the Tamil translation of the Old Testament, and in turn, his heir, Johann Philipp Fabricius, finalized a revised translation of the whole Bible and the Apocrypha (1777–1782).

[46] For further comprehension of Pietist missions, see Robert L. Gallagher, "Bartholomäus Ziegenbalg Models Holistic Missions: Pietism in Eighteenth-Century Southern India," in *The Past and Future of Evangelical Missions*, ed. Aminta Arrington, Kenneth R. Nehrbass, and Narry Santos, Evangelical Missiological Society Series, no. 29 (Pasadena, CA: William Carey Publishing, 2021), 42–63; and Robert L. Gallagher, "Encountering Pietist Missions," in John Mark Terry and Robert L. Gallagher, *Encountering the History of Missions: From the Early Church to Today* (Grand Rapids, MI: Baker Academic, 2017), 173–98, esp. Bartholomäus Ziegenbalg, 180–87.

Moravian missionaries,[47] the Leipzig Evangelical Lutheran Mission, and the Copenhagen Mission Society, which sponsored the Greenland mission begun in 1721 by Hans Egede, a Dano-Norwegian Lutheran missionary. In reflecting on Ziegenbalg's heritage, Stephen C. Neill acknowledges, "A new epoch in the history of the Christian mission had begun."[48] Daniel Jeyaraj reinforces this notion by declaring him "the true father of the modern Protestant missionary movement."[49]

MY IDENTITY IN THE STORY OF CHRIST

The biblical and historical stories in *Christ among the Nations* are important. Stories connect us. They inspire and encourage us, giving us hope and expectation of a better day. They give life perspective, provide glimpses of wisdom into our existence, and enlighten changing experiences that shape us. They join us together as human beings.[50] Stories join families and the people of a nation together. We live by telling our stories. If we do not tell our stories, we are not living—at least not living life to the fullest.

---

[47] For a further understanding of Moravian missions, see Robert L. Gallagher, "Encountering Moravian Missions," in Terry and Gallagher, *Encountering the History of Missions*, 199–223, esp. Nicolaus von Zinzendorf, 200–21; Robert L. Gallagher, "The Integration of Mission Theology and Practice: Zinzendorf and the Early Moravians," *Mission Studies: Journal of the International Association for Mission Studies* 25, no. 2 (2008): 185–210; and Robert L. Gallagher, "Zinzendorf and the Early Moravians: Pioneers in Leadership Selection and Training," *Missiology: An International Review* 36, no. 2 (2008): 237–44.

[48] Stephen C. Neill, *A History of Christianity in India: 1707–1858* (New York: Cambridge University Press, 1985), 28.

[49] Daniel Jeyaraj, *Bartholomäus Ziegenbalg: The Father of Modern Protestant Mission—An Indian Assessment* (New Delhi, India: The Indian Society for Promoting Christian Knowledge, and Chennai, India: The Gurukul Lutheran Theological College and Research Institute, 2006), 9.

[50] On Oprah Winfrey's CBS interview with Prince Harry and Meghan Markle (March 4, 2021), Markle, in speaking of the Archewell Foundation, a nonprofit she and her husband started in 2020 to listen to people and their communities, help them tell their stories, and put action behind their words, stated, "Life is about storytelling—about the stories we tell ourselves, stories we are told. What we buy into and for us, [it is] about storytelling through a truthful lens that is hopefully uplifting . . . able to give a voice to a lot of people who are unrepresented, and who are not heard."

My family upbringing was largely devoid of story. Since life is story and without telling our story we do not really live, this absence became a major issue in the formation of my identity within a noncommunicative, unromantic, and stoic Australian upbringing. A part of this challenge stemmed from the fact that I was twelve to fifteen years younger than anyone else in the entire family. I was five years old before I realized that I had an older brother and sister who were away at college. As such, I trained myself to be invisible in order to live safely in a society that cuts you down to size if you draw attention to yourself and in an era when children could only "be seen and not heard."

My parents were born before the First World War, and lived as young adults through the Great Depression and World War Two. Growing up in my home, there was love and peace. Yet ours was a home of the Depression. I do not remember visitors coming to the house. There was no music played. My bedroom had one chair, one table, and one bed without any decorations on the wall, and a two-foot-wide wardrobe of clothes alongside one pair of functional shoes and sneakers.

Imagination Paves a Way

"Runk" was my imaginary friend who lived in the backyard. We told stories together via the blind cord on the back veranda that became our telephone extension. Radio provided an opportunity to stimulate my creativity through listening to children's stories as I lay on the lounge-room carpet after school. Saturday afternoon pictures at the Regent Theatre also provided yarns of inspiration that I reenacted on the patio lawn, which became catalysts for fanciful games in the neighborhood. I was ten when I saw my first television screen. A new world of American propaganda consequently unfolded on the table of my juvenile mind: hamburgers and pizzas; ten-pin-bowling and gridiron football; and Roy Rogers and Hopalong Cassidy became a part of my childhood vocabulary, even if I was unsure of their full meaning.

Around the family dinner table there was little conversation other than debates about the legal nuances of lawn bowls. My father spoke five words—per year. Father's rural family was geographically distant. On visiting his kinfolk, he would come alive, however. Away from his administrative responsibilities and the drudgery of distractions, Dad spent the nights sitting in front of the large open fire of the farmhouse kitchen playing cribbage and yarning with his older brothers. They told tales of the past, blurring reality into fiction as the hours rolled away into anecdotes stretched like cellophane over a jar of homemade butter.

The town I grew up in was less than eight thousand people, situated some fifty miles north of Sydney, tottering on the eastern edge of the continent. My mother's family were prominent business and regional leaders. There was a measured interaction among my aunts and uncles. I did attend a few family weddings, as evidenced by photos of me still in shorts clinging to my mother and wearing a shy smile. There was one family reunion with my mother's siblings. At that function, the multiplicity of bottles sitting on the table ready for consumption mesmerized me. I did not attend any funerals of my aunties, uncles, cousins, or grandmother. My mother did not allow it. The only funerals I attended were of my mother and father, and my older siblings closed those occasions to the public. I missed hearing the eulogies reflecting on the lives of my parents even though they were state and national influencers. There were no stories about character or accomplishments—only a hymn, Psalm 23 read in a whisper, and a few noble sentences from the unknown vicar. In my childhood, there were no stories at clan gatherings, weddings, or funerals to pass on the collective memory of my family. Who am I apart from my family? I am an individual unmoored from story, swimming in life without a line of connection.

We Are Our Stories

There were a few fleeting exceptions. In my early teens, I enjoyed a two-year window in which I visited my only living grandparent. My maternal grandmother lived in a turn-of-the-century cottage in the middle of our village. Walking home from high school, I often visited my "Mumma," listening to her stringing stories in common with her friends over cups of tea and biscuits. For example, Miss Fry telling the story of her pioneer father floating ironbark logs down Narara Creek to load onto the steamships bound for Sydney. Amid the chronicles of Mumma, I found a sense of historical connection.

There were also other tales of influence. In the late afternoons of grade four, Mr. Tate read Dorothy Wall's *Adventures of Blinky Bill*, the little Australian koala bear who always got his hand stuck in the honey tin.[51] My first reader was Arthur S. Maxwell's *Uncle Arthur's Bedtime Stories* regarding moral lessons and stories of Jesus. Moreover, Mr. McIntyre, my Presbyterian Sunday-school teacher, told of Toyohiko Kagawa, the Japanese social activist who lived in the slums of Kobe. Currently sifting through the family memorabilia, I am only now beginning to appreciate my epic in the stories of my grandmother, mother, and father, together with my siblings and extended family via the cuttings from my hometown newspaper.

We are our history. We are our story. Our history is our story. We need to know the legends that shape us as individuals, in addition to the collective chronicles of our family, region, state, nation, ethnic group, religious affiliation (Protestant, Catholic, or Orthodox), and the institution for which we work—business, college, denomination, or ministry association. Our identity and belonging are in our history—our shared story. If we do not hear our account, then we do not know our history—who we are as an individual, family, or people. Our identity becomes truncated, and subsequently we can flounder and struggle with who we are and our attachments. We live our story. Our telling of our legend is life. If we do not know our history, we drift into the future. History, our story, gives us hopeful direction toward the yet to come. History of our past buttresses our present, and shapes our prospects.

Enhancing Our Mission Story

How do we go forward in enhancing our mission story? How do we see our story in God's bigger narrative? And who will listen? Slowing down our pace of life, unplugging from technology,

---

[51] Robert L. Gallagher, "Blinky Bill Rides Again: An Australian Folk Tale's Impact," *Theology, News, and Notes* 44, no. 4 (1997): 14–15.

and welcoming Sabbath rest enhances opportunities for stories as these spiritual practices carve spaces to listen and talk to God and each other. That is why road trips, long walks, and hugging steaming lattes away from the crippling invasion of social media and stifling performance pressures move us toward listening and telling stories.

In my early days of following Christ while working at the Wollongong steel works, every lunchtime for two years was spent sitting at the kitchen table of Pastor Bill and Joan Beard—eating Joan's delicious hot offerings and listening to Bill tell evangelistic stories of pioneering days. Bill's best sermons were at that kitchen table. In attending the Beards' fledgling church, central to our worship was robust singing of God's glory from the King James Bible, people standing in the congregation declaring living testimonies of Christ's work, and missionaries witnessing the Spirit's goodness in exotic places. Unfortunately, the congregation was ahistorical. The story of God's kingdom expansion through history was missing. The feeling that was propagated was that we discovered the Holy Spirit who had been absent in the human saga from Acts 28 until the 1904 Welch revival.

I found my story by telling about Jesus. I spoke of Christ to my parents after long drives home following Friday-night youth group. My aging parents graciously listened. My father turned toward Christ as Savior, and experienced the Lord's gift of healing. My mother asked for the blessed Holy Spirit sitting on the bed in my brother's room. The Spirit of Christ embraced her with such gentleness as she expressed her love to God in a prayer language. On my mum's deathbed, Christ appeared as her eternal hope. Others in the family were not as receptive to the message of Christ our Savior, Empowerer, Healer, and Hope.

The art of personal storytelling is waning. Our current Western society is passively listening to what others are spoon feeding us through mass and social media. Stories and metaphors shaped my first Christian adventures through the preaching of Bill Beard, Leo Harris, Jack Hayford, Bob Mumford, David Pawson, and Malcolm Smith. For instance, in 1971 Judson Cornwell came to our struggling Wollongong church plant and devoted an entire sermon telling about a stray dog who lived in the long grass of his backyard, whom he eventually enticed—through food and love—into his home. Then one day the little dog jumped onto Judson's lap, and God spoke to the preacher about the Father's deep care and concern for the people of this world by giving his one and only Son.

FINALE

In my family there was little story. The difference in my age certainly crippled the opportunity for discussion. But the barriers of control and protection also hindered a nurturing of transformative anecdotes. And because I knew little about my people, I could only tell little. I still have nothing much to say through lack of knowledge. Little story—little message.

How then can people call on Christ, whom they have not believed in? Moreover, how can they believe in Jesus, whom they have not heard? And how can they hear without someone telling them the story? In proclaiming Christ as Savior, Empowerer, Healer, and Hope in today's world, we have an overflow of messengers, methods, means, and motivations. However, what about our message? Do we know the narratives of God's Word, so that we may speak boldly under the anointing of the Holy Spirit to proclaim Christ? Should we remain ignorant of the modern-day global happenings of Christ's ministry among the nations? We have a responsibility to communicate the transforming global mission of Christ through story: biblical, historical, and contemporary stories.

We all have mission stories to tell as we participate in the story of God. Love your children, grandchildren, and neighbors by telling your mission story of Christ's love in your life. Allow me to end with the following poem, which is my narrative in Christ—our narrative in Christ—where humanity's story intersects with the mission story of God.

OUR JANUARY SIX

Here we are
    calling on the forces of nature
        turmoil in our minds
            adjusted compromise
                emboldened by a plea to freedom
                raising our defiant arms
                    in insignificant unity.

* * *

Blood-soiled Love
    placed in compromise
        huddled in servitude
            worn between two worlds
                resting in resolute arms
                    lying between moments of sweetness.

* * *

"Where is your sting
    where is your servitude?"

* * *

Rest now
    fainted warrior
        wise in peace
            seedbed of unity
                triumphant in glory.

* * *

About the Authors

Sarita Gallagher Edwards (PhD, Fuller Theological Seminary) is a professor of religion at George Fox University in Newberg, Oregon. Sarita served as a missionary with CRC Churches International in Papua New Guinea and Australia, and teaches in the areas of biblical theology, intercultural studies, world religions, and world Christianity. Her most recent publications include *Breaking through the Boundaries: God's Mission from the Outside In* (Orbis Books, 2019) and *Abrahamic Blessing: A Missiological Narrative of Revival in Papua New Guinea* (Pickwick, 2014), as well as numerous other chapters and articles.

Robert L. Gallagher (PhD, Fuller Theological Seminary) is a professor emeritus of intercultural studies at Wheaton College Graduate School in Chicago, where he has taught since 1998. He previously served as the president of the American Society of Missiology (2010–11), an executive pastor in Australia (1979–90), and a theological educator in Oceania since 1984. His most recent publications include coediting *Contemporary Mission Theology: Engaging the Nations* (Orbis Books, 2017) and *Sixteenth-century Mission: Explorations in Protestant and Roman Catholic Theology and Practice* (Lexham Press, 2021), as well as coauthoring *Encountering the History of Missions: From the Early Church to Today* (Baker Academic, 2017) and *Breaking through the Boundaries: God's Mission from the Outside In* (Orbis Books, 2019).

About the Authors

Paul W. Lewis (PhD, Baylor University) is an associate dean and professor of historical theology and intercultural studies at the Assemblies of God Theological Seminary at Evangel University in Springfield, Missouri. He and his wife, Eveline, were missionaries with the Assemblies of God World Missions (USA) to Asia and the Pacific Rim for over twenty-two years. His most recent publications include coediting *A Light to the World: Explorations in Ecumenism, Missions, and Pentecostalism* (Pickwick, 2017), *Missiological Research: Interdisciplinary Foundations, Methods, and Integration* (William Carey Publishers, 2018), and *Asia-Pacific Pentecostalism* (Brill, 2019).

DeLonn L. Rance (PhD, Fuller Theological Seminary) serves as a professor of missions and intercultural studies at the Assemblies of God Theological Seminary in Springfield, Missouri, and as the missiologist for the Missions Commissions of both the World Assemblies of God Fellowship and the Pentecostal World Fellowship. In his thirty-six years as a missionary, his passion and calling have focused on mobilizing the global church to missions and equipping missionaries from all nations, to all nations. A member of the Assemblies of God World Missions (USA) Latin America and Caribbean regional team, he facilitates missionary training both in the region and globally.

Previously Published in
The American Society of Missiology Series

1. *Protestant Pioneers in Korea*, Everett Nichols Hunt Jr.
2. *Catholic Politics in China and Korea*, Eric O. Hanson
3. *From the Rising of the Sun: Christians and Society in Contemporary Japan*, James M. Phillips
4. *Meaning across Cultures*, Eugene A. Nida and William D. Reyburn
5. *The Island Churches of the Pacific*, Charles W. Forman
6. *Henry Venn: Missionary Statesman*, Wilbert R. Shenk
7. *No Other Name? Christianity and Other World Religions*, Paul F. Knitter
8. *Toward a New Age in Christian Theology*, Richard Henry Drummond
9. *The Expectation of the Poor: Latin American Base Ecclesial Communities in Protest*, Guillermo Cook
10. *Eastern Orthodox Mission Theology Today*, James J. Stamoolis
11. *Confucius, the Buddha, and Christ: A History of the Gospel in China*, Ralph R. Covell
12. *The Church and Cultures: New Perspectives in Missiological Anthropology*, Louis J. Luzbetak, SVD
13. *Translating the Message: The Missionary Impact on Culture*, Lamin Sanneh
14. *An African Tree of Life*, Thomas G. Christensen
15. *Missions and Money: Affluence as a Western Missionary Problem . . . Revisited* (Second Edition), Jonathan J. Bonk
16. *Transforming Mission: Paradigm Shifts in Theology of Mission*, David J. Bosch
17. *Bread for the Journey: The Mission and Transformation of Mission*, Anthony J. Gittins, CSSp
18. *New Face of the Church in Latin America: Between Tradition and Change*, edited by Guillermo Cook
19. *Mission Legacies: Biographical Studies of Leaders of the Modern Missionary Movement*, edited by Gerald H. Anderson, Robert T. Coote, Norman A. Horner, and James M. Phillips
20. *Classic Texts in Mission and World Christianity*, edited by Norman E. Thomas
21. *Christian Mission: A Case Study Approach*, Alan Neely
22. *Understanding Spiritual Power: A Forgotten Dimension of Cross-Cultural Mission and Ministry*, Marguerite G. Kraft

23. *Missiological Education for the 21st Century: The Book, the Circle, and the Sandals*, edited by J. Dudley Woodberry, Charles Van Engen, and Edgar J. Elliston
24. *Dictionary of Mission: Theology, History, Perspectives*, edited by Karl Müller, SVD, Theo Sundermeier, Stephen B. Bevans, SVD, and Richard H. Bliese
25. *Earthen Vessels and Transcendent Power: American Presbyterians in China, 1837–1952*, G. Thompson Brown
26. *The Missionary Movement in American Catholic History*, Angelyn Dries, OSF
27. *Mission in the New Testament: An Evangelical Approach*, edited by William J. Larkin Jr. and Joel W. Williams
28. *Changing Frontiers of Mission*, Wilbert R. Shenk
29. *In the Light of the Word: Divine Word Missionaries of North America*, Ernest Brandewie
30. *Constants in Context: A Theology of Mission for Today*, Stephen B. Bevans, SVD, and Roger P. Schroeder, SVD
31. *Changing Tides: Latin America and World Mission Today*, Samuel Escobar
32. *Gospel Bearers, Gender Barriers: Missionary Women in the Twentieth Century*, edited by Dana L. Robert
33. *Church: Community for the Kingdom*, John Fuellenbach, SVD
34. *Mission in Acts: Ancient Narratives in Contemporary Context*, edited by Robert L. Gallagher and Paul Hertig
35. *A History of Christianity in Asia: Volume I, Beginnings to 1500*, Samuel Hugh Moffett
36. *A History of Christianity in Asia: Volume II, 1500–1900*, Samuel Hugh Moffett
37. *A Reader's Guide to Transforming Mission*, Stan Nussbaum
38. *The Evangelization of Slaves and Catholic Origins in Eastern Africa*, Paul V. Kollman, CSC
39. *Israel and the Nations: A Mission Theology of the Old Testament*, James Chukwuma Okoye, CSSp
40. *Women in Mission: From the New Testament to Today*, Susan E. Smith
41. *Reconstructing Christianity in China: K. H. Ting and the Chinese Church*, Philip L. Wickeri
42. *Translating the Message: The Missionary Impact on Culture* (second edition), Lamin Sanneh
43. *Landmark Essays in Mission and World Christianity*, edited by Robert L. Gallagher and Paul Hertig
44. *World Mission in the Wesleyan Spirit*, Darrell L. Whiteman and Gerald H. Anderson (published by Province House, Franklin, TN)

45. *Miracles, Missions, & American Pentecostalism*, Gary B. McGee
46. *The Gospel among the Nations: A Documentary History of Inculturation*, Robert A. Hunt
47. *Missions and Unity: Lessons from History, 1792–2010*, Norman E. Thomas (published by Wipf & Stock, Eugene, OR)
48. *Mission and Culture: The Louis J. Luzbetak Lectures*, edited by Stephen B. Bevans
49. *Comprehending Mission: The Questions, Methods, Themes, Problems, and Prospects of Missiology*, Stanley H. Skreslet
50. *Christian Mission among the Peoples of Asia*, Jonathan Y. Tan
51. *Sent Forth: African Missionary Work in the West*, Harvey C. Kwiyani
52. *Mangoes or Bananas: The Quest for an Authentic Asian Christian Theology*, Hwa Yung
53. *Contemporary Mission Theology: Engaging the Nations: Essays in Honor of Charles E. Van Engen*, edited by Robert L. Gallagher and Paul Hertig
54. *African Christian Leadership: Realities, Opportunities, and Impact*, edited by Kirimi Barine and Robert Priest
55. *Women Leaders in the Student Christian Movement: 1880–1920*, Thomas Russell
56. *Traditional Ritual as Christian Worship: Dangerous Syncretism or Necessary Hybridity?* R. Daniel Shaw and William R. Burrows
57. *Christian Mission, Contextual Theology, Prophetic Dialogue: Essays in Honor of Stephen B. Bevans, SVD*, edited by Dale T. Irvin and Peter C. Phan
58. *"Go Forth": Toward a Community of Missionary Disciples*, Pope Francis, selected with commentary by William P. Gregory
59. *Breaking through the Boundaries: Biblical Perspectives on Mission from the Outside In*, Paul Hertig, Young Lee Hertig, Sarita Gallagher Edwards, and Robert L. Gallagher
60. *A Long Walk, A Gradual Ascent: The Story of the Bolivian Friends Church in its Context of Conflict*, Nancy J. Thomas (published by Wipf & Stock, Eugene, OR)
61. *The Missionary Spirit: Evangelism and Social Action in Pentecostal Missiology*, Jerry M. Ireland